Contemporary Photographic Art from Moscow

Zeitgenössische Fotokunst aus Moskau

2995
995
A1
4
AF592988

Contemporary Photographic Art from Moscow

Zeitgenössische Fotokunst aus Moskau

Edited by
Herausgegeben von
Alexander Tolnay

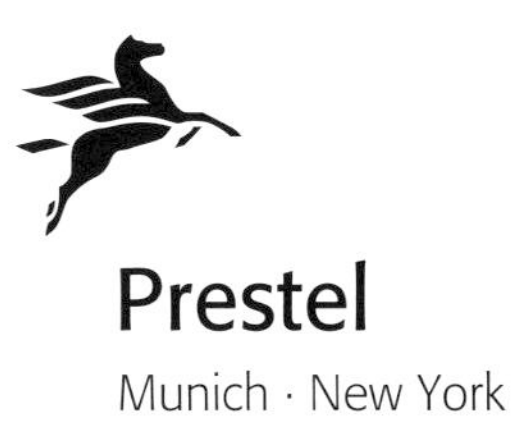

Prestel
Munich · New York

This book was published on the occasion of the exhibition 'Contemporary Photographic Art from Moscow' at the Akademie der Künste im Marstall, Berlin (29 September to 29 October 1995), ifa-Galerie, Berlin (29 September to 5 November 1995), and Neuer Berliner Kunstverein, Berlin (29 September to 12 November 1995)

Dieses Buch erschien anläßlich der Ausstellung „Zeitgenössische Fotokunst aus Moskau" in der Akademie der Künste im Marstall, Berlin (29. September bis 29. Oktober 1995), der ifa-Galerie, Berlin (29. September bis 5. November 1995), und dem Neuen Berliner Kunstverein, Berlin, (29. September bis 12. November 1995)

Translated from Russian into German by Friedrich Hübner (Dyogot)
(Übersetzungen Russisch-Deutsch von Friedrich Hübner)

Translated from German into English by Elizabeth Clegg (Foreword, Barsch and Lammert) and Fiona Elliott (Becker, Dyogot and Tolnay)
(Übersetzungen Deutsch-Englisch von Elizabeth Clegg und Fiona Elliott)
English texts copyedited by Nicholas Hardyman

Front cover: Boris Mikhailov, from the series 'Ground Bound' *(Aus der Serie „Bodenständig"),* 1991 (see cat. 54)
Back cover: Anatoli Shuravlev, 'Untitled' *(Ohne Titel),* 1992 (see cat. 71)

© by Prestel-Verlag, Munich · New York 1995
© of works illustrated by the artists

Photograph credits appear on p. 128

Die Deutsche Bibliothek – CIP-Einheitsaufnahme:
Contemporary photographic art from Moscow / Zeitgenössische Fotokunst aus Moskau: [this book was published on the occasion of the exhibition 'Contemporary Photographic Art from Moscow' at the Akademie der Künste im Marstall, Berlin (29 September to 29 October 1995), ifa-Galerie, Berlin (29 September to 5 November 1995), and Neuer Berliner Kunstverein, Berlin (29 September to 12 November 1995)] / ed. Alexander Tolnay. – München · New York: Prestel, 1995

Prestel-Verlag
Mandlstraße 26, D-80802 Munich, Germany
Tel. (+49-89) 38 17 09-0; Fax (+49-89) 38 17 09-35 and
16 West 22nd Street, New York, NY 10010, USA
Tel. (212) 627-81 99; Fax (212) 627-98 66

Prestel books are available worldwide. Please contact your nearest bookseller or write to either of the above addresses for information concerning your local distributor.

Cover design by Rainer Lienemann, Munich
Designed by Konturwerk, Helga Schörnig, Munich
Lithography by Fotolito Longo, Frangart
Typeset by Max Vornehm GmbH, Munich
Printed and bound by Schoder Druck, Gersthofen

Printed in Germany

ISBN 3-7913-1607-9

Contents
Inhaltsverzeichnis

Acknowledgements
Danksagung

Irina Bazileva (Moskau)
Eliana Beynaert (ZENO X Galerie, Antwerpen)
Wilfried Eckstein (Goethe-Institut, Moskau)
Dr. Peter Hahn (Berlin)
Michael Kahn-Ackermann (Goethe-Institut, Moskau)
Stefanie Krumm (Landeskulturzentrum, Salzau)
Nina Kurieva (Moskau)
Ollivier Morane (La Base – Centre d'Art Contemporain, Le Vallois)
Larisa Sadovnikova (Akademie der Künste, Moskau)
Silke und Manfred Schmalriede (Pforzheim)
Tatyana Shipulo (Moskau)
Renate Stolze (Akademie der Künste, Berlin)
Inge Zimmermann (Akademie der Künste, Berlin)
and many others *(und viele andere nicht genannte)*

ALEXANDER TOLNAY

Foreword

Vorwort

Die Moskauer Kunstszene befindet sich seit Mitte der achtziger Jahre in einer Aufbruchstimmung. In der Zeit der Perestroika (1987–1990) begann eine Phase der Anerkennung und Institutionalisierung der bis dato nichtoffiziellen Kunst, und die neue Moskauer Fotokunst ist ein Kind dieser Epoche. In diese Periode fällt die Gründung der Gruppe „Unmittelbare Fotografie" in einem der zahlreichen inoffiziellen Fotoclubs, mit dem viele der hier vorgestellten, verschiedenen Generationen zugehörigen Fotografen verbunden waren und dessen Stil und Programmatik sie entscheidend entwickelt haben. Diese Amateurfotoclubs spielten eine wichtige Rolle in der Entstehung der künstlerischen Fotografie in Moskau. Seit den siebziger Jahren entwickelte sich dort eine kritische Haltung gegenüber der bis dahin dominierenden ‚sozialen Fotografie' im Sinne eines sozialistisch-realistischen Bildjournalismus. Man wandte sich von ihrem dokumentarischen Stil ab und hin zu einer Subjektivität, die das Surreale und Groteske, die Verfremdung und die Montage als Methode der fotografischen Bildinszenierung einsetzte.

Seit Anfang der neunziger Jahre unterstützen neue Strukturen, professionelle Organisationen – wie das Institut für Zeitgenössische Kunst oder das Zentrum für Zeitgenössische Kunst – und private Galerien – wie Shcola und 1.0 – die Arbeit der Moskauer Fotokünstler. Ihr Medium, das noch immer unter der Nachwirkung der offiziellen Kulturpolitik der ehemaligen Sowjetunion leidet, die die Fotografie als Nicht-Kunst von anderen Kunstgattungen trennte, erfuhr damit eine ästhetische Aufwertung als gleichberechtigte Ausdrucksform neben Malerei, Grafik und Skulptur. Die Anerkennung der Fotografie als Kunst ging mit der zunehmenden Verbreitung der neuen Medien – Video und Computer – einher und paradoxerweise auch mit dem Beginn der gleichzeitigen Auflösung der Grenzen zwischen den einzelnen Medien. Dabei wurde die Fotografie oft gleichwertiger Teil multimedialer Installationen und dreidimensionaler Objekte, in denen die mediale Bedingtheit des zweidimensionalen Lichtbildes reflektiert wird.

Im Medium Fotografie werden in vielfältiger Weise die weit gefächerten künstlerischen Ansätze der Moskauer Fotokünstler thematisiert: Untersuchung des realen und des imaginären Raumes, Dekonstruktion von Symbolen und Zeichen der sowjetischen Staatsideologie, Infragestellung der individuellen und kollektiven Erinnerung, Selbstidentifikation und Selbst-

The Moscow art scene has been caught up in change since the mid 1980s. Hitherto unofficial art began to receive recognition and acceptance by the establishment during the days of Perestroika (1987–90); and New Moscow photography is a child of that time. It was also the period that saw the founding of the Immediate Photography Group in one of the then numerous amateur photography clubs. Many of the photographers featured here, elder and younger alike, were associated with this group and significantly influenced the evolution of its style and artistic programme. The amateur photography clubs played an important part in the development of art photography in Moscow. Since the late 1970s and early 1980s there had been growing criticism of the so-called 'social photography' of social-realist photojournalism which had been dominant in Moscow until that point. There was now a move away from the documentary to the subjective, with photographers using the surreal and grotesque, alienation and montage, to stage their compositions.

New structures and professional organizations, such as the Institute for Contemporary Art and the Center for Contemporary Art, or private galleries such as Shcola and 1.0, have been supporting the work of Moscow artist-photographers since the early 1990s. This has greatly improved the status of photography as an aesthetic form, setting it on an equal footing with painting, graphics and sculpture (for even today photography is suffering the after-effects of the official cultural policies of the former Soviet Union, which categorized it as 'non-art' and segregated it from other art forms). The recognition that photography is indeed an art form came with the spread of the new media – video and computer-generated images – but also, paradoxically, with the concomitant disintegration of the boundaries between the various media. For the use of the new media meant that photography often become an equal player in multi-media installations and three-dimensional objects, which also demonstrated the inherent limitations of the photographic image as a two-dimensional medium.

Photography now serves the many artistic interests of Moscow artist-photographers in a multiplicity of ways: investigating real and imaginary spaces; deconstructing the symbols and signals of Soviet ideology; questioning memory, both collective and individual; establishing a sense of self, and presenting the self in the light of a new physical awareness of the human body; contextualizing the digital image and mass-culture; and processing the conceptual notions of the 1980s. Quite aside from various attempts to find common ground, what in fact connects these artists is, firstly their use of photographic means to explore the image as constructed reality, and secondly the way their work reveals the falseness of the expectations of reality that are associated with photographic presentation. Thus contemporary art-photography in Moscow would define itself as diametrically opposed, aesthetically and historically, to the erstwhile realistic reportage-photography from which it grew in the first place.

This book presents current works by the leading figures in this new realm of photography. The main part of the book is devoted to showing the work of eighteen selected photographers and groups in the context of three exhibitions running concurrently in Berlin. Detailed texts by the distinguished writers Yekaterina Dyogot (Moscow) and Kathrin Becker (Berlin), portray the development and current state of photography in Moscow. Three essays by the organizers of the Berlin exhibitions, Barbara Barsch (ifa-Galerie), Angela Lammert (Akademie der Künste) and Alexander Tolnay (Neuer Berliner Kunstverein) broaden the perspective to include further considerations that have emerged from their work as curators. The full picture is completed with biographies and prose portraits of the artist-photographers by Irina Bazileva (Moscow), and a select bibliography to inspire future interest.

inszenierung im Lichte einer neuen Körpererfahrung, Kontextualisierung des digitalisierten Bildes und der Massenkultur sowie Verarbeitung der konzeptuellen Tradition der achtziger Jahre. Trotz der verschiedenen Annäherungsmethoden verbindet alle diese Künstler die Tatsache, daß in ihren Arbeiten der Einsatz von fotografischen Mitteln der Beschäftigung mit dem Bild als konstruierte Realität dient und die von der fotografischen Präsentation erwartete Wirklichkeitsdarstellung als Fiktion entlarvt wird. Somit definiert sich die zeitgenössische Fotokunst in Moskau ästhetisch und historisch als Gegenpol zur einstigen realistischen Reportagefotografie, aus der sie letztlich hervorging.

Im vorliegenden Buch werden die wichtigsten Vertreter dieser neuen Fotokunst mit aktuellen Werken vorgestellt. Das Bildmaterial von 18 ausgewählten Fotografen und Künstlergruppen, das sich auf drei begleitende Berliner Ausstellungen bezieht, bildet den Hauptteil des Buches. Ausführliche Texte zweier renommierter Autorinnen, Yekaterina Dyogot (Moskau) und Kathrin Becker (Berlin), beschreiben die Entwicklung und die gegenwärtige Situation des Mediums Fotografie in Moskau. Drei Aufsätze von den Veranstaltern der Berliner Ausstellungen, Barbara Barsch (ifa-Galerie), Angela Lammert (Akademie der Künste) und Alexander Tolnay (Neuer Berliner Kunstverein), erweitern den Blickwinkel um einzelne Aspekte, die sich aus ihrer kuratorischen Arbeit ergeben haben. Die von Irina Bazileva (Moskau) erstellten Biografien und Kurzbeschreibungen der Fotokünstler sowie eine weiterführende ausgewählte Bibliografie zum Thema runden das Informationsangebot dieser Publikation ab.

YEKATERINA DYOGOT

New Moscow Photography: Pictures of Utopia and Scepticism

Die neue Moskauer Fotografie: Bilder der Utopie und der Skepsis

1 *Die neue Moskauer Fotografie ist ein Kind der Perestroika-Epoche 1987–1990: Gerade in jener Zeit entstanden (und zerfielen bald) die Klubs, aus denen die heutige Generation von Fotokünstlern hervorgegangen ist. Der Fotoveteran Boris Mikhailov, der etwas jüngere Vladimir Kupriyanov und die sehr viel jüngeren Igor Moukhin, Sergei Leontiev, Vladislav Efimov, Maria Serebriakova, Ilya Piganov und Anatoli Shuravlev sind alle auf irgendeine Art mit der Gruppe „Unmittelbare Fotografie" verbunden, die sich 1987 im Rahmen der halboffiziellen Ausstellungsvereinigung „Eremitage" bildete. „Unmittelbare Fotografie" war ein Klub von Fotoamateuren, die sich, anders als in den meisten Klubs dieser Art, durch ein künstlerisches Programm verbunden fühlten. Dieses Programm sah Fotos ohne Voreingenommenheit und ideologische Klischees vor. Die generelle Möglichkeit der Unmittelbarkeit wurde für die Moskauer Fotografen allerdings bald zum Gegenstand von Zweifel und von Reflexion.*

Schon Ende der achtziger Jahre legten einige Mitglieder von „Unmittelbare Fotografie" ihre Fotoapparate beiseite und begannen, auf Flohmärkten nach fremden Fotos zu suchen. Diejenigen nun, die ein klein wenig später zur Arbeit mit dem Foto gekommen sind (Olga Chernysheva, Vadim Fishkin, AES, Gor Chahal, Fenso, IV. Vysota und viele andere), neigen noch viel weniger dazu, selbst ins Objektiv zu schauen, sondern vielmehr dazu, mit Fotografie zu operieren. Mehr noch: Selbst wenn das Foto, mit dem der Künstler arbeitet, von ihm selbst stammt, so camoufliert er zuweilen diesen Umstand; in jedem Fall wird das Foto als Readymade benutzt, hinter dem kein individueller Blick steht, sondern die Fotografie als eine Form der Praxis, zu der sich moderne Kunst definiert.

Die sogenannte „konzeptuelle Fotografie", die ständig Zweifel an ihrer eigenen Zuverlässigkeit sät, da sie sich als eine künstlerische Ausdrucksweise der Kunst analysiert, ist eine Form der Selbstanalyse der Kunst schlechthin. Da die Hauptlinie der Moskauer Kunst seit Beginn der siebziger Jahre der Konzeptualismus war, also der Skeptizismus nicht nur gegenüber der offiziellen Ideologie, sondern gegenüber jeglicher Sprache und damit auch gegenüber der Kunst selbst, hatte die „konzeptuelle Fotografie" leichtes Spiel. Und obwohl nur Mikhailov (der in engem Austausch mit Kabakov stand) und teilweise Kupriyanov in irgendeiner Form mit der Moskauer konzeptuellen Tradition verbunden sind, vollzogen fast alle neuen Moskauer

1 New Moscow photography is a child of the days of Perestroika from 1987 to 1990, for it was this period that saw the growth, and rapid decline, of the clubs which nurtured the present generation of artist-photographers. The veteran photographer Boris Mikhailov, the somewhat younger Vladimir Kupriyanov and the much younger Igor Moukhin, Sergei Leontiev, Vladislav Efimov, Maria Serebriakova, Ilya Piganov and Anatoli Shuravlev have all been connected in some way with the Immediate Photography Group, which was set up in 1987 under the auspices of the Hermitage Group, a semi-official exhibition organisation. Immediate Photography was a club for amateur photographers whose members – unlike those of most other clubs of this kind – shared a common artistic programme. The programme's aim was photography free of prejudice and ideological cliché. But the viability of immediacy was soon to become the subject of doubt and reflection among Moscow photographers.

By the late 1980s some members of Immediate Photography had already laid their cameras aside and were beginning to seek out photographs in jumble sales. Those who came to photography a little later (Olga Chernysheva, Vadim Fishkin, the AES-Group, Gor Chahal, the Fenso-Group, IV Vysota and many others) were even less likely to be looking through the viewfinder themselves, preferring to operate with existing photography. Furthermore, even if artists have produced the photographs they themselves are using, they will often disguise this fact. Whatever the case, the photograph is used as a ready-made object, which owes its existence not to any individual's perception but to photography as a praxis against which modern art defines itself.

So-called Conceptual Photography, seeing itself as one of the languages of art and thus constantly sowing the seeds of doubt as to its own reliability, is in fact a form of self-analysis by art itself. Conceptualism had dominated art in Moscow since the early 1970s, disseminating scepticism not only with regard to official ideology but towards any kind of language and hence towards art itself, with the result that Conceptual Photography easily found a foothold. And although only Mikhailov (working closely with Kabakov) and, to a certain extent, Kupriyanov, have any real connections with Conceptualism in Moscow, in the early 1990s almost all the New Moscow photographers abandoned their hitherto uncritical pictorial approach,

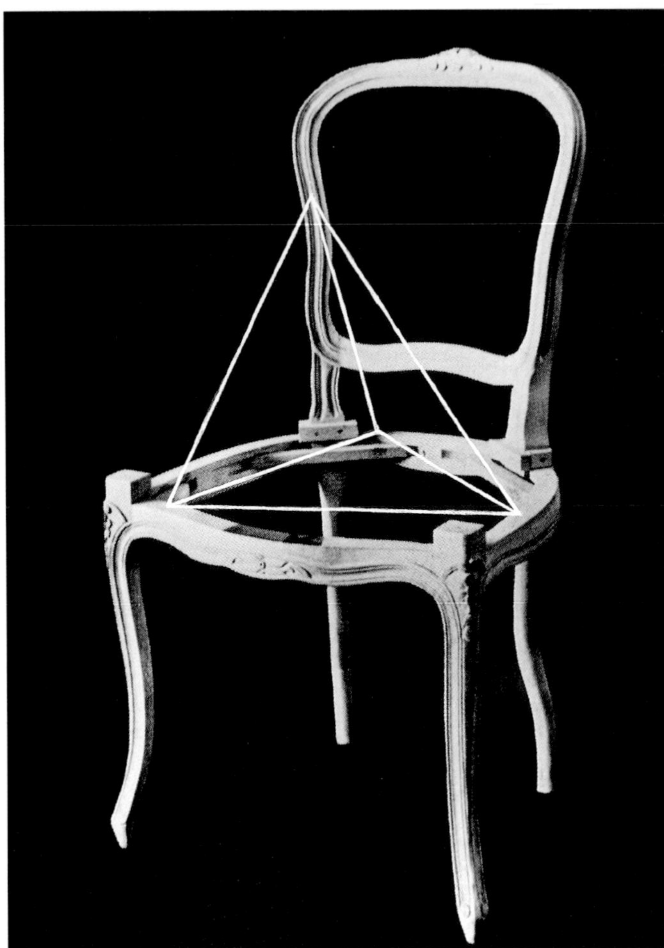

MARIA SEREBRIAKOVA, Untitled *(Ohne Titel)*, 1990

turning their attention instead to the very being of their own artistic language and to discovering its limits. In so doing they were of necessity forced into defining their own position regarding the historic choice made by the avant-garde of Soviet photography in the 1920s, when the decision had gone in favour of photography that was spontaneous and documentary in nature.

In his widely read text 'Against the Synthetic Portrait – In Favour of the Spontaneous' (in the journal *Novyj LEF*, 1928) Alexander Rodchenko held up the 'synthetic', which was in his view a falsifying, painterly portrait (the photo-portrait simply imitating painting) against the precision of the spontaneous shot. The example that in Rodchenko's opinion clinched the argument in favour of spontaneity was a folio of photographs of Lenin, which he felt were much to be preferred to any portraits of him. 'Everyone saw this folio and none, even without knowing why, will now accept artistic lies about Lenin.'[1] For Rodchenko the spontaneous shot is the guarantor of truth, giving the 'painterly lie' short shrift, and at the same time fulfilling a repressive function. It is well known that right from its earliest days photography has been used for repressive purposes because of its very precision (for example for the

Fotografen am Anfang der neunziger Jahre den Übergang von der unkritischen Bildhaftigkeit zur Herausarbeitung des Wesens und der Grenzen der eigenen Sprache. Notwendigerweise mußten sie dabei ihre eigene Einstellung zu jener historischen Wahl definieren, die die sowjetische Fotoavantgarde der zwanziger Jahre getroffen hatte, zur Entscheidung für dokumentarischen Charakter und Momentaufnahme.

In seinem bekannten Text „Gegen das ‚synthetische' Porträt – für die Momentaufnahme" (Zeitschrift „Novyj LEF", 1928) stellte Alexander Rodchenko dem „synthetischen", d. h. aus seiner Sicht verfälschenden, malerischen Porträt (und dem die Malerei imitierenden Fotoporträt) die Genauigkeit der Momentaufnahme gegenüber. Das Beispiel, das nach Rodchenkos Meinung endgültig die Priorität der Momentaufnahme beweisen konnte, war eine Mappe mit Leninfotos, die dessen malerischen Porträts unbedingt vorzuziehen war: „Diese Mappe hat jeder gesehen, und keiner, auch wenn er es selbst nicht bemerkt, wird eine künstlerische Lüge über den ewigen Lenin akzeptieren."[1] Die Momentaufnahme ist für Rodchenko der Garant der Wahrheit, der der Existenz der „malerischen Lüge" keinen Raum läßt, der also eine repressive Funktion ausübt. Es ist bekannt, daß die Fotografie schon im Augenblick ihres Entstehens gerade wegen ihrer Präzision zu repressiven Zwecken benutzt wurde, z. B. zur erkennungsdienstlichen Behandlung von Kriminellen. Bei Rodchenko liegt die begrenzende Funktion der Momentaufnahme als integraler Bestandteil ihrer Ästhetik – die im Foto festgehaltene Variante schließt die übrigen Varianten aus – einem Projekt der totalen Kontrolle zugrunde, das gerade die Fotografie als Trägerin des kollektiven Sehvermögens über die individuellen Varianten der Wirklichkeitsdarstellung ausübt: „Jeglicher künstlerischen Darstellung eines Menschen, die von einem Menschen geschaffen wurde, kann man mit einer Fotografie und anderen Dokumenten den Nimbus nehmen."[2]

Für russische Fotokünstler der postutopischen Epoche ist es offenkundig, daß die Dokumentarfotografie überhaupt keine Garantie dafür bietet, daß hinter ihr die Realität steht, und daß sich dies gerade am Beispiel der Aufnahmen Rodchenkos erweist. Die neue Moskauer Fotografie ist in einem Land großgeworden, in dem nicht die Fotoaufnahmen selbst, sondern gerade die Tatsache ihrer Verfälschung und ihrer Ausnutzung für ideologische Manipulationen zu Wegweisern in der Geschichte von Politik und Kunst wurden. Die Skepsis gegenüber der Zuverlässigkeit von Dokumentarfotografie, die der neuen russischen Fotografie insgesamt eigen ist, ermöglicht zwei unterschiedliche ästhetische Lösungen: Die erste besteht in dem Bemühen, im Foto die „Wahrheit" zu restaurieren; die zweite besteht in der radikalen Kritik am Anspruch des Fotos auf dokumentarischen Wahrheitscharakter generell.

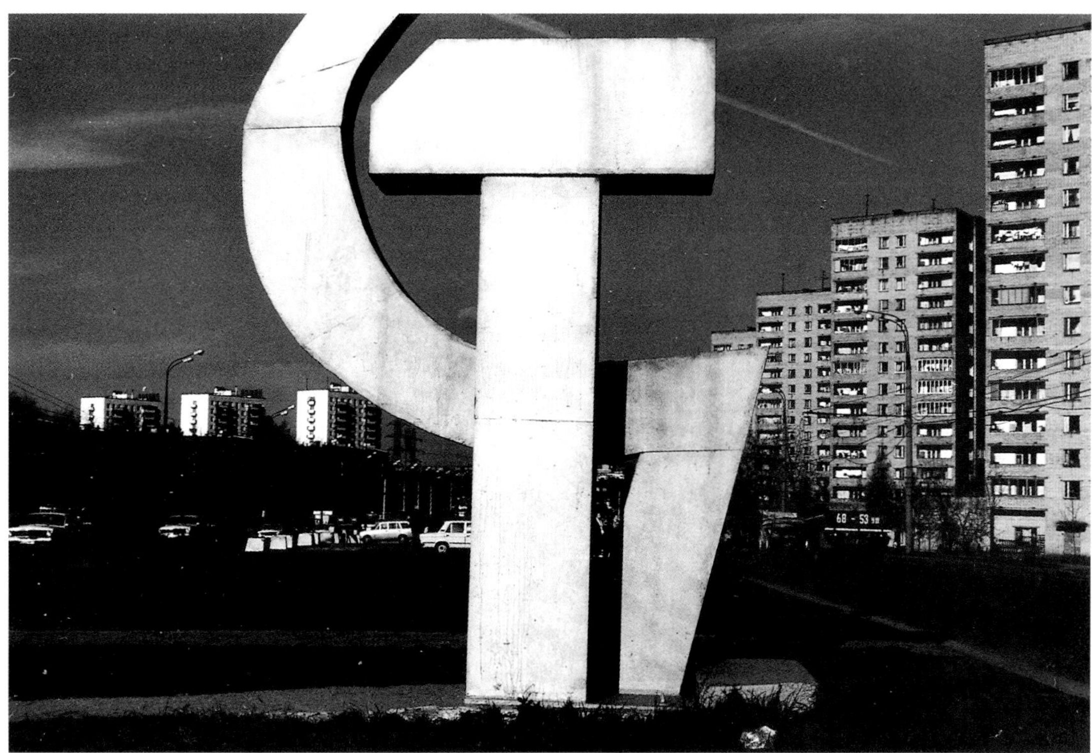

IGOR MOUKHIN, from the series 'Last Soviet Monumental Art' *(Aus der Serie „Letzte sowjetische Monumentalkunst")*, Schelesnowodsk, 1989

identification of criminals). As far as Rodchenko was concerned, the limiting function of the spontaneous shot, seen as an integral part of the aesthetic (because the variant captured within the picture naturally excludes all other variants), is at the very roots of a drive towards total control. This is practised by photography as the keeper of our collective vision as opposed to other, more individual modes of representing reality: 'A photograph and a few other documents will readily remove the nimbus from any representation of a person, made by another person'.[2]

For Russian photo-artists of the post-utopian period it is perfectly clear that documentary photography offers absolutely no guarantees as to its reality and that this is proved by photographs by none other than Rodchenko himself. The New Moscow photographers have grown up in a land where it was not the pictures themselves but rather the fact of their falsification and exploitation for ideological manipulation that became markers in the history of politics and art. The scepticism regarding the reliability of documentary photography which pervades all of new Russian photography leads to two rather different aesthetic solutions. One is to be found in efforts to restore 'truth' to photography; the other takes the form of radical criticism of the claims of photography to be dealing, by and large, in documentary truth.

2 *Die erste Lösung zwingt den Künstler vor allem dazu, der Gleichsetzung seiner Tätigkeit mit der „direkten" Aufnahme des Sujets Widerstand entgegenzusetzen. Die zeitgenössische Moskauer Fotografie, die sich als „künstlerisch" begreift, definiert sich selbst in erheblichem Maße – ästhetisch wie auch institutionell – als Gegenpol zur Reportagefotografie. Dies aber führt notwendigerweise zu einer außerordentlich großen Abschwächung oder Camouflage des Momentcharakters der Aufnahme. Schon der Gruppenname „Unmittelbare Fotografie" verwies keineswegs auf den Augenblick der Aufnahme, im Gegenteil: Die ersten Arbeiten der Gruppenmitglieder und auch von Alexander Slyusarev, der viele von ihnen ausbildete, zeichneten sich durch den Aspekt meditativer Zeiterweiterung aus. Um den Augenblick zu dehnen, hoffte der Fotograf gleichsam auf einen Beitrag zur Zeit durch den sich in die Fotoarbeit versenkenden Betrachter. Später allerdings bevorzugten die Künstler eine zuverlässige Variante und begannen, ihre eigene Zeit in die Fotografie zu investieren. Um das manipulierte ideologische Foto zu vermeiden, nimmt der Künstler paradoxerweise Zuflucht zu verschiedenartigen Manipulationen der Fotografie. Gerade in ihnen ist seine individuelle Geste enthalten: Er klebt ein Blättchen Zigarettenpapier oder ein Stück Mullbinde auf, nimmt mit der Hand Beschriftungen vor oder deckt ein Stück Plexiglas darüber.*

Maria Serebriakova zeichnet den Häusern auf einem gefundenen Foto Stelzenbeine an und läßt damit den Raum der Landschaft zwiespältig werden – je nach

2 The first solution forces the artist above all to resist his or her work being seen in the same light as a 'direct' shot of the subject matter. Contemporary Russian photography which sees itself as 'artistic' largely defines itself – both on an aesthetic and an institutional level – as going in the opposite direction to reportage photography. This, however, results of necessity in the momentary nature of the shot being watered down or camouflaged as far as possible. The very name 'Immediate Photography' is in no sense a reference to the momentary nature of the photographs in question. On the contrary, early works by the group's members, similar to that of Alexander Slyusarev who taught many of them, are in fact characterized by a meditational stretching of time. And to achieve this stretching of the moment, the photographer would hope for the viewer's input as he or she is naturally absorbed into the picture. Later, however, artists preferred a more reliable method and began to invest their own time in the photography. In order to avoid manipulated, ideological images, artists would take refuge, paradoxically enough, in various forms of manipulation of the photographs themselves. And in so doing artists would stamp their own individuality on a work – by sticking a piece of cigarette paper or a bit of gauze bandage on to the surface, writing on it or covering it with a piece of Plexiglas.

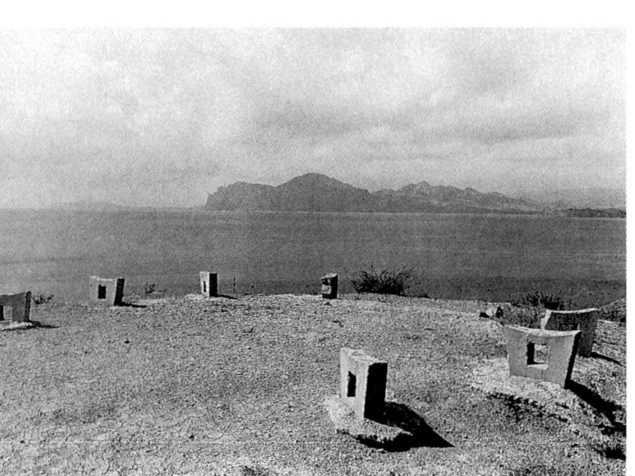

IGOR MOUKHIN, *Bench (Bank)*, 1993

Maria Serebriakova adds stilts to the houses on her found photographs, causing the landscape to split in two. Depending on how one views the picture, a house appears either to be contained within or outside the landscape – a way of assuring that the reception of the image goes on endlessly. She achieves the same effect by using words, or for example by adding a text to a landscape photograph, such as: 'The liar says: Everything I say is a lie', a text which will in fact not lead to any even remotely logical conclusion. Both of these prevent any clear interpretation of the photographs, weakening the intrinsically repressive nature of photography by introducing and integrating different versions of reality. Since the repressiveness of photography is a condition of its momentary nature, the aim of these devices is nothing less than to slow down the fleeting nature of photography.

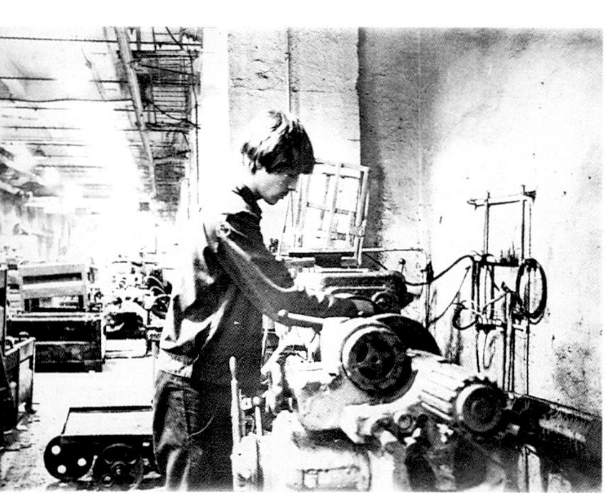

VLADIMIR KUPRIYANOV, *Factory (Fabrik)*, 1987

A technique from the earlier days of photography uses the effect of space to soften and even remove the harsh instantaneity of a shot – stereo photography. Vladimir Kupriyanov uses various means in his work to maintain a continuous stereoscopic effect: he mounts life-sized portraits *(The Rodionovs)* under Plexiglas prisms, prints photographs from the *Family Album* on

„Ausrichtung" unseres Blickes scheint sich das Haus innerhalb oder außerhalb der Landschaft zu befinden –, und dies ist ein Verfahren, um die Rezeption der Fotografie ewig anhalten zu lassen. Das gleiche Ziel erreicht sie mit verbalen Mitteln, indem sie einem Landschaftsfoto den Text „Der Lügner sagt: Alles, was ich sage, ist gelogen" hinzufügt, einen Text, dessen Verstehen im Prinzip nicht bei einem auch nur einigermaßen logischen Ergebnis verharren kann. Sowohl das eine wie das andere Verfahren schließt eine eindeutige Rezeption des Fotos aus, schwächt damit die natürliche Repressivität der Fotografie ab und vermag dadurch getrennte Varianten der Realität in ihr zu integrieren. Und da die Repressivität der Fotografie durch die Momentaufnahme bedingt ist, ist das Ziel dieser Gesten nichts anderes als das Retardieren des Augenblickscharakters der Fotografie.

Aus der Geschichte der Fotografie ist eine Technik bekannt, in der der harte Augenblickscharakter der Aufnahme mit Hilfe eines räumlichen Effekts gemildert und aufgelöst wird: die Stereofotografie. Vladimir Kupriyanov deklariert in seinen Arbeiten mit Hilfe unterschiedlicher Mittel ständig das Vorhandensein eines stereoskopischen Effekts: Er bringt lebensgroße Porträts („Die Rodionovs") im Innern von Plexiglasprismen unter; er zieht die Fotografien des „Familienalbums" auf zerknittertem Fotopapier ab (was den Abdruck weniger flach macht); er wiederholt in einer polyfiguralen Komposition („Verwirf mich nicht von deinem Angesicht") einzelne Figuren mehrmals; er legt in einem Foto-Objekt mehrere Glasscheiben mit gleichen Darstellungen aufeinander. Binokularität allerdings verwendet er nie – die sich wiederholenden Fragmente sind immer gleich, und die Stereoskopie ist nicht optischen, sondern ästhetischen Charakters. Der Anspruch auf Räumlichkeit (der vom Künstler immer betont wird) soll auf Kosten der Fotografie selbst erzielt werden, die unter dem Blickwinkel des Raumes Variationsbreite und damit Zeitvorrat gewinnt.

Eine weitere Variante des Injizierens von Zeit in die Momentaufnahme repräsentieren die Arbeiten von Vladislav Efimov: ‚Porträts' unbestimmter Objekte, die von ihm vor der Aufnahme eigens vorbereitet oder präpariert wurden. Fast bis zur biologischen Einheit verschmilzt Efimov unterschiedliche Gegenstände und Materialien, oft Kadaver, Knochen oder Bälge verstorbener Tiere; in seinen letzten Arbeiten hat er banale Lebensmittel (Hühnerbeine, Möhren, Bananen) so mumifiziert, daß sie an Fragmente menschlicher Körper erinnerten. Der Gegenstand sieht letztlich nicht wie eine Schöpfung von Menschenhand aus, er ist eigentlich mehr ein Denkmal der Zerstörung als des Schaffens. Aber gerade dadurch enthält er in sich einen explosiven Vorrat an zeitlicher Erweiterung. Die den Schaffensprozeß abschließende Fotografie scheint unter Zuhilfenahme einer lang andauernden Exposition gemacht worden zu sein, die gerade dazu in der Lage ist, langsame, mikroskopische Transformationen in der

Realität einzufangen. Vadim Fishkin integriert in seinen Aufnahmen Moskauer Hochhäuser, auf denen er ‚entzündete' Silhouetten von Engeln plaziert, ebenfalls den Effekt langer Exposition in die Fotografie, was es ihm erlaubt, mit bloßen Augen Nicht-Sichtbares festzustellen.

Einige der erwähnten Arbeiten sind unikal, andere könnten theoretisch vervielfältigt werden und wiederum andere werden tatsächlich vervielfältigt, ihre Poetik aber widerstrebt dennoch grundsätzlich einer Verbreitung. Das lange Andauern der Fotoexposition widerspricht dem medialen Exponieren der Fotografie – auf einer Ausstellung oder in der Presse –, d. h. ihrer augenblicklichen Vervielfältigung. Bei Rodchenko zieht die kurze Fotoexposition, d. h. die maximale Geschwindigkeit der Aufnahme, maximale Geschwindigkeit der medialen Verbreitung und ungeheure Auflagenhöhe nach sich. Die Wurzeln der Kunst der meisten Moskauer Fotokünstler ist jene Art von Fotografie, die, im Unterschied zur professionellen Fotojournalistik, sehr viel weniger mit der Auflagenhöhe verbunden ist und die Brisanz der Einzigartigkeit besitzt: das Amateurfoto, vom ‚touristischen' Schnappschuß bis zum Kitschporträt aus dem provinziellen Fotoatelier. Diese Fotos werden selbst dann nicht verbreitet, wenn sie vervielfältigt werden, sondern bleiben an ihrem Platz. Selbst wenn sie in einem Fotoatelier hergestellt sind, bleibt das Negativ beim professionellen Hersteller. Noch stärker unikal sind die handkolorierten „Luriks" und andere Kitschfotografien, mit denen besonders Boris Mikhailov in der Mitte der achtziger Jahre arbeitete. Und Einzelwerke im buchstäblichen Sinn sind schließlich die gefundenen Fotos, deren Negativ verlorengegangen ist.

Das ‚Ursprungsmilieu' der neuen Moskauer Fotografie ist nicht das öffentliche medienbezogene Fotoarchiv, das bei Rodchenko beständig die Varianten der Wirklichkeitsdarstellung kontrolliert, sondern das persönliche, sehr viel weniger anschauliche und überschaubare Archiv. Die extreme Ausprägung eines solchen Archivs ist das gedachte: der Raum des Gedächtnisses. Wenn Vladislav Efimov eine Fotografie innerhalb einer kleinen Schachtel oder eines ziemlich hohen Schachtes plaziert, wo immer nur ein Mensch hineinschauen kann, dann präsentiert und plaziert er sie als unabänderlich im Innern des individuellen Bewußtseins eingeschlossen. Eine derartige Vorstellung von Fotografie ist mit der Utopie der betont individualistischen Rezeption verbunden, im Gegensatz zur Kollektivität der Fotos ‚à la Rodchenko'. Gerade als ‚individuelle Halluzinationen' werden solche Fotos Efimovs völlig natürlich in die Videotechnik überführt. In ihrer Videovariante erlangen die Fotografien Bewegungsfähigkeit, was paradoxerweise eine zusätzliche Garantie für ein Retardieren der Darstellung ist – es bannt die Gefahr des augenblicklichen Abgleichens. Das sich Bewegende ist langsamer als das Augenblickliche. Dem gleichen Ziel dienen auch die Fotos, auf denen Anatoli

crumpled photographic paper (making the print less flat), he repeats certain figures many times in a multi-figured composition *(Turn not your countenance from me)* and he creates a photo-object containing several pieces of glass on top of each other with each bearing the same image. In doing this, however, he never uses binocularity: the repeated fragments are always identical and the stereoscopy is aesthetic rather than optical. These pretensions of space (always emphasized by the artist) are achieved at the cost of the photography itself which, however, with this spatial aspect then gains in breadth of variety and hence in time.

A further variation on the theme of injecting time into what was a momentary shot can be seen in the works of Vladislav Efimov, in his *Portraits* of indeterminate objects which he himself has either prepared or made for the purposes of the shot. Efimov merges diverse objects and materials into what becomes an almost organic whole, often using the carcasses, bones or pelts of dead animals. In his latest works he has mummified banal items of food (chicken bones, carrots, bananas) until they would seem to be reminiscent of human body parts. In the end the objects do not resemble anything created by human hand, they are more a testimonial to destruction than creation. But it is precisely in this that they acquire an explosive measure of extended time. The act of photography, coming as it does at the end of the process of creation, seems to be the result of a lengthy exposure time, which would appear to be able to capture microscopic, infinitely slow changes in reality. Vadim Fishkin also integrates the effects of lengthy exposure into his photographs of Moscow high-rise buildings, with 'flaming' silhouettes of angels on the roofs, as though he is able to see the unseeable with his naked eye.

Some of the works referred to here are one-offs, others could theoretically be reproduced and some are in fact reproduced, but the poetry of their being fundamentally resists reproduction. The lengthy process of exposing a photograph is a contradiction of the exposure of photography by the media, that is to say its instantaneous reproduction in an exhibition or in the press. According to Rodchenko, a short exposure time produces the fastest possible distribution time amongst the media and high print runs. But far removed from photo-journalists' concerns over print runs, the work of most Moscow photo-artists is a form of photography that lives by the volatility of the unique: amateur photography, from the 'tourist's' snapshot to the kitsch portraits from provincial photographers' studios. These photographs are not distributed even when they are copied. They stay where they belong. Even if they are from a photographic studio, the negatives stay with the professional photographer. An even stronger one-off quality is to be seen in the hand-tinted 'luriks' and other kitsch photographs used in particular by Boris Mikhailov in the mid 1980s. And last amongst the one-offs are the found photographs – photographs for which the negatives have been lost. The 'breeding ground' for New Moscow photography is not the public media photo-archive, which Rodchenko sees as controlling potential representations of reality, but instead the personal archive, which is both less vivid and less manageable. The extreme version of this kind of archive is in the mind, within the realms of memory. When Vladislav Efimov places a photograph inside a small box or down a deep shaft so that only one person can view it at a time, he interiorises his photographs, presenting them as irrevocably locked within the individual consciousness. Any such notion of photography is bound up in the utopia of absolute individual reception, quite the opposite to the collective imperative of photographs produced by Rodchenko and his followers. These photographs by Efimov transfer, in fact, completely naturally into video form – specifically as 'individual hallucinations'. In their video version these photographs acquire the capacity for movement, which paradoxically serves as a further guarantee for the slowing up of their presentation by preventing the danger of instant comprehension. Anything that moves is by definition slower than the momentary. Anatoli Shuravlev is working towards the same goal in his photographs showing computer-assisted images of antique sculptures in which the statues take on different poses. In work of this kind it is easy to see how the artists can claim to be portraying a reality that, as well as embracing the dimension of time, is independent both of artist and viewer.

These tendencies in Moscow photography can be read as attempts at restoring and resanctifying the notion of depths, which would long since appear to have been discredited in the art of the twentieth century. If Rodchenko's understanding of photography presents us with the utopia of some absolute mediator, as universal as Esperanto and devoid of 'truth' as an intrinsic value, then New Moscow photography has given life to a quite different utopia, where photography constitutes an absolute reality of its own. Photographs understood in these terms, unlike painting, have the potential for completeness. They contain everything that is needed to reveal any imaginable details, only limited by our own inadequate powers of perception. And this is exactly the construct around photography in Antonioni's film *Blow Up*. Here photography is credited with the power to reveal a secret (a secret of nature's, for the hero discovers a dead body on an enlarged landscape photo), but only if a photograph has been taken for its own sake, without any ulterior purpose (the hero is a professional photographer in advertising, requiring young women to hold still for long periods in unnatural poses; in the end he is punished for using nature in this way and loses the dead body he had found, that is to say he loses the meaning in nature). Photography centred on a utopian revelation of truth will always give pride of place to the shots by amateur photographers.

Shuravlev Computertransformationen antiker Skulpturen abbildete: Die Statuen ändern ihre Posen. In solchen Arbeiten tritt klar der Anspruch des Künstlers zutage, eine weder von ihm noch vom Betrachter abhängige Realität zu zeigen, die dazu auch noch über eine zeitliche Dimension verfügt.

Man kann diese Tendenzen in der Moskauer Fotografie als Versuche zur Restauration und Resakralisierung der Idee der Tiefe deuten, die in der Kunst des 20. Jahrhunderts längst diskreditiert zu sein schien. Wenn die Vorstellungen Rodchenkos von Fotografie vor uns die Utopie eines absoluten Mittlers erstehen lassen, der universell wie das Esperanto ist und dabei nicht den Eigenwert einer ‚Wahrheit' in sich trägt, so läßt die neue Moskauer Fotografie eine andere Utopie wieder aufleben – die Utopie von Fotografie als einem absoluten Resultat. Fotografie besitzt in diesen Vorstellungen, anders als das Bild, potentielle Vollständigkeit. In ihr ist alles gegeben; zur Aufdeckung aller beliebigen Details und Möglichkeiten mangelt es nur an der aufschließenden Fähigkeit unseres Sehvermögens. Gerade dies ist der Mythos der Fotografie in Antonionis Film „Blow-Up", in der ihr die Fähigkeit zugeschrieben wird, ein Geheimnis zu enthüllen (das Geheimnis der Natur, da der Held eine Leiche auf der vergrößerten Fotografie einer Landschaft entdeckt), aber nur in dem Fall, wenn die Fotografie um ihrer selbst willen gemacht ist, ohne Ziel und Zweck (der Held beschäftigt sich auch noch mit dem professionellen Aufnehmen von Werbefotos, wobei er junge Frauen dazu zwingt, lange Zeit in unnatürlichen Posen zu erstarren; für diese Gewalt gegenüber der Natur wird er schließlich bestraft und verliert die gefundene Leiche, also den Sinn der Natur). Die Fotografie, die sich an der Utopie der Wahrheitsenthüllung orientiert, wird immer der Amateuraufnahme den privilegierten Platz einräumen.

3 *Fotografen, die den romantischen Glauben an irgendein Geheimnis hinter der Realität teilen, neigen, wie schon Rodchenko bemerkte, zu einer malerischen Unbestimmtheit der Darstellung, um so die unsichtbare Wahrheit zu begünstigen. Aber wenn ein Künstler eine kritische Position wählt, dann wird nicht der Anspruch auf das Geheimnis, sondern die Enttäuschung über dessen Nichtvorhandensein zum Leitmotiv des Werks. In diesem Fall erhält optische Unklarheit eine gegenteilige Bedeutung: So stellt die Serie von Fotografien Anatoli Shuravlevs, die Ansichten der ägyptischen Pyramiden und Sphinxe präsentieren, wie sie vor 200 Jahren ausgesehen haben – der Künstler hat sie neu auf Cibachrom aufgenommen, stark vergrößert und in die Rahmen Stiche des 18. Jahrhunderts eingeschlossen – gerade die Ironisierung des ‚absoluten Sehvermögens' im Foto dar. Auf den ersten Blick besitzen diese Fotografien eine solche Fülle, daß der Betrachter bei einer bestimmten Anspannung des Auges in der*

Lage ist, kleinste Details genau zu betrachten; nach einiger Zeit ist jedoch klar, daß der Blick wie an einer Wand zerbrochen wird, und zwar durch den Genauigkeitsgrad in der Darstellung, der von dem ursprünglichen Stich vorgegeben ist. Die gleiche Erfahrung von Hoffnung und Enttäuschung, geknüpft an die Fähigkeit des Fotos, Realität wiederzugeben, beschreibt Roland Barthes in seinem Buch „Die helle Kammer": Beim Suchen nach seiner Mutter auf fotografischen Darstellungen vergrößert er die Aufnahme, aber er erhält damit nur die Rasterpunkte des Abzugs.[3] *Die Möglichkeit des „blow-up", der Vergrößerung, des ‚Aufblasens' eines Fotos zugunsten einer offenbar in ihm verborgenen Wahrheit wird von ihm, anders als von Michelangelo Antonioni, mit dem Skeptizismus aufgenommen, der auch den radikalen Strömungen der zeitgenössischen Kunst eigen ist.*

Ähnlich wie Shuravlev demonstiert auch Olga Chernysheva die Unmöglichkeit, sich auf die ‚Aura' eines Fotos zu verlassen. In einer Serie von Arbeiten montiert sie Kinderfotografien einer Mutter und einer Tochter im gleichen Alter zusammen: Dieser Traum von der Vereinigung verschiedener Zeiten in einem Raum, von der Aufhebung der Irreversibilität der Momentaufnahme wird durch die Offenkundigkeit der Montage abgekühlt. Auch in weiteren Arbeiten bedient sich Chernysheva des Kunstgriffs einer naiven Dokumentenfälschung, so wenn sie mit Hilfe von Schere und Retuschen unpräzise Landschaftsfotos in üppig dekorierte Torten verwandelt und damit gleichsam die Vorstellung vom alten Amateurfoto als einem Träger von Einzigartigkeit, Originalität und demzufolge Wahrheit betont. Aber die Tortenlandschaft, die Anspruch auf handwerklich gefertigte Unwiederholbarkeit erhebt, ist unverkennbar aus einer vervielfältigten Fotoaufnahme gemacht, die aus einer in Massenauflage erscheinenden Zeitschrift ausgeschnitten wurde. Man kann diese Arbeiten übrigens als ironische Dekonstruktion aller Ansprüche des Fotos interpretieren – nicht nur auf Wahrheitscharakter des Dargestellten, sondern auch auf dokumentarischen Charakter: Sträucher auf einem Landschaftsfoto sind Werke eines Fotografen, genau wie Sträucher auf einer Torte der Kunstfertigkeit eines Konditors entspringen.

Die Kritik der dokumentarischen Möglichkeiten der Fotografie enthält dann besonders intensive Reflexion, wenn der Fotograf das Dokumentarische als Kunstbegriff begreift, das noch auf die konstruktivistische Fotografie zurückgeht. So hat Igor Moukhin seine Serie „Monumente" (einen Katalog von monumentalen Denkmälern aus sowjetischer Zeit) im Stil der Fotos der zwanziger Jahre aufgenommen, mit paradoxen Perspektiven und unerwarteten Standpunkten, und damit den ‚Blick Rodchenkos' als ein Readymade benutzt. Aber Rodchenkos Modelle – Sportler, Jungpioniere, Schriftsteller – sind bei Moukhin durch Fußballer aus Gips und einen Gagarin aus Metall ersetzt worden: Der durch und durch ideologische Charakter

3 Photographers who hold to the Romantic belief in some secret behind reality, tend (as Rodchenko observes) towards a degree of painterly imprecision in their work in order to open the way for that invisible truth. But where an artist adopts a critical stance, then the work is determined not by the secret but by disappointment at its absence, and in this case optical imprecision takes on the opposite function. The series of photographs by Anatoli Shuravlev showing views of the pyramids and sphinxes of Egypt as they looked two hundred years ago (rephotographed by him onto cibachrome, greatly enlarged and framed along with eighteenth-century prints) can thus be seen as an ironic presentation of 'absolute powers of perception'. At first sight these photographs display such wealth of detail that the viewer, by looking in a particular way, is able to see the minutest details very clearly. After a while, however, it becomes clear that this act of seeing is being broken up as though against a wall – in fact by the very exactness of the detail provided by the original print. In his *Camera Lucida*, Roland Barthes describes the same experience of hope and disappointment in photography's capacity to convey truth: in the search for photographic images of his mother he enlarges a shot but is rewarded only with the matrix of dots of the print itself.[3] The possibilities of enlargement, of 'blowing up' a photograph to find in it some hidden truth, are viewed by him, unlike Antonioni, with the same scepticism as is found in the radical movements in contemporary art.

Like Shuravlev, Olga Chernysheva also demonstrates the utter impossibility of relying on a photograph's 'aura'. In one particular series of works she mounts together childhood photographs of a mother and daughter at the same age; but the obviousness of the montage militates against the dream of uniting different times and of denying the irreversibility of the spontaneous shot. In other works Chernysheva again employs the device of the apparently naïve falsification of documents, retouching and taking scissors to vague landscape photographs, turning them into richly decorated 'cakes'. She is thereby emphasizing the idea of the old amateur photograph as being unique, original and therefore truthful. But the cake landscape which might seem to lay claim to being hand-created and unreproducible is clearly not made from a one-off photograph but from a photograph cut out of a mass-produced magazine. One can interpret these photographs as an ironic deconstruction of any pretensions to truthfulness or documentary accuracy that photography might have: the foliage in a landscape photograph is the work of the photographer just as the leaves decorating a cake are a product of the pastry-cook's skill.

Criticism of the documentary potential of photography becomes particularly intense when the photographer, going back to the Constructivists, uses the documentary itself as his or her device, as does Igor Moukhin in his series 'Monuments'. This is a collection of monumental sculptures from the Soviet era (both well known and less well known) taken in the style of photographs from the 1920s but with odd perspectives and unexpected viewpoints, thereby using 'Rodchenko's view' as a readymade. But Rodchenko's models – sportsmen, young pioneers, writers – have been replaced by Moukhin with plaster casts of footballers and a metal Yuri Gagarin: the wholly ideological quality of Rodchenko's work is laid bare and the poetics of Constructivism are exposed as a rhetoric really no different from the rhetoric of Stalinist art.

Boris Mikhailov is a photo-artist who has for a long time now been working consistently with the idea of falsified photographs. Among the artists of the recent avant-garde he carries the most authority. He lives in Kharkov but exhibits in Moscow. As early as 1980 he took ideological montage as the theme of his piece *About Loneliness* which also included plans for future falsification. As the commentary informs the viewer: a photograph of two young women is to be cut into two pieces and the right-hand figure should then be mounted first with one man and then with another. In the same way as Kabakov's albums are filled with reflections by him on his activities as a book-illustrator operating with signs and meanings, so too this purely Conceptual work by Mikhailov is determined by his own experience as a retoucher in a photographic studio. This experience equips Mikhailov to uncover the manipulative aspect and utter inauthenticity not only in

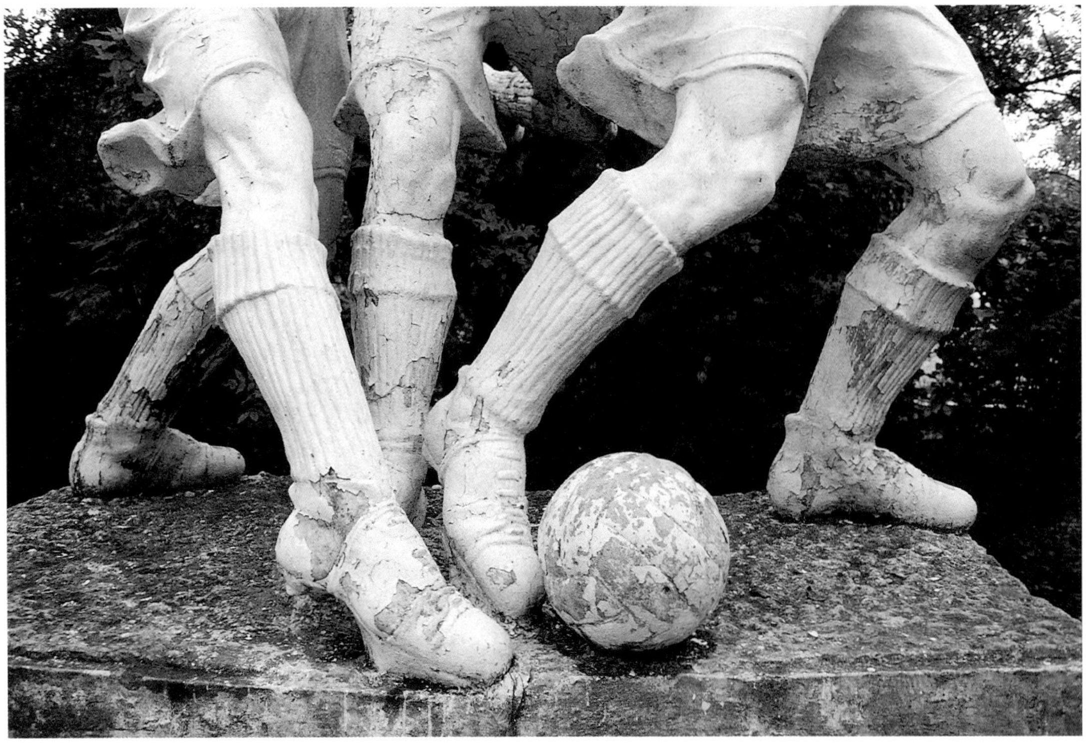

IGOR MOUKHIN, from the series 'Last Soviet Monumental Art' *(Aus der Serie „Letzte sowjetische Monumentalkunst")*, Schelesnowodsk, 1992

von Rodchenkos Aufnahmen offenbart sich, und die konstruktivistische Poetik wird als eine Rhetorik entlarvt, die der Bildsprache Stalinscher Kunst ähnelt.

Boris Mikhailov ist ein Fotokünstler, der schon lange mit großer Konsequenz das Motiv des gefälschten Fotos bearbeitet. Von den Künstlern der neuesten Fotoavantgarde ist er derjenige mit der größten Autorität. Er lebt in Kharkov, stellt aber in Moskau aus. Schon seine frühe Arbeit „Über die Einsamkeit" (1980) hatte die ideologische Montage zum Thema: Sie stellte den Plan einer noch zukünftigen Fälschung dar. Die Fotografie zweier junger Frauen sollte – wie aus dem Kommentar hervorgeht – in zwei Teile zerschnitten und die rechte Figur konsequent erst mit einem Mann und dann mit einem zweiten Mann zusammenmontiert werden. Wie die Alben Kabakovs von dessen Reflexion über die eigene Tätigkeit als Buchillustrator, der mit Zeichen und Bedeutung operiert, durchzogen waren, so ist auch diese rein konzeptuelle Arbeit Mikhailovs von seiner Analyse der eigenen Arbeitserfahrung als Retuscheur im Fotoatelier bestimmt. Diese Erfahrung ermöglichte es ihm, den manipulativen Charakter und die umfassende Inauthentizität nicht nur in ideologisierten Reportageaufnahmen, sondern auch in naiven, halb amateurhaften Fotografien aufzudecken. Alle folgenden Arbeiten Mikhailovs entlarven auf unterschiedliche Art und Weise jeglichen Gedanken an Fotografie als Mittel zur Dokumentation der Realität als Fiktion. In der Serie „Spaziergänge mit Borja", in der er banale Ansichten von einer Provinzstadt mit Kommentaren ergänzt, die intime Erinnerungen und Gefühle des Künstlers beschreiben, füllt er das Foto nicht mit ‚wahrem Leben' an – was einer utopischen Geste gleichkäme –, sondern er zwingt eher dazu, dessen Leere zu fühlen sowie die Bereitschaft, Illustration einer beliebigen Erinnerung zu sein. ‚Fiktive Erinnerungen' schafft er in der neuen Serie „Wenn ich Deutscher gewesen wäre", in der er die Möglichkeiten offener Inszenierung erforscht. Mikhailov demonstriert hier seine Variante des Verhältnisses zwischen Nazioffizieren – einer wird vom Künstler selber dargestellt – und der Bevölkerung in der besetzten Ukraine, eine fantastische und recht provokative Variante, die keinen Bezug zur historischen

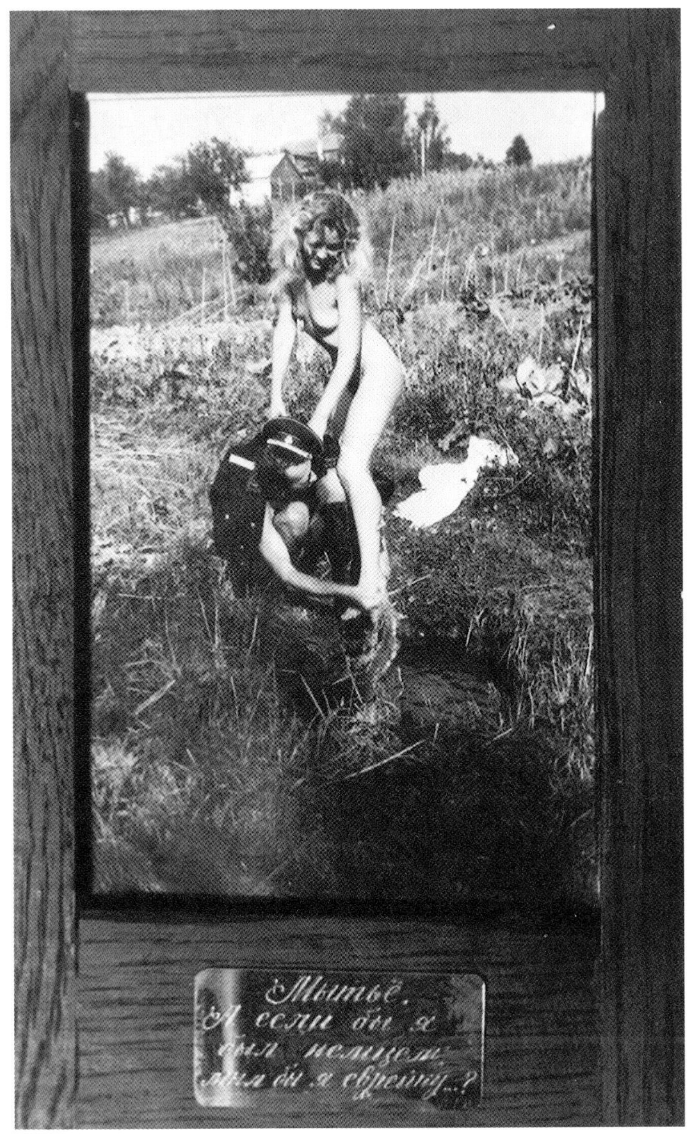

BORIS MIKHAILOV, from the series 'If I had been a German': *The Foot Bath (Aus der Serie „Wenn ich Deutscher gewesen wäre": Fußwaschung)*, 1995

Realität hat. Wenn Mikhailov das Alltagsvertrauen des Betrachters in das Fotodokument radikal in Frage stellt, setzt er seine Geste in Verbindung zur Praxis der Geschichtsfälschung mit Hilfe der Fotografie, was jedes totalitäre Regime auszeichnete.

Eine noch komplexere Variante der Simulation dokumentarischer Echtheit ist die Serie „Bodenständig". Sie besteht scheinbar aus erlesenen gestellten Fotografien im Geiste einer Werbeästhetik, die dokumentarischen Charakter vorspiegelt: Panoramaoptik, Brauntönung, ausgeklügelt zufällige Komposition, Kleidungsstücke, die entfernt an die dreißiger Jahre erinnern, eine Ästhetik der Zerstörung. Tatsächlich jedoch ist diese Serie mit einer ‚authentischen' Zufallsmethode aufgenommen, mit einer Kamera, die Mikhailov in Brusthöhe hielt, ohne ins Objektiv zu schauen. Was der Autor simuliert, ist gerade die Simulation. Da der reflektierende Künstler in unseren Tagen den Glauben an die Wahrhaftigkeit und an die dokumentarische

the photography of ideological reportage but equally in naïve, semi-amateur work. All Mikhailov's subsequent work is by one means or another exposing any notions of photography as a method of documenting reality. In the series 'Walks with Borja', in which Mikhailov takes banal views of a provincial town and adds a commentary describing his own intimate memories and feelings, he does not fill the photograph with 'true life' (which in itself would be something of a utopian gesture) but rather underlines the very emptiness of the images which are apparently there to be used to illustrate whatever memory one might care to choose. In his new series 'If I had been a German' he creates 'fictive memories', exploring the possibilities of openly staging shots. Mikhailov here gives his version of the relationship between Nazi officers (one played by himself) and the population in the occupied Ukraine, a fantastic and highly provocative version with no bearing whatsoever on historical reality. When Mikhailov kicks aside the viewer's customary trust in documentary photography, he is of course aligning his own actions with the practice of re-writing history through photography which is the norm for any totalitarian regime.

An even more complex variant of simulated documentary accuracy is the series 'Ground Bound'. It consists – or so it would appear – of high-quality posed photographs bearing all the hallmarks of advertising: panoramic views, sepia tones, cleverly devised chance compositions, items of clothing vaguely reminiscent of the 1930s and 1940s; an aesthetic of destruction. And yet this series was in fact made using 'real' chance methods, that is to say with a camera which Mikhailov held at chest height without looking through the viewfinder. For here the author of the works is simulating simulation. Since artists who reflect on their work are these days losing any faith they might once have had in the truthfulness and documentary accuracy of photography (even if they know they have taken the photographs themselves), the only way left to comment on this truth is by reference to its absence. In his day Rodchenko, disappointed with painting, turned with enthusiasm to photography; artists today have no more avenues of hope to pursue, and yet they do have the compensation of much greater freedom of choice in *how* they carry out their work.

Olga Chernysheva has inherited the aesthetics of black and white from the Moscow Conceptualists, but not their tendency to verbalise their art. This does, however, oblige her to redefine the nature of her creativity in each of her works – creativity in an age which has lost any illusions about the notion of absolute, original creating. And she not infrequently draws on the idea of the work of the pastry-cook as a model for creativity. In her work Chernysheva is constantly striving to find a balance between a 'positive approach' (the original, creative act, natural and authentic) and scepticism regarding the potential of the former. In these works she often uses found photographs which, after authorial retouching, take on an indeterminate, anonymous character.

Genauigkeit der Fotografie verliert (sogar wenn er weiß, daß er diese selbst gemacht hat), besteht der einzige Weg, etwas über diese Wahrheit zu sagen, im Hinweis auf ihr Fehlen. Rodchenko wandte sich seinerzeit, enttäuscht von der Malerei, begeistert der Fotografie zu; der heutige Künstler hat nichts mehr, worauf er seine Hoffnung stützen könnte, aber dies gibt ihm auch mehr Freiheit in der Wahl seiner Mittel.

Notes

1 Alexander M. Rodtschenko and Warwara F. Stepanowa [Alexander Rodchenko and Warwara Stepanova], *Die Zukunft ist unser einziges Ziel...*, exhibition catalogue, ed. Peter Noever, Österreichisches Museum für angewandte Kunst, (Munich, 1991), p. 234

2 Ibid.

3 Roland Barthes, *Camera Lucida: Reflections on Photography*, (New York), p. 100

Anmerkungen

1 Peter Noever (Hrsg.): Alexander M. Rodtschenko, Warwara F. Stepanova. Die Zukunft ist unser einziges Ziel, *München 1991, S. 234*

2 Ibid

3 Roland Barthes, Die helle Kammer. Bemerkungen zur Photographie, *Frankfurt a. M. 1985, S. 119*

KATHRIN BECKER

Photography versus Art – Art and Photography

Fotografie versus Kunst – Kunst mit Fotografie

1 *Mein letzter Aufenthalt in Moskau im April 1995 begann wie üblich mit einer Taxifahrt vom Moskauer Flughafen Sheremetyevo 2 in das Stadtinnere. Auf dem Weg fiel mir auf, daß eine Vielzahl der Fahrzeuge auf der Hutablage ein Objekt aufwies, das ich früher nicht bemerkt hatte. Es war dies eine kleine goldene Krone mit einem weinroten, samtartigen Kissen in der Mitte. Meine Frage, ob es sich bei diesem Gegenstand um eine politische Bekundung des Fahrzeuginhabers, um das Zeichen für die russischen Monarchisten handelte, rief augenblickliche Heiterkeit bei dem Taxifahrer hervor. Er erklärte mir, daß es sich bei der Krone um ein aus der Türkei importiertes Fahrzeugdeodorant handelte, das den deutschen ‚Wunderbaum' als Lufterfrischer abgelöst habe.*

Augenscheinlich war meine Annahme von der Erfahrung dominiert, daß das Territorium der Sowjetunion bis in die Details der Alltagskultur hinein von primär ideologischen Zeichen durchsetzt war. Diesen Zeichen entsprach ihre ideologisch gestimmte Deutung, die die Zeichen (auch im Bereich der künstlerischen Artefakte) in systemkonform und nonkonform einzuteilen vermochte. Für den Bereich der Fotografie in der Sowjetunion galt, daß diese im Verlaufe der dreißiger Jahre eine durchgreifende ideologische Vereinnahmung erfuhr. Dem professionellen sozialistischen Fotojournalismus als einzige vorgesehene Existenzform der Fotografie war die Aufgabe zugeteilt, ein die Wirklichkeit ideologisch überhöhendes Bild der Sowjetunion zu entwerfen. Der Prozeß der Befreiung der Fotografie vom ideologischen Imperativ verlief in nur sehr langsamen Bahnen. Grundsätzlich hatte die Fotografie in der Sowjetunion bis in die Gegenwart hinein weder einen Marktwert noch wurde ihr überhaupt ein „Kunstcharakter", ein ästhetischer Wert zugesprochen. Die Fotografie war nicht Gegenstand der Kunstmuseen und öffentlichen Sammlungen.

Eine Beschäftigung mit Fotografie jenseits des utilitären Fotojournalismus war in den Amateurfotografen- und Kameraclubs vorgesehen. Seit dem Ende der fünfziger Jahre bildeten diese eine vom Regime unionsweit geförderte Maßnahme, die den Werktätigen die Erfahrung einer ‚Wirklichkeit in ihrer revolutionären Entwicklung' durch das Auge der Kamera ermöglichen sollte. Die Funktionalisierung der Fotografie und ihre Entprofessionalisierung jenseits der politischen repräsentativen Fotojournalistik fiel bereits in die Frühphase der Sowjetunion: „We should bring the

1 My last stay in Moscow in April 1995 began as usual with a taxi journey from the Sheremetyevo 2 airport into the city centre. On the way it struck me that a large number of vehicles had an object on the glove box that I had not seen before: a little golden crown with a wine-red, velvety cushion in its centre. I greatly amused the taxi driver when I asked if it was a statement of political allegiance on the part of the owner of the vehicle, perhaps a Russian monarchist symbol. He explained to me that it was an air-freshener for cars, imported from Turkey, and that it had ousted the German 'Miracle Tree'.

My supposition had quite clearly been heavily influenced by past experience that in the territory of the Soviet Union ideological symbols permeated through to the very last detail of daily life. And these ideological symbols corresponded to their ideologically determined meaning, in turn separating these symbols into those which did and did not conform to the system—with this applying as much in the realm of artistic output as anywhere else. One area, that of photography, was completely taken over for ideological purposes in the Soviet Union in the 1930s. Photography was only allowed to exist in the shape of professional photo-journalism and was required to create an image which elevated reality to a higher ideological plane. The process of freeing photography from its ideological imperative has made extremely slow progress. Underpinning this during the Soviet era and even into the present day has been the fact that photography neither had commercial value nor was even credited with having artistic qualities or aesthetic value. Photography was not for galleries and public collections.

Any photographic activity beyond utilitarian photo-journalism was provided for in the so-called amateur photography clubs and camera clubs. From the late 1950s onwards these were supported throughout the Union, with the intention of making it possible for working people to experience 'the revolutionary development of reality' through the eye of the camera. Photography, other than politically directed photo-journalism, was already being deprofessionalized and reduced to function alone in the early days of the Soviet Union: 'We should bring the boons of photography into the very thick of the masses... Like any progressive individual should have a watch, so he should be able to handle a camera'.[1] Obviously the idea of educating working people in camera clubs is supported ideologically by the notion of progress, and any aesthetic re-evaluation of photography as a medium was impossible simply because of the designation 'amateur', as opposed to the 'mastery' of the professional photographer. With the political thaw, above all in the late 1980s and early 1990s, came a first critical review of the contents of socialist photography on the initiative of social, in Western terms 'leftist', photographers. Their concern was with 'unprettified' everyday life as it really was under socialism and with uncovering social wrongs under the Soviet Regime.[2] Both official and critical, social photography are predisposed towards seeing the photographic image as being able to capture reality: these social photographers were thus countering the ideological 'correction' of reality, dictated for socialist, documentary photography by the regime, with their own correction of the corrected.

2 'I photograph to find out what the world looks like photographed.' (Garry Winogrand)

Where social or politicized images naturally raised questions concerning context of form, and about the conditions governing the medium and its representation, then photography itself, as an aesthetic category, became the subject of discourse. This was a consequence of the potential of the individuals and groups that broke away from the photo clubs in the 1970s and 1980s. As with Western 'author photographers' (such as Klaus Honnef) their goal was to work autonomously, freed from any kind of social function. A loosely connected group was to be found within the so-called Hermitage Group, which was founded in 1986 as a semi-official organisation of official and unofficial artists, art historians, architects, film-makers and photographers. Two members of the Hermitage Group, Alexei Shulgin and Ilya Piganov, subsequently founded the Immediate Photography Group (amongst others its members included Vladislav Efimov, Sergei Leontiev, Boris Mikhailov and Alexander Slyusarev). The creation of this group, as of Yuri Babich's group, The Letter Readers, completed the separation of documentary political and social photography from autonomous art photography. Thus the social and political aspects of photography receded into the background. There was a clear move amongst the members of Immediate Photography towards the themes and subject matter of their immediate surroundings[3] as well as towards innovative experiment with the photographic image and with the conditions of its technical production. The photographers Alexander Slyusarev (Moscow) and Boris Mikhailov (Kharkov) became the most important role models for the younger generation of photographers in Moscow, who then had a decisive influence on the developments leading to the autonomization of photography.

Alexander Slyusarev concentrated his efforts – innovative within the Moscow context – on establishing

boons of photography into the very thick of the masses… Like any progressive individual should have a watch, so he should be able to handle a camera."[1] Offensichtlich ist die Idee der Erziehung der Werktätigen in den Kameraclubs ideologisch vom Fortschrittsgedanken untermauert. Eine ästhetische Revision des Mediums Fotografie blieb allein durch die Etikettierung des ‚Amateurhaften', das der ‚Meisterschaft' der professionellen Fotografen gegenübersteht, ausgeschlossen. Eine erste kritische Reflexion der Inhalte der sozialistischen Fotografie unternahmen im Tauwetter, vor allem aber in den späten siebziger und frühen achtziger Jahren die Vertreter einer sozialen, im westlichen Sinne ‚linken' Fotografie. Sie widmeten sich dem ‚ungeschönten' Alltag im real existierenden Sozialismus und der Entlarvung sozialer Mißstände unter dem Sowjetregime.[2] Wie die offizielle Fotografie ist auch die kritische soziale Fotografie von der Auffassung beherrscht, daß das fotografische Bild in der Lage ist, die Wirklichkeit zu erfassen: Der ideologisch gestimmten ‚Korrektur' der Wirklichkeit nach den Bedürfnissen des Regimes in der sozialistischen dokumentarischen Fotografie stellten sie eine Korrektur des Korrigierten gegenüber.

2 *„I photograph to find out what the world looks like photographed." (Garry Winogrand)*

Der Diskurs der Fotografie als ästhetischer Kategorie, in dem sich auch für ein soziales oder politisiertes Image im gattungsmäßigen Kontext die Frage nach den Bedingungen des Mediums und seiner Repräsentation selbst stellt, ging aus dem Potential von Einzelpersonen und Gruppen von Fotografen hervor, die sich aus den Vereinigungen der Fotoclubs in den siebziger und achtziger Jahren abspalteten. Im Sinne der westlichen „Autorenfotografie" (Klaus Honnef) strebten diese nach einer von jeder gesellschaftlichen Aufgabe befreiten, autonomen Arbeit. Ein loser Zusammenschluß dieser Fotografen fand sich innerhalb der ‚Ermitage-Vereinigung', die 1986 als halboffizielle Organisation von offiziellen und inoffiziellen Künstlern, Kunsthistorikern, Architekten, Filmemachern und Fotografen gegründet wurde. Zwei Mitglieder der Ermitage-Gruppe, Alexei Shulgin und Ilya Piganov, gründeten in der Folge die Gruppe der „Unmittelbaren Fotografie" (Mitglieder: Vladislav Efimov, Sergei Leontiev, Boris Mikhailov, Alexander Slyusarev u. a.). Mit der Entstehung dieser Gruppe wie auch der Gruppe der ‚Briefleser' durch Yuri Babich hatte sich ein Schritt vollzogen, der die dokumentarische politische und soziale Fotografie endgültig von der sich autonomisierenden künstlerischen Fotografie trennte. Die sozialen und politischen Aspekte der Fotografie gerieten in der Folge in den Hintergrund. Im Falle der Mitglieder der ‚Unmittelbaren Fotografie' läßt sich eine Zuwendung zu den Themen und Gegenständen der unmittelbar umgebenden Welt[3] wie zu dem Versuch der Innovation des fotografischen Bildes und seiner technischen Entstehungsbedingungen beobachten. Die Fotografen Alexander Slyusarev (Moskau) und Boris Mikhailov (Kharkov) wurden zu den wichtigsten Vorbildern der jungen Fotografengeneration in Moskau, die die Entwicklungsprozesse der Autonomisierung der Fotografie entscheidend beeinflußten.

Alexander Slyusarev verlegte seine im Moskauer Kontext innovativen Bestrebungen auf die Hervorbringung eines subjektiven fotografischen Standpunkts, der der offiziellen Version von Fotografie als Übermittlerin einer objektiv erfaßbaren Wirklichkeit diametral entgegensteht. Jedes Objekt kann Gegenstand der subjektiven Fotografie Slyusarevs sein, die sich immer der Thematisierung des Verhältnisses von Fotograf und Objekt widmet. Die kritische Distanz Boris Mikhailovs zur Rolle des fotografischen Mediums für die Vergegenwärtigung der Wirklichkeit vollzieht sich in vielfältiger Form. Dabei bedient er sich der Methoden des ‚Moskauer Konzeptualismus', indem er fiktive ‚Personagen' erfindet, die vorgeblich Werke schaffen, die nicht von Mikhailov selbst stammen wie er auch seinen teilweise auf archiviertem amateurfotografischem Material basierenden narrativen Werken fiktive Erinnerungen und Ereignisse unterlegt. Gleichzeitig bearbeitet Mikhailov die Oberfläche des Abzugs oder Negativs durch Übermalungen, wie dies auch die jüngeren Vertreter der Moskauer Fotografie wie Katya Golitsyna in ihren Arbeiten anwenden. Die verwendete Farbe in den Kolorierungen und Übermalungen läßt sich als Designat für die ironische Distanz, die Mikhailov zum ‚Wahrheitsgehalt' der Fotografie einnimmt, einordnen.

Im wesentlichen verlegten sich die Entwicklungsprozesse innerhalb der Moskauer künstlerischen Fotografie auf bildimmanente Innovationsbestrebungen des fotografischen Bildes einerseits (Alexei Goga, Sergei Leontiev, Tatyana Liberman, Igor Moukhin u. a.) und ‚externe' Kontextualisierungsstrategien des Bildes andererseits (Vladislav Efimov, Vladimir Kupriyanov, Ilya Piganov, Alexei Shulgin u. a.). Die Fotografieszene bildet dabei bis in die späten achtziger Jahre hinein einen im Verhältnis zur Kunstszene relativ hermetischen Kreis wie auch das fotografische Image in den Werken der Bildenden Kunst relativ wenig direkte Verwendung findet. (Ausnahmen wären etwa die fotografischen ‚Faktographien' der Gruppe „Kollektive Aktionen" um Andrei Monastyrsky, die Fotografien der Aktionskünstler Rimma und Valeri Gerlovin oder die Arbeiten Francesco Infantes). In gewissem Sinne setzte sich die von der Kulturpolitik der Sowjetunion verfolgte Trennung in die Gattungen von Malerei als Kunst und Fotografie als Nicht-Kunst in diesem Sinne bis in die jüngste Vergangenheit hinein fort.

Die Fotoserie Leontievs ‚Versuche in harter Fotografie' zeigt unter Zuhilfenahme von Blitzlicht entstandene Porträts nächtlicher Flaneure auf Moskaus Arbat. Die Porträts werden in der Reihenfolge ihrer

a subjective, photographic standpoint diametrically opposed to the official version of photography as the purveyor of objectively graspable reality. Anything whatsoever can be the object of Slyusarev's subjective photography, which is above all concerned with the thematization of the relationship between the photographer and his subject matter. This critical distance towards the role of photography as a medium for recreating reality is set up by Boris Mikhailov in a whole variety of ways. He draws on the methods of the Moscow Conceptualists, creating fictive 'personas' who supposedly produce his works. Similarly, he attributes fictive memories and events to certain of his narrative works which are based in part on archive material by amateur photographers. At the same time Mikhailov overpaints the surface of the prints or negatives, as do younger Moscow photographers such as Katya Golitsyna. The paint used in the colorations and overpainting can be taken to stand for the ironic distance with which Mikhailov views the 'truth content' of photography.

On the one hand developments in Moscow art photography largely took the form of a striving towards internal innovation within the photographic image itself (the work of Alexei Goga, Sergei Leontiev, Tatyana Liberman, Igor Moukhin and others). On the other hand there were also those photographers interested in 'external' strategies to contextualize the image (Vladislav Efimov, Vladimir Kupriyanov, Ilya Piganov, Alexei Shulgin and others). Right up until the late 1980s the photographers formed a relatively hermetic circle as opposed to the rest of the art scene, just as the photographic image appears relatively rarely as a component in the visual arts. (Exceptions would be the 'factographs' made by the Collective Action Group led by Andrei Monastyrsky, the photographs by the action-artists Rimma and Valery Gerlovin, or the works by Francesco Infante.) To a certain extent the split created by the Soviet cultural authorities between painting as art and photography as non-art has lasted until very recently.

Sergei Leontiev's series of photographs 'Study in Hard Photography' shows flash-assisted portraits of night-time strollers on Moscow's Arbat. The portraits are numbered in sequence as they were taken. They are concerned with the relationship between the portrayer and the portrayed that results from the technical parameters of the series as dictated by the photographer, as well as from the element of chance in the night-time encounters. The interpretations which Leontiev wished to elicit form his series depend both on the emotional involvement of the viewer, who finds him or herself confronted with 'immediate' photographic representation, and on the viewer following through the textual relations between the figures portrayed.

Igor Moukhin also explores the theme of photographic representation, working as he does with the signs and symbols of socialist government power. In so far as the cultural symbols of the Soviet Union are in the process of dissolving and disappearing, so too in Moukhin's work they are losing their ideological significance: they have been robbed of their function as ballast for the system and are being stripped of their erstwhile aura and monumentality. The destabilization of these symbols is a result of the perspective Moukhin adopts towards his subject-matter: a perspective that is unstable and utterly opposed to the techniques of monumental composition. Moukhin's interest lies in the part that photography plays in the process of what Jan Assmann calls 'the cultural formation' of symbols. Symbols representing the power of the state (such as monuments and memorials) descend during the course of the historical process of changing power structures into the lower levels of any society's cultural consciousness. Following the loss of their utilitarian and didactic function they are then open to radical re-interpretation. They transmute from positive role model to negative anti-model, seen in the light of changed circumstances. Photography has the capacity to represent one and the same symbol as power-laden, or as an expression of the loss of that same power. In Moukhin's work the subject-matter is trivialized, descending from 'high' to 'low', from greater to lesser significance.

Alexei Goga's work, based on the existence of movement inherent in the photographic subject, may be seen in terms of the crisis in the human perception of time (Virilio). The contradiction between the potential for movement of the (human) photographic subject and the immobility of photographic representation is linked for Goga with the question of the possibility of presenting (and perceiving) the photographic subject as a unified whole. Goga's works concentrate on the many-sidedness of the person portrayed, showing the moving photographic subject by means of photography which is itself governed by time-controlled technical factors.

Goga, Leontiev and Moukhin in their interest in the medialization of photography can be seen as representatives of a current in art photography that is concerned with photographic representation as an intrinsic questioning of the image itself. Vladislav Efimov, Ilya Piganov, Alexei Shulgin and Vladimir Kupriyanov are all pursuing 'external' strategies to contextualize the photographic image – above all in their critical stance regarding the question of authorship and in their attempts to fit the image syntactically into external artistic structures. As a result lines of formal demarcation between art and photography begin to dissolve.

In the late 1980s Alexei Shulgin began working with found negatives from a design archive. In his appropriation of shots of industrial objects, the products of painstaking work by unknown authors, Shulgin addresses the question of the relationship between the photographer and the photographic subject, as does Boris Mikhailov in his 'Personage' photographs. Both cases illustrate the dependence on context of the photo-

Entstehung mit einer Numerierung versehen. Sie widmen sich der Beziehung zwischen dem Porträtierenden und dem Porträtierten, die sich durch die vom Fotografen vorherbestimmten technischen Entstehungsbedingungen der Serie und die Zufälligkeit der nächtlichen Begegnung ergibt. Die von Leontiev intendierte Interpretationserwartung der Serie richtet sich auf die emotionale Einbindung des Betrachters, der sich mit einer ‚unmittelbaren' fotografischen Repräsentation konfrontiert sieht, und auch auf das Nachvollziehen der textuellen Relationen zwischen den Porträtierten.

Dem Thema der fotografischen Repräsentation widmet sich auch Igor Moukhin, der mit den Zeichen und Symbolen der sozialistischen Staatsmacht arbeitet. Insofern die kulturellen Zeichen der Sowjetunion in der Auflösung und im Verschwinden begriffen sind, lösen sie sich in den Arbeiten Moukhins aus ihren ideologischen Bezügen; sie sind ihrer systemstabilisierenden Funktion beraubt und erfahren eine Entauratisierung und Entmonumentalisierung. Die Destabilisierung der Zeichen erfolgt über die Einnahme einer instabilen, der monumentalisierenden Kompositionstechnik entgegenstehenden Perspektive des Produzenten auf das Objekt. Moukhin widmet sich dem Anteil, den die fotografische Repräsentation an dem Prozeß der „kulturellen Formung" (Jan Assmann) der Zeichen innehat. Dabei sinken die die Staatsmacht repräsentierenden Zeichen (Monumente, Denkmäler etc.) im Verlaufe der historischen Prozesse von Machtwechseln in die tieferen Schichten des kulturellen Bewußtseins einer Gesellschaft ab und erfahren im Zuge des Verlustes ihrer utilitären und didaktischen Funktion eine gänzlich neue Interpretation. Sie wandeln sich vom positiven Identifikationsmodell zum (im Verhältnis zum Neuentstandenen) negativen Gegenmodell. Das fotografische Bild ermöglicht, ein und dasselbe Zeichen als Träger der Macht und als Ausdruck des Machtverlustes zu präsentieren. Das Objekt erfährt in den Arbeiten Moukhins eine Trivialisierung von ‚high' zu ‚low', vom hohen zum niedrigen Bedeutungswert.

Alexei Gogas Arbeiten auf der Grundlage der Bewegungshaftigkeit des fotografischen Objekts läßt sich mit der Krise der menschlichen Zeitwahrnehmung (Paul Virilio) in Verbindung bringen. Der Widerspruch zwischen der potentiellen Bewegungshaftigkeit des (menschlichen) fotografischen Objekts und der Statik der fotografischen Repräsentation verknüpft sich für Goga mit der Frage nach der Möglichkeit der Darstellung – und Wahrnehmung – des fotografischen Objekts als Ganzheit. Gogas Arbeiten widmen sich der Allansichtigkeit des Porträtierten, die sich aus der Wiedergabe des bewegten fotografischen Objekts in der fotografischen Repräsentation entwickelt, die ihrerseits zeitabhängigen technischen Faktoren unterworfen ist.

Goga, Leontiev und Moukhin figurieren im Zusammenhang der Medialisierung der Fotografie als Vertreter einer Richtung der künstlerischen Fotografie, die sich mit der fotografischen Repräsentation als bild-

immanenter Fragestellung beschäftigt. Vladislav Efimov, Ilya Piganov, Alexei Shulgin und Vladimir Kupriyanov verfolgen ‚externe' Kontextualisierungsstrategien des fotografischen Bildes, die sich vor allem als kritisches Verhältnis zur Frage nach der Autorenschaft wie auch als Versuch der syntaktischen Einbindung des Bildes in ein äußeres Wirkungsgefüge darstellt. Dabei beginnen sich die gattungsmäßigen Grenzen von Bildender Kunst und Fotografie aufzulösen.

Alexei Shulgin arbeitete am Ende der achtziger Jahre mit gefundenen Negativen aus einem Designarchiv. Die Appropriation der Aufnahmen von Industrieobjekten als Resultat der langwierigen Arbeit unbekannter Autoren im Werk Shulgins geht – ähnlich wie im Falle der ‚Personagen'-Fotografien von Boris Mikhailov – dem Verhältnis von fotografischem Subjekt und Objekt nach und illustriert die Kontextabhängigkeit des fotografischen Bildes, das sich unabhängig von seiner ursprünglichen Intention in einer Wertetransformation aus dem utilitären Zusammenhang der Gebrauchsfotografie in den Kunstkontext überführen läßt. In einem anderen Werkzusammenhang bedient sich Shulgin dem Medium des Fernsehens. Dabei fotografiert er meist ‚ungegenständliche' Bilder unmittelbar vom Fernsehbildschirm ab und isoliert sie somit aus einem Informationsgefüge aus unzähligen Einzelbildern, die das träge menschliche Auge zu unterscheiden nicht in der Lage ist. Das so gewonnene fotografische Bild präsentiert Shulgin in Fernsehgeräten ähnlichen Rahmungen und Formaten. Das ‚ungegenständliche' fotografische Fernsehbild erfährt eine Auratisierung und gleichzeitig eine Sinnentleerung, zu der es nur durch die statische fotografische Repräsentation gelangen kann. Die „Rotating Old Photographs" Shulgins schließlich zeigen gerahmte, gefundene alte Fotografien, die mit einem Elektromotor und einem Bewegungsmelder ausgestattet sind, so daß sie bei der Annäherung durch den Betrachter in Schwingungen versetzt werden. Die verhinderte visuelle Fixierung des fotografischen Bildes durch den Betrachter illustriert eine Verunsicherung der fotografischen Repräsentation als Mechanismus eines Informationstransfers.

Einem ähnlichen Aspekt geht auch Ilya Piganov in seinen im Collageverfahren zusammengesetzten fotografischen Tableaus nach. Die in maschineller Massenproduktion vervielfältigten Fotografien werden zu Ornamenten zusammengesetzt, die das fotografische Bild aus seiner Inhaltlichkeit lösen und dekorativen Gesichtspunkten unterwerfen. Ausgehend von der Einschätzung einer fundamentalen Krise des Künstlers im zeitgenössischen Rußland führt Piganov eine Erschütterung der fotografischen Repräsentation in bezug auf die Gesetzmäßigkeiten des Kommunikationsmodells herbei, indem sie ‚nichts' repräsentiert, sondern als von inhaltlichen Bestimmungen losgelöste visuelle Information funktioniert: „The attempt to disorient the thoughtful viewer by the apparent lack of artistic intention is achieved through the neutralization of the

graphic image which, removed from its original function, can then be transposed from the utilitarian parameters of functional photography into the realms of art. In another area of his work Shulgin makes use of television, photographing largely 'abstract' images directly from the screen and thereby isolating them from a web of information composed of countless individual pictures, which the slow-moving human eye is unable to discern individually. Shulgin then shows the resulting pictures in frames and in a format resembling the television sets from whence they came. Thus 'abstract' photographed television pictures both acquire their own aura and lose actual meaning, in a way that is only possible as a result of their being shown in a static form. And lastly there are Shulgin's 'Rotating Old Photographs': old, found photographs that have been framed and fitted with an electric motor and a movement sensor, so that they are set in motion whenever a viewer approaches. The viewer's preventing the picture from remaining immobile demonstrates the undermining of photographic representation as a mechanism for information transfer.

A similar theme is to be found in the photographic tableaus of Ilya Piganov, which he constructs as collages. Mechanically mass-reproduced photographs are combined for their decorative qualities, with the result that purely decorative considerations supplant content. Responding to what he sees as a fundamental crisis for artists in contemporary Russia, Piganov seriously questions the laws of communication as they apply to photographic representation, by showing it as representing 'nothing', functioning on a purely visual level devoid of all content:

> The attempt to disorient the thoughtful viewer by the apparent lack of artistic intention is achieved through the neutralisation of the personal qualities of each individual 'beautiful' work by uniting them into a single series merely on the basis of common tone and format.[4]

An important step in the destruction of formal boundaries between art and photography was the move away from the two-dimensional, with photography conquering space by virtue of the spatial, staged manner of its presentation and by combining photographic images with other elements to create installations. This step only properly occurred in Moscow in the late 1980s and early 1990s. Vladimir Kupriyanov played a decisive part in these developments. Kupriyanov's early work focuses on the deconstruction of the formulas behind the political rituals of mass culture, handed down from previous generations, which he transposes into new contexts and profanes by means of citation and repetition. He also directs his attention to the objects and events of daily life, the incidental and insignificant, raising them to a higher level in his compositions. The use of transparent film (duratrans) for the photographic image and the layering of two or more of these inside one wooden frame both clouds the question of photographic representation and increases the aura surrounding it. At the same time space advances more or less of its own accord into the photograph in so far as the distance between the duratrans is the necessary prerequisite for the intended clouding of the photographic image. The framed duratrans display the characteristics of an object which requires representation in actual space, needing light to be shone through it. Other than here, duratrans are used in the wholly spatial, monumental installations by Kupriyanov, which are to a certain extent a response to architectural form. As ideological symbols disappear with the dissolution of the Soviet Union, there are ever fewer references in his work to the formulas of socialism in all their pathos:

> In the choice of motifs, in the mode of expression of the pictures and in their atmosphere, particularly the last two groups of works in the nineties are characterised by a confrontation with German Romanticism. Everything about the photographic document that is trivial, everyday, or due to chance is transformed by Kupriyanov in the course of his work into a work of art which ranges through the dramatic and tragic, from bathos to the sublime.[5]

In Vladislav Efimov's works the third dimension makes its entry via objects which he creates purely for the purposes of photographic representation: mechanical apparatus, amorphous sculptural objects and arrangements of diverse objects in small boxes. Once the objects have been photographed they are destroyed, because they only serve Efimov as the formal means to realise his surreal compositions and have no other functional significance than this. In his search for a suitable photographic form Efimov employs the old method of stereo-photography. He also shows slides in stereo speakers lit from the inside, which are installed either hanging or lying on their sides. In Efimov's work the third dimension comes into being on the one hand through the simulation of depth in the speakers which are themselves a physically inseparable element of the photographic composition, and on the other hand through the boxes themselves, which take on sculptural characters by virtue of their presentation in space, either hanging or lying.

3 Efimov, Kupriyanov, Piganov, Shulgin and others belong to the generation of Moscow photographers that has advanced the autonomy of the medium. They demonstrated the possibilities of using the medium of photography, crossing between different forms to create 'art using photographic means'.[6] With the blurring of

personal qualities of each individual's ‚beautiful' work by uniting them into a single series merely on the basis of common tone and format."[4]

Einen bedeutenden Schritt in der Sprengung der gattungsmäßigen Grenzen von Kunst und Fotografie bildet der Ausbruch aus der zweiten Dimension, die Eroberung des Raums durch die Fotografie in Form von Inszenierungen des fotografischen Bildes im Raum und der Zusammenfügung von fotografischen Bildern und anderen Elementen zu Installationen. Im wesentlichen vollzog sich dieser Schritt in Moskau erst am Ende der achtziger und zu Beginn der neunziger Jahre. Einen bedeutenden Anteil an dieser Entwicklung hatte Vladimir Kupriyanov. Sein frühes Werk ist an der Dekonstruktion der überkommenen Formeln der politischen Rituale der Massenkultur orientiert, die er durch die Versetzung in neue kontextuelle Bezüge, durch Zitieren und Wiederholen profanisiert. Gleichermaßen richtet er seinen Blick auf die Gegenstände und Erscheinungen des Alltagslebens, auf Nebensächliches und Belangloses, dem er in seinen Kompositionen Erhabenheit verleiht. Die Verwendung von Transparentfilm für das fotografische Bild und die Präsentation zweier oder mehrerer übereinanderliegender Schichten von Transparentfilmen in einem Holzrahmen führen zu einem Undeutlichmachen der fotografischen Repräsentation, die ihrer auratischen Überhöhung dient. Gleichzeitig führt sich in dieser Form der Präsentation der Raum gewissermaßen selbst in die Fotografie ein, insofern der Zwischenraum zwischen den beiden Schichten der Transparentfilme unabdingbare Voraussetzung für die intendierte Verunklärung des Bildes ist. Die gerahmten Transparentfilme weisen einen Objektcharakter auf, der nach einer Präsentation im Raum verlangt, die ein Durchscheinen des Lichts durch die Transparentfilmobjekte fördert. Darüberhinaus findet der Transparentfilm in den raumgreifenden, monumentalen Installationen Kupriyanovs Verwendung, die in Teilen von einer Auseinandersetzung mit architektonischen Formen geprägt sind. Der Bezug zu den Pathosformeln des Sozialismus tritt in seinem Werk mit dem Verschwinden der ideologischen Zeichen nach der Auflösung der UdSSR zunehmend zurück: „In der Wahl der Motive, der Bilddramaturgie und in den Stimmungsqualitäten sind gerade die letzten der beiden Werkgruppen der neunziger Jahre von einer Auseinandersetzung mit der deutschen Romantik geprägt. Das Zufällige, Alltägliche und Triviale des photographischen Dokuments wird im Prozeß der Bearbeitung von Kupriyanov transformiert (...) in ein Kunstwerk mit dramatischen, tragischen pathetischen und erhabenen Ausdrucksqualitäten."[5]

In den Arbeiten Vladislav Efimovs gelangt die dritte Dimension über Objekte in das Werk, die er eigens für die fotografische Repräsentation schafft: mechanische Gerätschaften, amorphe skulpturale Objekte und Arrangements verschiedener Gegenstände in kleinen Kästen. Nach der fotografischen Aufnahme der Objekte werden diese zerstört, insofern sie Efimov lediglich als formale Mittel zur Hervorbringung seiner surrealen Kompositionen dienen und keinen anderen als diesen funktionalen Bedeutungswert haben. Auf der Suche nach einer adäquaten Präsentationsform für die fotografische Repräsentation arbeitet Efimov mit den historischen Methoden der Stereofotografie und einer Präsentationsform des Diapositivs in von innen beleuchteten Stereoboxen. Die fotografischen Objekte der Stereoboxen werden im Raum hängend oder liegend installiert. Die dritte Dimension erscheint in den Arbeiten Efimovs einerseits in der Vortäuschung eines Tiefeneffekts innerhalb der Boxen, die gleichzeitig räumlicher, untrennbarer Bestandteil der fotografischen Komposition sind; andererseits nehmen die Boxen selbst durch ihre hängende oder liegende Präsentation im Raum skulpturalen Charakter an.

3 *Efimov, Kupriyanov, Piganov, Shulgin und andere gehören zu der Generation Moskauer Fotografen, die die Autonomisierung des Mediums weiter vorangetrieben haben. Sie zeigten die Möglichkeiten der Benutzung des Mediums Fotografie in gattungsübergreifenden Zusammenhängen für die Entstehung einer „Kunst mit fotografischen Mitteln."*[6] *Im Rahmen der Verwischung der Grenzen zwischen der Selbstdefinition des Produzenten als „Fotograf" oder „Künstler", die von den traditionellen Fotografen nicht immer ohne Mißtrauen beäugt wird, ist eine junge Moskauer Künstlergeneration in der Lage, das Medium der Fotografie als eine Möglichkeit der künstlerischen Ausdrucksform zu verwenden. Der Medienseparatismus beginnt sich aufzulösen, wie etwa Tatyana Dobers und Alexander Alexeevs Installation „Das Licht eines Fernen Sterns", die unter Verwendung von Film, Video und übermalter Fotografie entstand, zeigen kann. Mit dem Zugriff auf Labortechniken westlichen Standards und die Eröffnung der Möglichkeiten einer höher entwickelten Farbprint-Technik verliert das abzubildende fotografische Image zunehmend an Raum. Das inszenierte Bild als Ausdruck einer konstruierten Wirklichkeit in Anlehnung an die inszenierten Bildwelten der Fernsehshow, von Werbung und Video-Clip gewinnt in Moskau an Bedeutung.*

In ihren Fotoserien separiert Maria Serebriakova Gegenstände, die etwas Fremdes, Seltsames innerhalb der Wirklichkeit der gefundenen fotografischen Bilder aus den Printmedien veranschaulichen. Die Separation erfolgt durch Übermalungen von Details des fotografischen Bildes, durch das Hinzufügen von ungewöhnlichen und scheinbar sinnlosen Details. Dabei öffnet sich innerhalb der Oberfläche des fotografischen Bildes ein separater Raum, der auf diesen Gegenstand bezogen ist und die Gesetzmäßigkeiten des fotografischen Bildes in seiner Gesamtheit unterminiert. Das ‚Eigenleben' der Bilder, die keine „a priori Mythologien" (Margarita Tupitsyn) aufweisen, transponiert sich in

self-imposed designations such as 'artist' or 'photographer' – a situation viewed by traditional photographers more often than not with a degree of suspicion – a whole generation of young Moscow artists is now in a position simply to draw on photography as a means of artistic expression. The divisions between various media are beginning to disappear, as can be seen in the installation *The Light of a Faraway Star* by Tatyana Dober and Alexander Alexeev, which was created using film, video and overpainted photographs. With access to laboratory techniques on a par with those in the West, and with the possibility of more advanced colour printing techniques, the representational photographic image is increasingly losing ground, whereas the staged picture as an expression of constructed reality along the lines of the constructed visual worlds of the television show, advertising and videoclips is rapidly gaining ground.

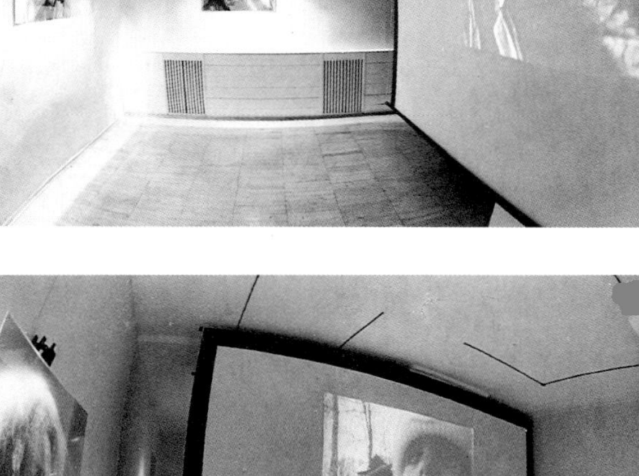

TATYANA DOBER, ALEXANDER ALEXEEV, Installation: *The Light of a Faraway Star*, Shcola Gallery, Moscow *(Installation „Das Licht eines fernen Sterns", Galerie Shcola, Moskau)*, 1994

In her photo series Maria Serebriakova isolates objects which illustrate the odd and strange within the context of the reality of found photographic images from various print media. She does this by overpainting certain details on the photograph and by adding other unusual, apparently meaningless, details. Thus a separate region is opened up on the surface of the photographic image which relates to the object in question at the same time as undermining the underlying principles of a photographic image. The pictures thereby acquire a 'life of their own', which is not dependent on 'a priori mythologies' (Margarita Tupitsyn) and which enters deeper into the space created in Serebriakova's installations, where the photographic 'picture in its own right' becomes part of inter-relationships quite at odds with its own nature and being.

Photographic means can be used, as in the case of the orbit projects by Vadim Fishkin, to illustrate a situation in which the photographic image is being used to illustrate hypotheses which have little to do any more with the immediacy of photographic representation. Photography under these circumstances is no longer analogous to reality but becomes a consciously constructed metaphor for schematic models of the processes of being and existence on this earth. An orbit, the path traced by a satellite or a rocket round a planet, serves Fishkin as a model for the phenomenon of being: the prerequisite for accepting the notion of an orbit being the existence of a centre. The path of the orbit itself describes a route of approach to the centre. The model of an orbit relates to the creative and existential conditions of the artist as creator, which Fishkin in elemental acts of constructive creativity explores as a model for the universe itself. Meanwhile the use of simulative photographic correspondence reduces the utopian dimension of the universe to the banal.[7]

In his photographic works Anatoli Shuravlev investigates the phenomenon of historical knowledge and its dependence on forms of representation, the 'politics of representation'.[8] Shuravlev's 'Egypt Series' is based on engravings of historic excavation sites in Egypt made by French artists at the end of the eighteenth century. Using photographic processes Shuravlev eradicates all traces of manual production, thereby creating 'impossible' photographic images: photographic impressions of places from a time when photography did not yet exist. The 'indexical link' (André Bazin) of photography to its object has been destroyed, with photography now introducing an area of theoretical discourse into the pictures.[9] Shuravlev's series of portraits from antiquity was based on illustrations (from books) of ancient sculptures from which he made slides. By then producing a colour print of two slides lying on top of each other Shuravlev generated a new 'fictive' portrait. The new portraits reveal three levels of representation: the sculptural representation of antiquity, the published photographic illustration and the synthetic portrait itself. For Shuravlev history takes the form of layers of time *and* of representation; historical knowledge is dependent on the way that history conveys itself.

Closely connected with the loss of the Soviet 'collective body' as an abstract construct disseminating the notion of collective identity, which was of lasting significance in the ontological reflection of Moscow Conceptualism, the thematization of the human body as a physical entity has become one of the most important points of reference for artists in Moscow today, and photography plays a major part in this. In the post-modern, neo-classical photographic work by Inna and Dmitri Topolsky the body is seen as an ideal form, potentially able to express classical notions of beauty.

In contrast, in the installation *The Scar,* based as it is on photography, the AES-Group presents the damaged human body. The work was created from a shot of a patient in a Moscow hospital with scars from stitches down the centre of his body from the breastbone to the abdomen. AES multiplied this partial view of a human

den Raum von Serebriakovas Installationen, in denen das fotografische ‚Bild an sich' Teil ihm selbst wesensfremder Relationen wird.

Der Einsatz von fotografischen Mitteln kann, wie im Fall der Orbit-Projekte Vadim Fishkins, Voraussetzungen unterworfen sein, die das fotografische Bild zur Illustration modellhafter Vorstellungen verwenden, die nicht mehr an die Unmittelbarkeit fotografischer Repräsentation appellieren. Die Fotografie verhält sich dabei nicht mehr analog zur Wirklichkeit, sondern erscheint als konstruierte Metapher für schematische Vorstellungen von globalen seinsmäßigen Prozessen. Der Orbit, die Umlaufbahn eines Satelliten oder einer Rakete um einen Planeten, dient Fishkin als Vorstellungsmodell von Phänomen des Seins: Voraussetzung für die Annahme eines Orbits ist die Existenz eines Zentrums. Die Umlaufbahnen beschreiben Wege der Annäherung an das Zentrum. Das Modell des Orbit steht im Zusammenhang mit den Seins- und Schaffensbedingungen des Künstlers als Demiurgen, denen Fishkin in der Vollziehung elementarer, konstruktiver Akte als Modell für das Universum nachgeht. Die utopische Dimension des Universums erfährt in der simulativen fotografischen Entsprechung dabei eine Banalisierung.[7]

Dem Phänomen des historischen Wissens und seiner Abhängigkeit von den Formen der Repräsentation, der ‚Politik der Repräsentation', geht Anatoli Shuravlev in seinen Fotoarbeiten nach.[8] *Die ‚Ägypten-Serie' Shuravlevs basiert auf Gravuren historischer Ausgrabungsorte in Ägypten, die französische Künstler am Ende des 18. Jahrhunderts anfertigten. In einem fototechnischen Verfahren tilgt Shuravlev die Spuren der manuellen Reproduktionsgraphik und schafft auf diese Weise ‚unmögliche' fotografische Images, fotografische Eindrücke von Orten aus jener Zeit, als die Fotografie noch nicht existierte. Der „indexale Bezug" (André Bazin) der Fotografie zu seinem Objekt ist gestört, die Fotografie transportiert nunmehr einen theoretischen Diskurs in Bildern.*[9] *Die antike Porträtserie Shuravlevs entstand auf der Grundlage von Buchreproduktionen antiker Skulpturen, die Shuravlev auf Diapositiven abfotografierte. Durch den Farbabzug zweier einander überlagernder Diapositive generiert Shuravlev ein neues ‚fiktives' Porträt. In den neugeschaffenen Porträts Shuravlevs lassen sich drei Ebenen der Repräsentation konstatieren: die antike skulpturale, die fotografische Buchreproduktion der Skulptur und schließlich die Repräsentation des synthetischen Porträts. Geschichte erscheint Shuravlev als einander überlagernder Zeit-* und *Repräsentationsschichten; das historische Wissen steht in Abhängigkeit von der Art und Weise, wie sich uns Geschichte vermittelt.*

Im Zusammenhang mit dem Verlust des sowjetischen ‚kollektiven Körpers' als ein kollektive Identität propagierendes, immaterielles Konstrukt, das in den ontologischen Reflexionen des Moskauer Konzeptualismus von nachhaltiger Wichtigkeit war, gerät die Thematisierung des menschlichen Körpers in seinen physischen Erscheinungsformen zu einem der bedeutendsten Bezugspunkte der aktuellen Moskauer Kunstszene. Dabei spielt die Verwendung fotografischer Mittel eine wesentliche Rolle. In den von einem postmodernen Neoklassizismus beherrschten Fotoarbeiten von Inna und Dmitri Topolsky erscheint der Körper im Sinne einer idealen Form als Ausdrucksmöglichkeit eines klassischen Schönheitsideals.

Den verletzten menschlichen Körper führt die Gruppe AES in der auf Fotografie basierenden Installation „Die Narbe" (The Scar) vor. Die Arbeit entstand durch die Aufnahme eines Patienten in einem Moskauer Krankenhaus, der in seiner Körpermitte vom Brustbein bis zum Unterbauch eine vernarbte Naht aufwies. AES multiplizieren die Teilansicht des menschlichen Körpers mit der Naht zu einer Endlosnarbe und präsentieren diese als Oberfläche einer säulen- oder röhrenartigen Struktur im Raum. Es ist nicht das Anliegen von AES, im Sinne der amerikanischen Erscheinung der ‚Victim art' das Leiden eines Schwerkranken vorzuführen. Der versehrte menschliche Körper dient ihnen als Metapher für den „sozialen Körper des neuen Rußland",[10] dem sie eine visuelle Entsprechung geben. AES thematisieren den Körper jenseits geschlechtsspezifischer oder ethnischer Fragen. Die Narbe ist als Folge einer durchlebten Verletzung eine Metapher für das erlittene Trauma des Individuums unter dem Sowjetregime und während des Zerfalls der UdSSR. Die körperbezogenen Projekte von AES beziehen sich auf eine ‚sensual provocation' des Rezipienten, dessen unmittelbare emotionale Involviertheit bedeutsamer sein soll als jede Interpretationsleistung. In Abgrenzung zu den Erscheinungen des Moskauer Konzeptualismus konstatieren AES eine Verlagerung des Diskurses vom Intellekt zum Körper wie auch das Ding selbst bedeutsamer sei als der Kommentar über das Ding.[11] In diesem Zusammenhang weiten AES ihre Installationen auf die Verwendung haptisch operierender Reize aus, wie etwa die Konstruktion von Korridoren mit heißer und kalter Luft, durch die der Betrachter schreitet, oder das Errichten einer schachbrettartigen Bodenstruktur, in der jedes zweite Feld mit einer Metallspitze gespickt ist, so daß der Betrachter beim Durchschreiten des Feldes seine Aufmerksamkeit auf seine eigenen Schritte zu lenken genötigt ist.

In einer der Gruppe AES verwandter Weise grenzen sich auch Aktionskünstler wie Oleg Kulik oder die Mitglieder der Gruppe ‚Nezesüdik' (Alexander Brener, Anatoli Osmolovsky u. a.) von der reflexiven Haltung des Moskauer Konzeptualismus ab. Kulik konstatiert ein Ende der Reflexion in der Moskauer Kunst und benutzt den eigenen Körper als Folie für die Darstellung des Verlustes von Kultiviertheit. Er stellt seine Verletzung, Beschmutzung und Erniedrigung zur Schau. Im Zusammenhang mit der Eröffnung der Ausstellung „Zeichen und Wunder" im Kunsthaus Zürich agierte Kulik in seiner Performance ‚Reservoir Dog' unbekleidet und angekettet auf allen Vieren vor dem

body with a line of stitches to form an endless scar that is presented as the outer surface of a pillar or tube-like structure standing in the exhibition space. AES is not aiming to demonstrate the suffering of the seriously ill, along the lines of so-called 'victim art' as in the United

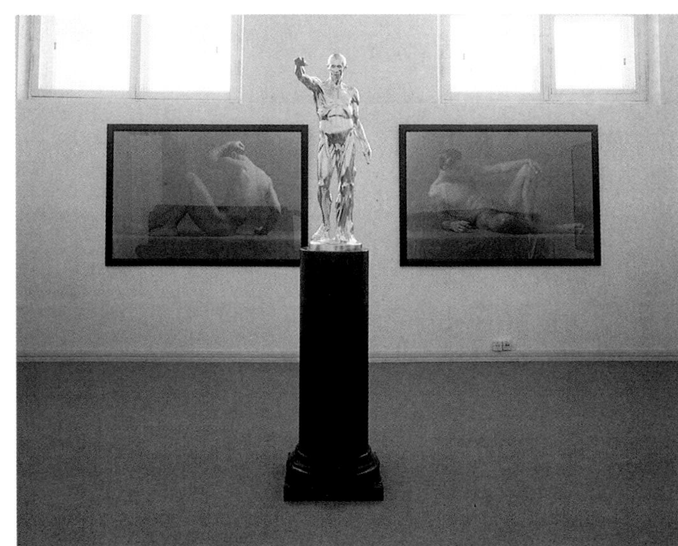

INNA TOPOLSKY, DMITRI TOPOLSKY, view of the exhibition, Aidan Gallery, Moscow *(Blick in die Ausstellung, Aidan-Galerie, Moskau),* March-April 1993

States. For them the damaged human body serves as the visual expression of a metaphor for the 'social body of the new Russia'.[10] AES thematizes the body without reference to questions of gender or ethnicity. The scar as the result of wounds is a metaphor for the traumas suffered by individuals under the Soviet regime as well as during the period of its dissolution. The body-based projects by AES are directed towards the 'sensual provocation' of the recipient, whose direct emotional involvement is more valuable than any intellectual feats of interpretation. Standing apart from the rest of the Moscow Conceptualists, the work of AES constitutes a shift in the discourse from the intellect to the body, with the thing itself seen as more important than any commentary on it.[11] With this in mind AES widens the scope of its installations to include tactile provocation by, for example, constructing corridors with hot and cold air for the viewer to pass through or by turning the floor into a kind of chessboard where every second square has a metal spike so that viewers are obliged to watch their step as they cross the area.

As with the AES-Group, action artists such as Oleg Kulik or the members of the Nezesüdik Group (Alexander Brener, Anatoli Osmolovsky and others) do not share the reflective stance of the Moscow Conceptualists. Kulik represents the end of reflection in Moscow art and uses his own body as a foil to present the loss of culture. He displays his own injuries, dirt and humiliation. At the opening of the exhibition 'Zeichen und Wunder' in the Kunsthaus in Zurich, Kulik put on his performance *Reservoir Dog*: naked and unchained and on all fours in front of the main entrance of the gallery, he barked like a dog and prevented visitors from going into the building for the opening by jumping up and trying to bite them, until he was taken into custody by the Swiss police. Yekaterina Dyogot has shown that the strategies of artists like Kulik were a consequence of their conviction that in Russia there was no room for an art-market along Western lines. In her view this accounts for a switch of interest in the Moscow art scene to the media market. According to its own estimation the market value of this scene could be measured against its 'market share', that is to say the extent to which these artists were reported in the media, hence the spectacular nature of their actions.[12] Taking up Dyogot's analysis it could be said that the photographic record of the action thereby plays an important part in the marketing strategy of the artist, although in the form of a press photograph in newspapers and magazines it is beyond his or her control as to its adequacy or media-effectiveness. In the 1960s the problem of the 'transformation' of actions through the photographic image was discussed with reference to the photographic documentation of performances. The discussion concerned questions of form in performance and how they would relate to photography. In Moscow action art in the 1990s the action is a means to achieving a publicised and publicly effective photographic image: an action is only fully realised when it appears as a mass media photographic image in the context of a newspaper article.

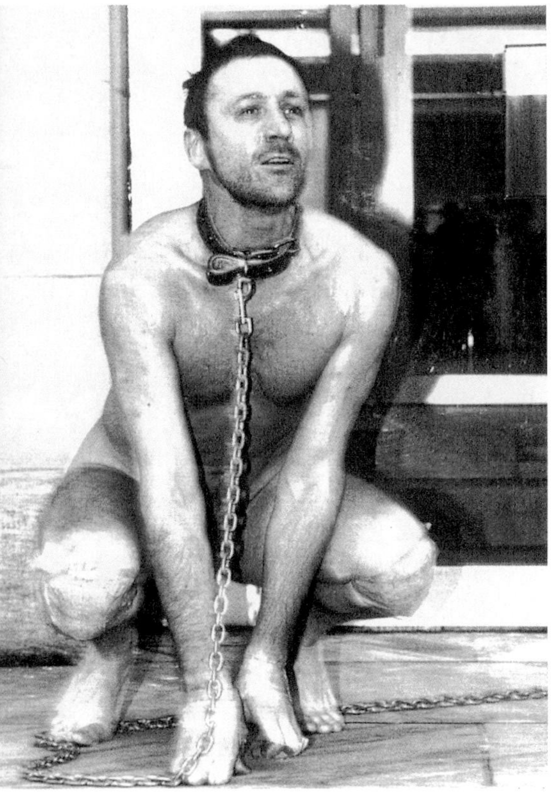

OLEG KULIK, *Reservoir Dog*, performance, Kunsthaus Zürich, 3 March 1995

Staged photographs, in which the artists themselves figure, form another important element in the Moscow art scene today. For Gor Chahal the photographic image would appear to be a foil for toying with his own identity. In his early works Chahal himself appears in everyday situations, generally with a female figure. The outer appearance of the figures, their body language and the evidence of the background seem to

Haupteingang des Ausstellungsortes, stieß dabei hundeartiges Gebell aus und hinderte die Vernissagenbesucher durch Anspringen und Beißversuche am Eintritt in das Gebäude, bis ihn eine Schweizer Polizeieinheit dem Gewahrsam zuführte. Yekaterina Dyogot führte aus, daß die Strategien von Künstlern wie Kulik der Auffassung entsprangen, daß sich in Rußland kein Kunstmarkt nach westlichem Vorbild etablieren konnte. Daher verlagere sich das Interesse eines Teils der Moskauer Kunstszene auf den Medienmarkt. Der Marktwert dieser Szene ließe sich nach eigenen Vorstellungen an ihrem „Marktanteil", d.h. an der Präsenz dieser Künstler in den Medien, messen, was den spektakulären Charakter der Aktionen bedinge.[12] In Anlehnung an die Aufführungen Dyogots ließe sich festhalten, daß das fotografische Bild der Aktion dabei einen entscheidenden Anteil an den Vermarktungsstrategien des Künstlers hat, das sich jedoch ohne seine Kontrolle auf Adäquatheit oder Medienwirksamkeit in Form einer Pressefotografie in den Zeitungen und Magazinen niederschlägt. In den sechziger Jahren ist hinsichtlich der fotografischen Dokumentation von Performances das Problem der ‚Transformation' der Aktion durch das fotografische Bild diskutiert worden. Diese Debatte betraf die Fragen gattungsbildender Aspekte der Performance im Verhältnis zur Fotografie. Im Falle der Moskauer Aktionskunst der neunziger Jahre erscheint die Aktion als Vehikel zur Erreichung eines öffentlichen und öffentlichkeitswirksamen (fotografischen) Bildes: Im massenmedial erzeugten fotografischen Bild im Kontext eines Zeitungsartikels realisiert sich die Aktion.

Die fotografische Selbstinszenierung bildet eine weitere wichtige Tendenz innerhalb der aktuellen Moskauer Kunstszene. Für Gor Chahal scheint das fotografische Image eine Folie für das Spiel mit Identitäten zu sein. In seinen frühen Arbeiten figuriert Chahal selbst in Alltagsszenen (meist gemeinsam mit einer weiblichen Person). Die äußeren Attribute der Figuren, ihre Körpersprache sowie die Angaben des Bildhintergrunds lassen auf die Zeit der vierziger Jahre schließen, wobei sich jedoch kaum Angaben zu einer lokalen Eingrenzung der Örtlichkeit finden lassen. Die Darstellung der Personen impliziert einen Handlungsverlauf, legt den Eindruck einer Sequenz aus einer Folge von Handlungen nahe, wobei diese jedoch in ihrer Vereinzelung nicht rekonstruierbar sind. Beim Vergleich der einzelnen Arbeiten aus dieser Phase, die nicht als Fotoserie angelegt sind, fällt auf, daß sich die Attribute der Personen gleichen. Die Arbeiten Chahals sind auf die Demontage des Narrativen hin angelegt; Chahal übernimmt die Rolle eines Schauspielers in zusammenhanglosen Geschehnissen, die der Stilisierung der Person dienen. In den neueren Arbeiten Chahals ist der Grad der Absurdität der künstlerischen Stilisierung gesteigert: Die Selbstdarstellung in roter Kappe und weißem Hemd vor einem Baumstamm trägt den Titel „Pilz", das fotografische (Selbst-)Bild ist Teil einer konstruierten Realität, deren semantische Dechiffrierung unmöglich ist.

Der Gruppe IV. Vysota dient das Kriegsgeschehen als Folie für ihre Selbstinszenierung: Das Projekt „Front-Freundinnen" zeigt die drei weiblichen Mitglieder der Gruppe in Militäruniformen im Zusammenhang mit Ereignissen, die als Kriegsvorgänge des Zweiten Weltkrieges interpretiert werden können. Das Bild des Krieges erscheint romantisiert; die Arbeiten widmen sich der Darstellung des engen Verhältnisses der drei Akteurinnen, die sich gegenseitig den Sitz der Uniform korrigieren, gemeinsam fröhlich vor der Kamera posieren oder mit dem Lesen eines Schriftstückes beschäftigt sind. Die einzelnen fotografischen Sequenzen der Serie „Front-Freundinnen" sind auf dreieckige Seidenwimpel gedruckt, die, von der Decke abgehängt, im Raum installiert werden. IV. Vysota appropriiert die totalitäre Kriegsberichterstattung, die das Verhältnis der Frontkämpfer als ‚eingeschworene Gemeinschaft' ideologisch überhöht, und unterzieht diese einer vollkommenen Ästhetisierung. Die Ästhetisierung des ‚Lyrischen' im Totalitären bildet die Zielsetzung der Arbeiten von IV. Vysota; die kitschige Inszenierung strebt dabei einer Sublimierung des Totalitären entgegen.

Die Arbeiten der Gruppe Fenso reflektieren die konstruierten Bilderwelten von Fernsehen, Werbung und Computerspiel. In dem Projekt „Fenso Lights" haben sich die Mitglieder der Gruppe unmittelbar in die Ebene des Computerspiels versetzt und erscheinen als ‚Science-Fiction-Ritter' in Kampfhandlungen in einer Waldlandschaft. Die fotografischen Darstellungen verhalten sich dabei analog zur Wirklichkeit, denn sie entstanden in einer realen Waldlandschaft und mit Hilfe von hausgemachten Rüstungen aus Alufolie. Wenn das Reale in Agonie verfallen ist (Jean Baudrillard) und sich die Wirklichkeit nurmehr daran messen läßt, inwieweit sie der Medienwelt entspricht, so simuliert Fenso die digitale und mediale Bilderwelt mit analogen Mitteln und treibt ein psychedelisches Spiel infantilen Größenwahns, das sie befähigt, sich direkt in den Raum der Maschine (des Computers) zu versetzen und von einer Bilderwelt zur anderen zu springen. Die Simulation des digitalen Bildes im Zusammenhang mit manuellen Fertigkeiten ist eine Erscheinung, die sich auch auf nicht-fotografische Objekte innerhalb der Moskauer Kunstszene überträgt. Die Porträtserie eines Kreises der Moskauer Kulturschaffenden von Yuri Albert beruht auf einer digitalen Auflösung des Bildes, setzt diese Auflösung jedoch in die als Kinderspiel konstruierte Mosaik-Technik des sog. Ministeck-Spiels um. Die Welt als psychedelischer Kinderspielplatz führt Fenso von der mystifizierten Ebene des Computer-Spiels auf die Ebene des coolen Reklamebildes: „Fenso & JVC". Der Name Fenso als Markenzeichen erscheint auf einem Kopfhörer, der unmittelbar mit einer einen ‚special-drink' enthaltenden Flasche mit dem Etikett von JVC (als Label eines Elektro-Konzern) verbunden

set the pictures in the 1940s, while at the same time there are few indications as to locality. The presentation of the figures implies a course of events, which give the impression of being part of a sequence of actions although these are now too fragmented to be reconstructed. When individual works from this phase are compared, although they are not presented as a series, it becomes noticeable that the figures portrayed share similar attributes. Chahal's work is aimed towards a breaking down of any narrative; he himself takes on the role of an actor in unlinked occurrences, which in fact serve to stylise the figure involved. In his more recent works Chahal has increased the level of absurdity of artistic stylization: he shows himself in a red cap and a white shirt in front of a tree trunk in a photographic (self-)portrait with the title *Mushroom,* part of a constructed reality that is semantically impossible to decipher.

The IV Vysota-Group uses scenes of war for their constructs around the self: the project 'Front Friends' shows three female members of the group in military uniform in surroundings which could be interpreted as a scene during the Second World War. The picture of war seems to have been romanticized; the works show the narrowness of the situation that the three female members of the cast are in, adjusting each other's uniforms, posing merrily in front of the camera as a group, or busy reading. The individual photographic sequences from the series are printed on three-cornered silk scarves, which are then installed hanging from the ceiling of the exhibition space. IV Vysota appropriates and completely aestheticizes totalitarian war reporting which, for ideological purpose, exaggerates the notion of the 'sworn comradeship' of the fighters at the front. This aestheticization of the 'lyrical' within the totalitarian is the goal of the works by IV Vysota with the pure kitsch of the tableau aiming at the sublimation of the totalitarian.

The works of the Fenso-Group reflect the constructed visual worlds of television, advertising and the computer game. In the project 'Fenso Lights' group members have seemingly entered the world of video games and appear as 'Science Fiction Knights' in battle scenes in a woodland setting. The photographic presentation seems to reflect reality, for the setting is a real woodland with home-made weapons and armour constructed out of aluminium foil. But if the real has fallen in agony (Baudrillard) and reality can now only be measured in so far as it corresponds to the media world, so Fenso, using analogy, simulate digital and medial visual worlds, playing a psychedelic game of childish delusions of grandeur which allows the group to enter directly into the territory of the machine (the computer) and jump from one visual world to another. The use of manual dexterity to simulate a digital image is also to be found applied to non-photographic subjects in the Moscow art scene. Yuri Albert's series of portraits of a circle of creative artists in Moscow is based

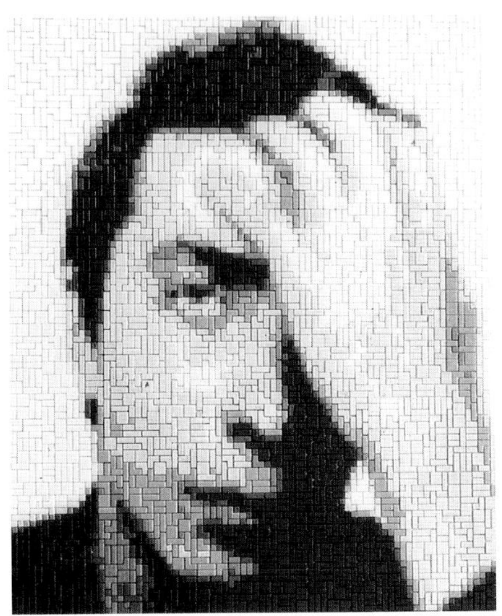
YURI ALBERT, *Portrait of V. Zakharov*, 1991

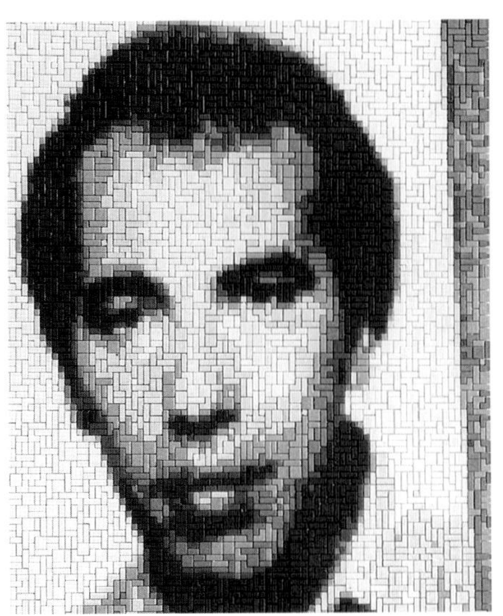
YURI ALBERT, *Self-Portrait (Selbstportrait)*, 1991

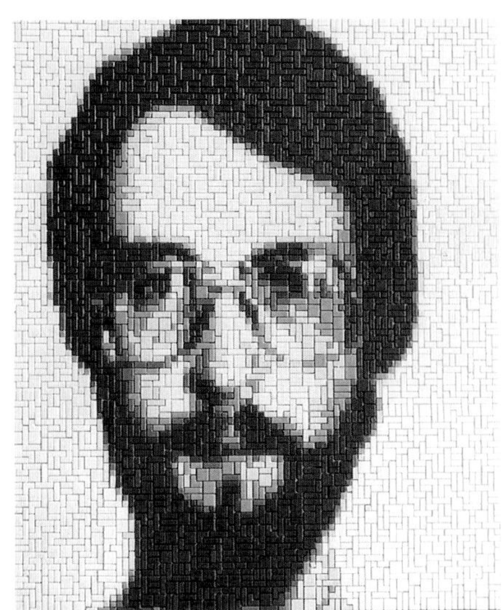
YURI ALBERT, *Portrait of S. Mironenko*, 1991

on the processes of digital dissolution, but here the image turns into no more than a mosaic similar to the pattern made by counters in a children's game. The world as a psychedelic playground leads Fenso from the mystification of computer games to the realm of the cool images of advertising: *Fenso & JVC*. The name Fenso as a brand name appears on headphones, linked directly to a bottle containing some 'special drink' and labelled JVC (the logo of a major electrical concern). In Fenso's case the simulation of the cult of the label (as is also found in concepts by Orlan, Ingold Airlines, Philipp Caszal and others) takes place along with a total openness as to artistic identity: Fenso as a Space Knight; Fenso as old men; Fenso as a brand name; the members of the group in a magazine advertisement for Fenso cigarettes; Fenso as guerrillas drinking Coca-Cola and milk.

Openness is a characteristic of the present day photographic 'landscape' in Moscow; it remains to be seen whether the blurring of boundaries between art and photography can really lead to a proper recognition of photography as a medium, or whether the use of photography simply as one medium amongst many will prove to have been no more than parasitic, in the long run only neutralising the photographic image itself.

ist. Die Simulation der Labelkultur (wie sie etwa auch in den Konzeptionen von Orlan, Ingold Airlines, Philipp Caszal u. a. anklingt) vollzieht sich bei Fenso im Zusammenhang mit einer totalen Offenheit der künstlerischen Identität: Fenso als Weltraumritter; Fenso als alte Männer; Fenso als Markenzeichen; die Mitglieder der Gruppe in einer Zigarettenwerbung der Marke Fenso in einem Journal; Fenso als Coca-Cola und Milch trinkende Guerillas.

Offenheit ist ein Kennzeichen der heutigen fotografischen ‚Landschaft' in Moskau; es bleibt abzuwarten, ob die Verwischung der Grenzen zwischen Bildender Kunst und Fotografie zu einer wirklichen Anerkennung des Mediums Fotografie führen kann oder ob die Verwendung von Fotografie als einem Medium unter vielen anderen sich als parasitär erweist und das fotografische Bild auf Dauer neutralisiert.

Notes

1 Anatoli Lunarcharsky (Soviet-Russian commissioner for Public Education 1917–1929), as quoted by Valery Stigneev in *Art of Contemporary Photography, Russia, Ukraine, Belarus*, exhibition catalogue (Moscow, 1994), p. 5.

2 See *Die Zeitgenössische Photographie in der Sowjetunion*, ed. Wiktor Misiano (Victor Misiano), (Schaffhausen, 1988).

Anmerkungen

1 *Anatoli Lunacharsky (russisch-sowjetischer Kommissar für Volksbildung 1917–1929), zitiert nach Valeri Stigneev in:* Art of Contemporary Photography. Russia, Ukraine, Belarus, *Kat., Moskau 1994, S. 5*

2 *Vgl. Wiktor Misiano (Victor Miziano):* Zeitgenössische Photographie in der Sowjetunion, *Schaffhausen 1988*

3 *Vgl. Tatyana Salzirn, zitiert bei John Jacob in:* The missing picture: Alternative contemporary photography from the Soviet Union, *Kat., MIT List Visual Arts Centre, Cambridge, Mass., 1990/1991, S. XIII*

4 *Tatyana Salzirn: „Solid Objects", in:* The missing picture: Alternative contemporary photography from the Soviet Union, *Kat. ebd., S. XXVII*

5 *Barbara Straka: „Eros und Agape – Das Pathos des Alltäglichen und die Profanität des Erhabenen im Werk Wladimir Kupriyanows", in:* Wladimir Kupriyanow. Fotoarbeiten 1981–1995, *Kat., Haus am Waldsee Berlin 1995, S. XLIX*

6 *Vgl. Enno Kaufhold: „Kunst mit fotografischen Mitteln: Fotoarbeiten Berliner KünstlerInnen", in:* Interferenzen: Kunst aus Westberlin 1960–1990, *Kat., Neue Gesellschaft für Bildende Kunst, Berlin 1991, S. 69–80*

7 *Vgl. Victor Miziano: „Soft Machines By Vadim Fishkin" in:* Vadim Fishkin – Orbita S., *Kat., Galerie XL, Moskau 1994*

8 *Vgl. Bojana Pejić in:* 22. Bienal Internacional de São Paulo, *Kat. 1994, S. 377 f. und Manuskript „Anatolij Shuravlev", Berlin 1995*

9 *Vgl. Rosalind Krauss: „Notes on the Index: Seventies Art in America", in:* October, The First Decade 1976–1986. *Hrsg. von A. Michelson, R. Krauss u. a., Cambridge, Mass., 1987, S. 9: „Every photograph is the result of a physical imprint transferred by light reflection onto a sensitive surface. The photograph is thus a type of icon, or visual likeness, which bears an indexical relation to its object."*

10 *Vgl. AES: The Scar, in:* Bad News from Russia, *Galerie Guelman Moskau, 1994*

11 *Vgl. die Exzerpte aus dem Interview zwischen Elena Selina, Sergey Khripun und AES „Body Space or Body Metaphysics" (Manuskript)*

12 *Vgl. den Vortrag von Yekaterina Dyogot im Rahmen der Ausstellung „Kräftemessen", Kunstverein München und Künstlerwerkstatt Lothringer Straße, München, 24. Juni 1995*

3 See Tatyana Salzirn as quoted by John Jacob in *The missing picture: Alternative contemporary photography from the Soviet Union,* exhibition catalogue, Cambridge Mass., MIT List Visual Arts Centre, 1990/1991, p. XIII.

4 Tatyana Salzirn, 'Solid Objects', in *The missing picture: Alternative contemporary photography from the Soviet Union,* op cit., p. XXVII.

5 Barbara Straka, 'Eros und Agape – Das Pathos des Alltäglichen und die Profanität des Erhabenen im Werk Wladimir Kuprijanows', in *Wladimir Kuprijanow: Fotoarbeiten 1981–1995,* exhibition catalogue, Berlin, Haus am Waldsee (Berlin, 1995), pp. XLIX.

6 See Enno Kaufhold, 'Kunst mit fotografischen Mitteln: Fotoarbeiten Berliner KünstlerInnen', in *Interferenzen: Kunst aus Westberlin 1960–1990,* exhibition catalogue, Berlin, Neue Gesellschaft für Bildende Kunst (Berlin, 1991), pp. 69–80.

7 See Victor Misiano, 'Soft Machines by Vadim Fishkin' in *Vadim Fishkin – Orbita S.,* exhibition catalogue, Moscow, XL Gallery (Moscow, 1994).

8 See Boyana Pejić in *22: Bienal Internacional de São Paolo,* exhibition catalogue (1994), p. 377 f, and (in manuscript), 'Anatoli Shuravlev' (Berlin, 1995).

9 See Rosalind Krauss, 'Notes on the Index: Seventies Art in America', in A. Michelson, R. Krauss, et al. (eds), *October: The First Decade 1976–1986* (Cambridge, Mass. 1987), p. 9: 'Every photograph is the result of a physical imprint transferred by light reflection onto a sensitive surface. The photograph is thus a type of icon, or visual likeness, which bears an indexical relation to its object'.

10 See 'AES: The Scar', in *Bad News from Russia,* exhibition catalogue, Moscow, Guelman Galerie (Moscow, 1994).

11 Excerpts from an interview between Elena Selina, Sergei Khripun and AES, 'Body Space or Body Metaphysics' (in manuscript).

12 Lecture by Yekaterina Dyogot as part of the project 'Kräftemessen' (Trials of Strength), Kunstverein München and Künstlerwerkstatt Lothringer Straße München, 24 June 1995.

Plates
Bildteil

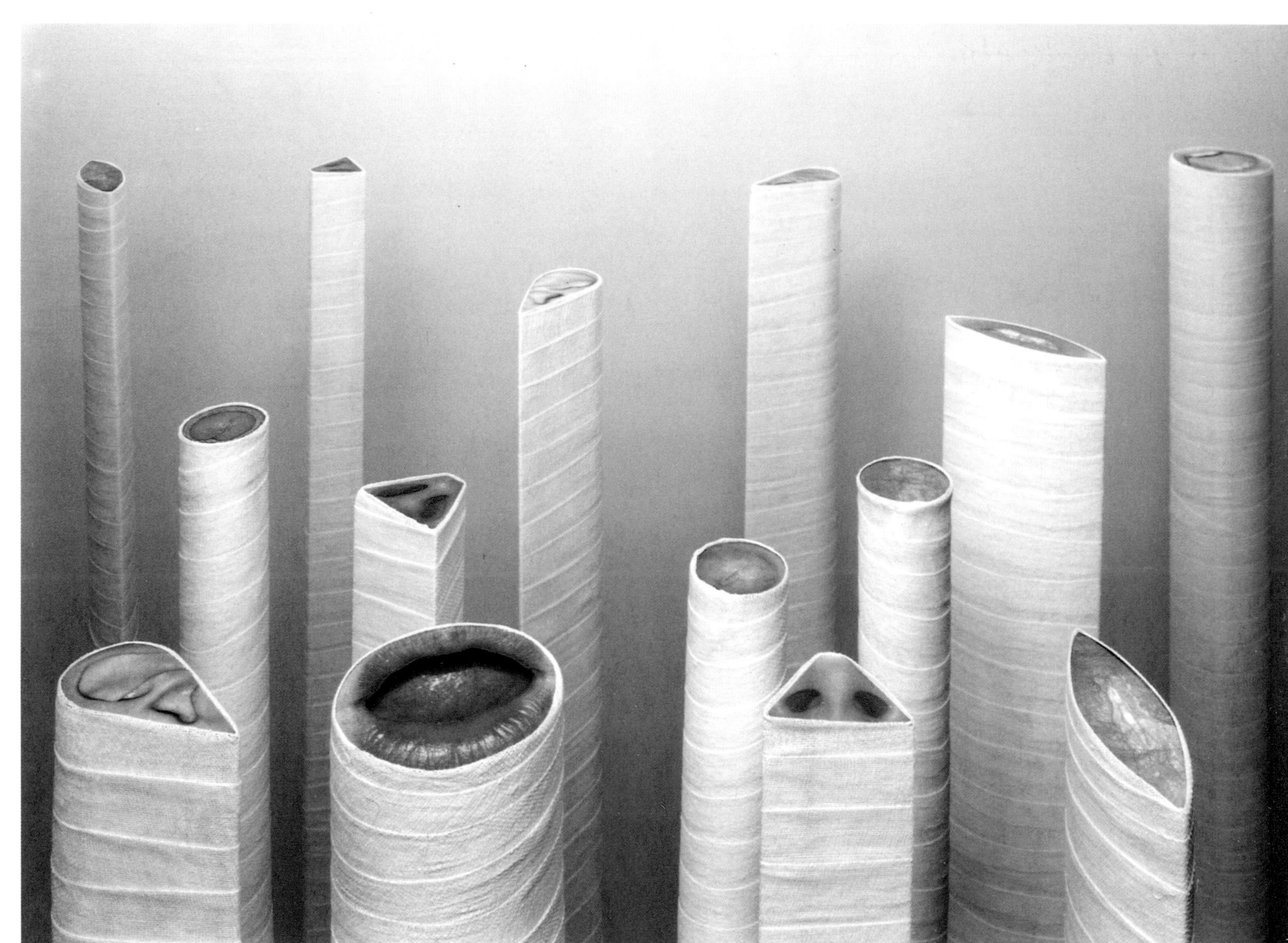

1 'Body Space' project: *Holes (Projekt „Körperraum": Löcher),* 1995

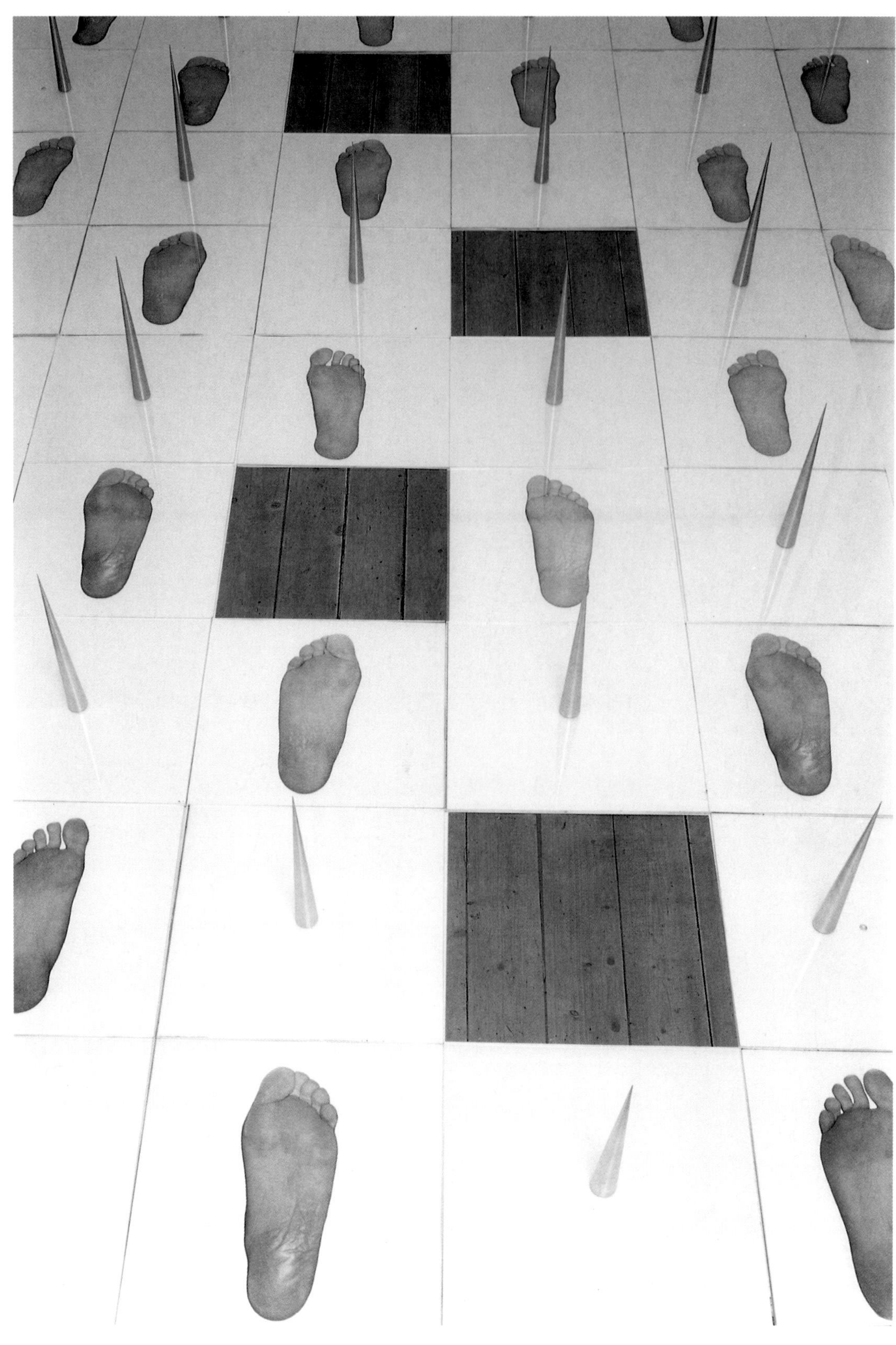

2 'Body Space' project: *Feet (Projekt „Körperraum": Füße)*, 1994

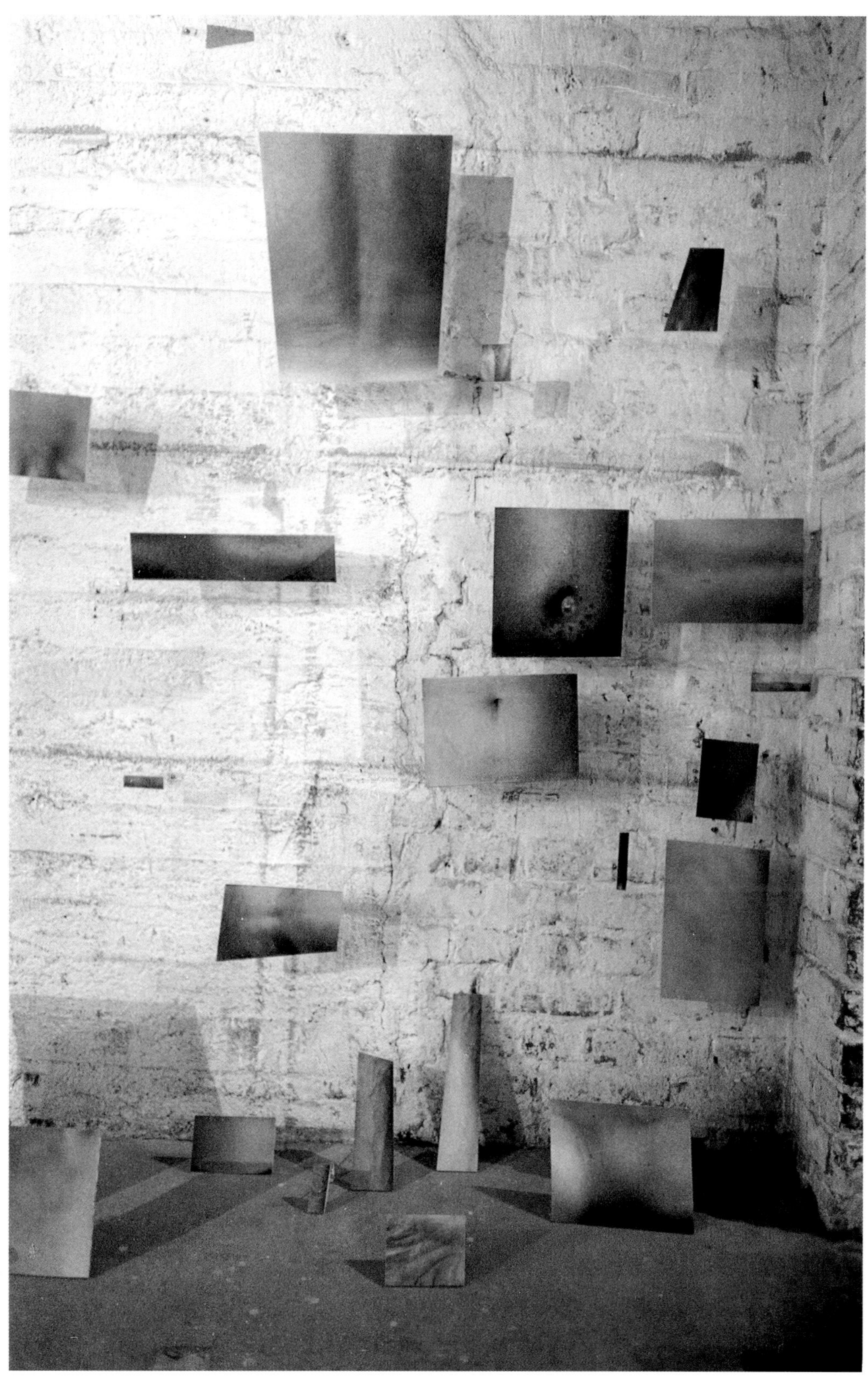

3 'Body Space' project: *Skin-Body Surface (Projekt „Körperraum": Haut, Oberfläche des Körpers)*, 1993

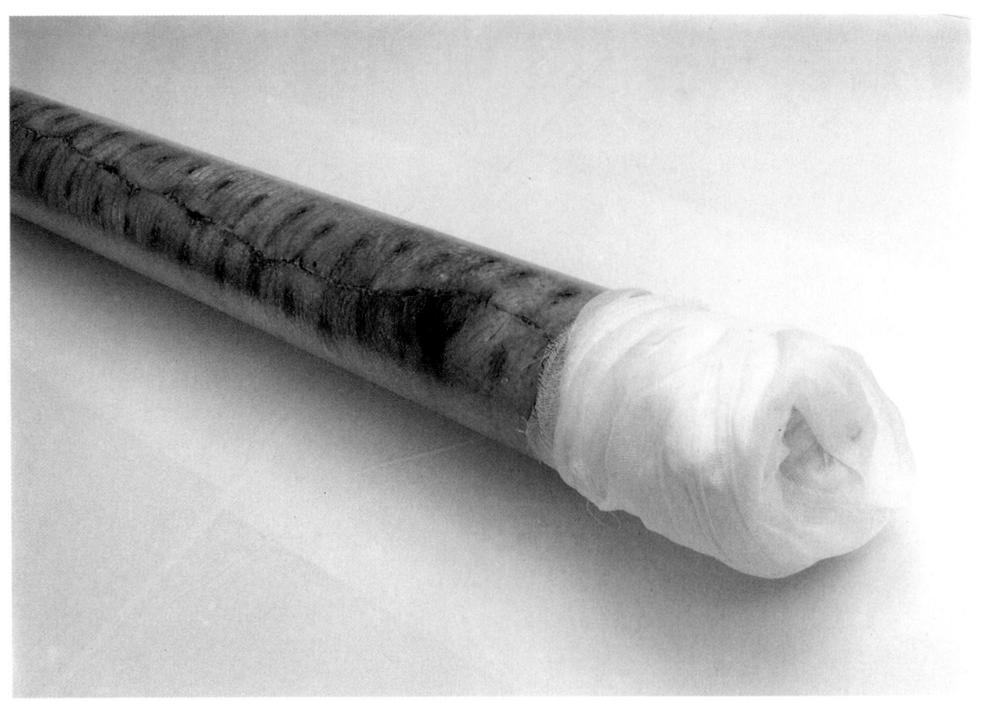

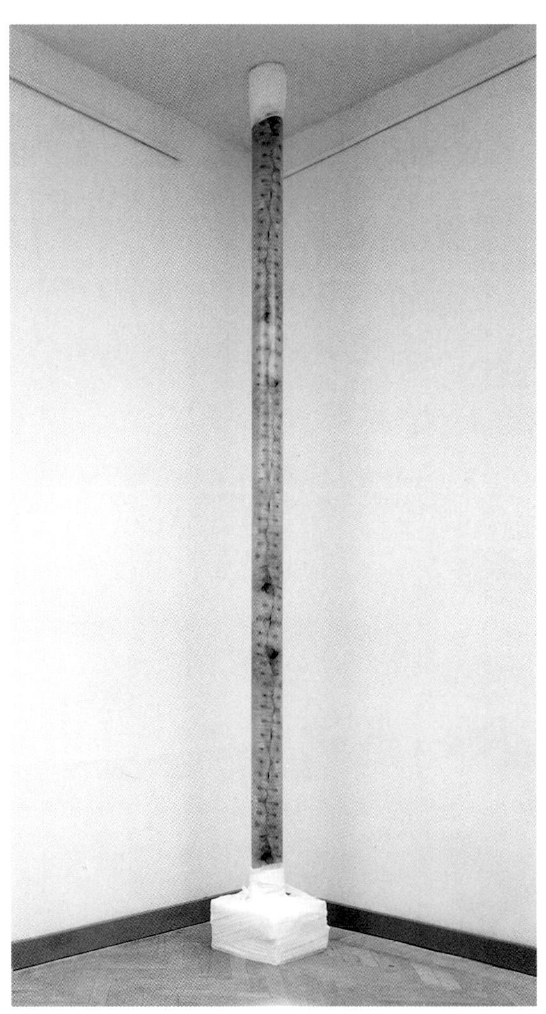

4 'Body Space' project: *The Scar (Projekt „Körperraum": Narbe),* 1995 (detail)

5 'Body Space' project: *The Scar (Projekt „Körperraum": Narbe), 1995*

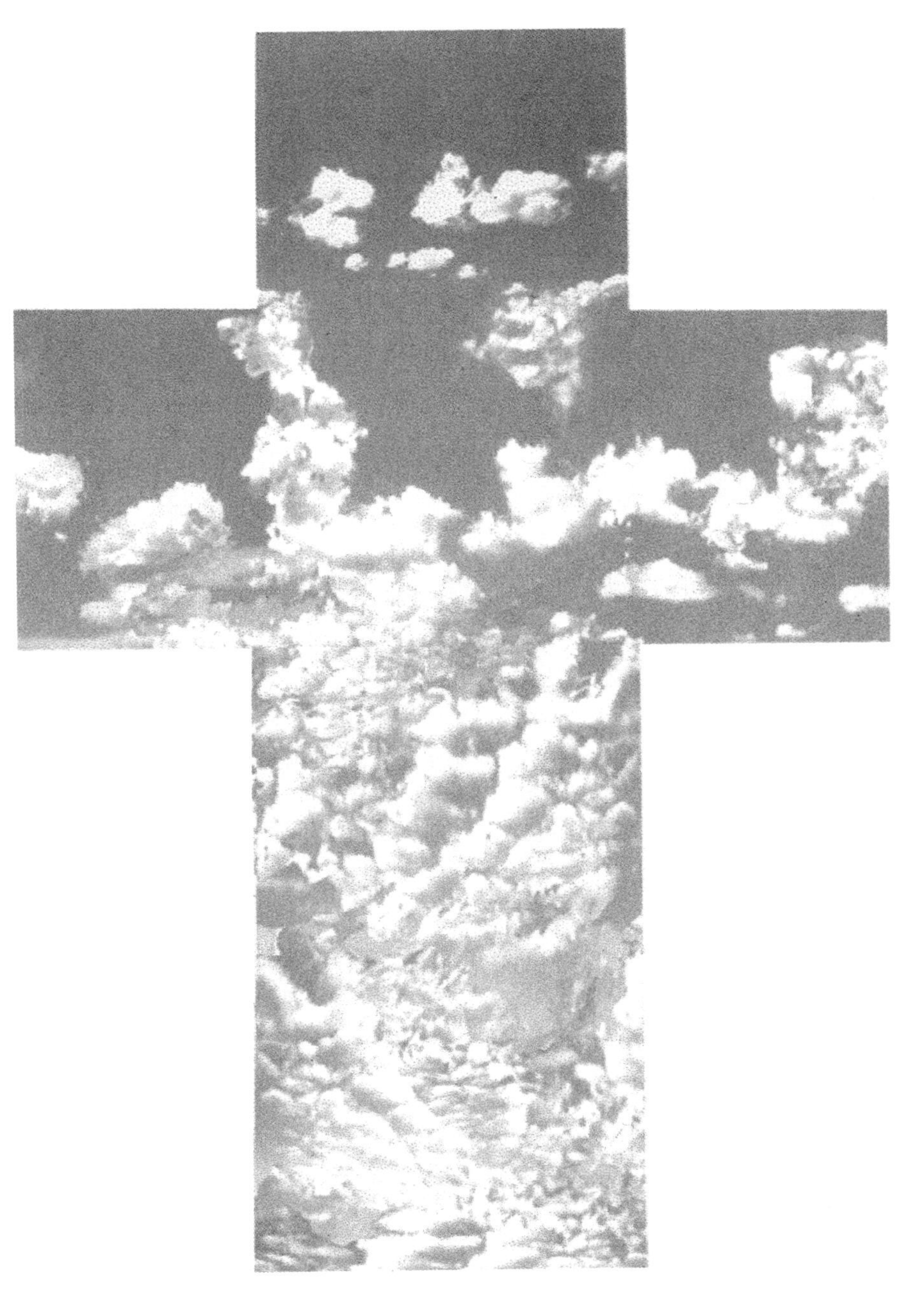

6 From the series 'Boxes' *(Aus der Serie „Schachteln“)*, 1995

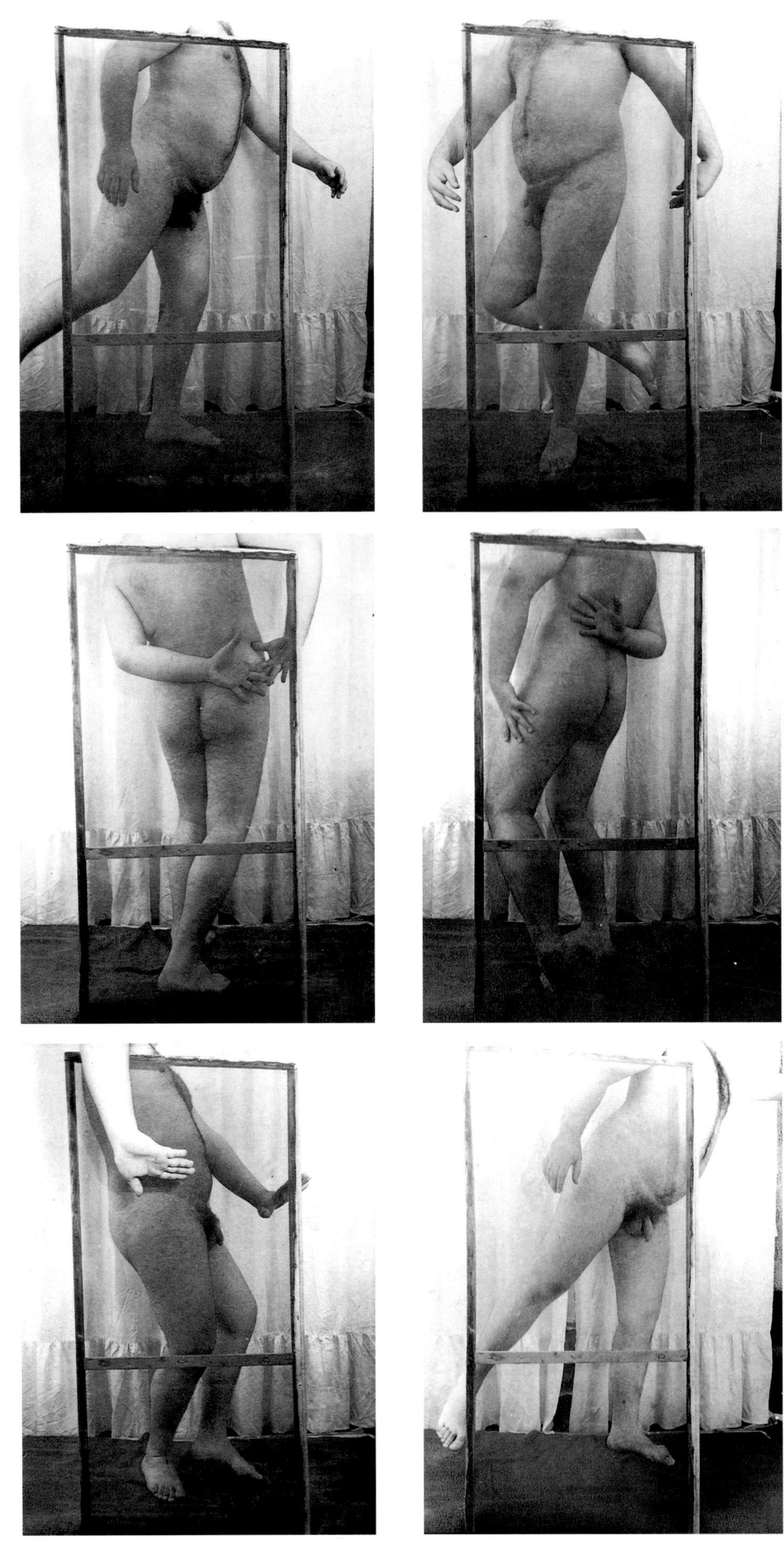

7 From the series 'Ballet' *(Aus der Serie „Ballett")*, 1994

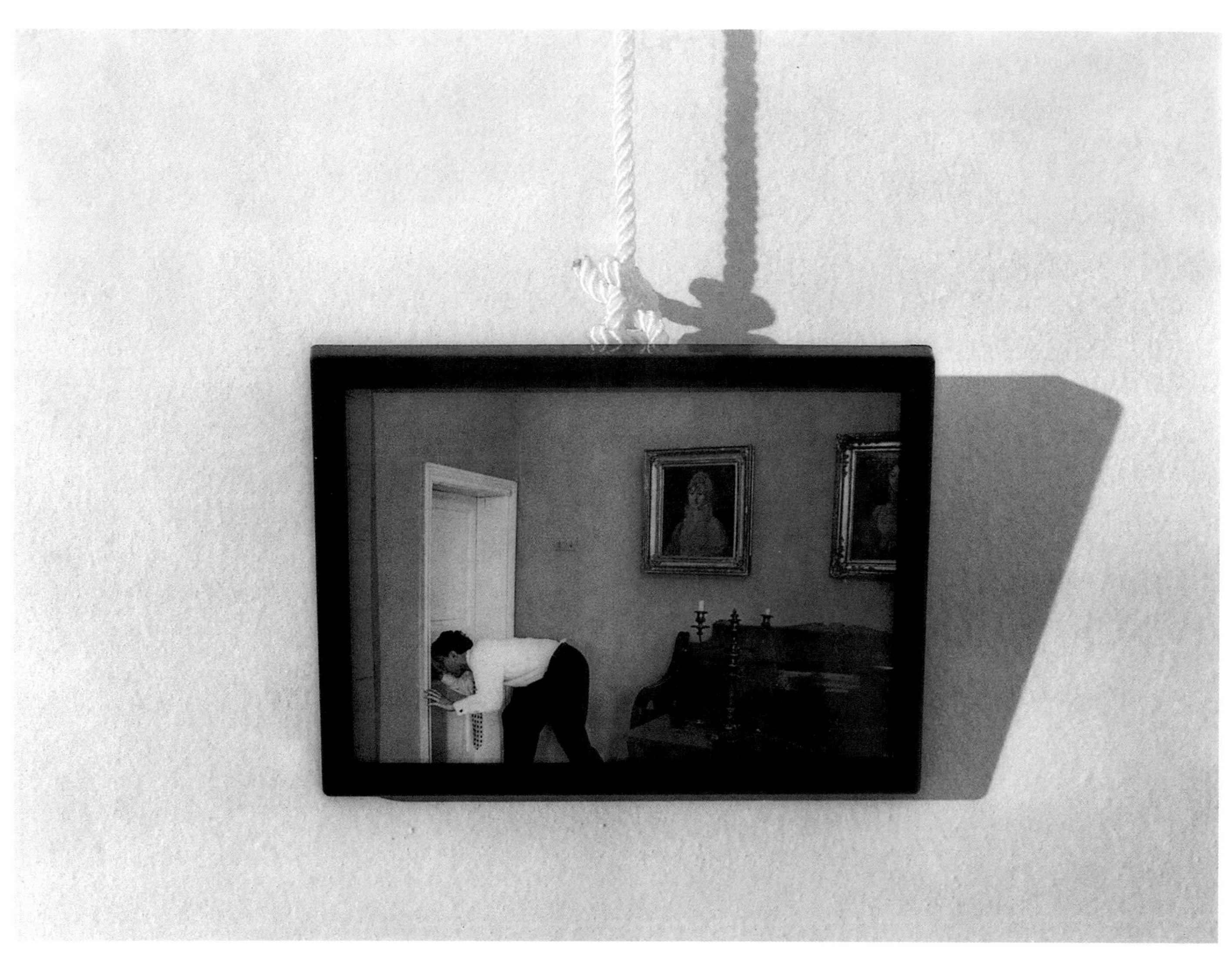

8 *When the Poets are not Sleeping (Wenn die Dichter nicht schlafen)*, 1991

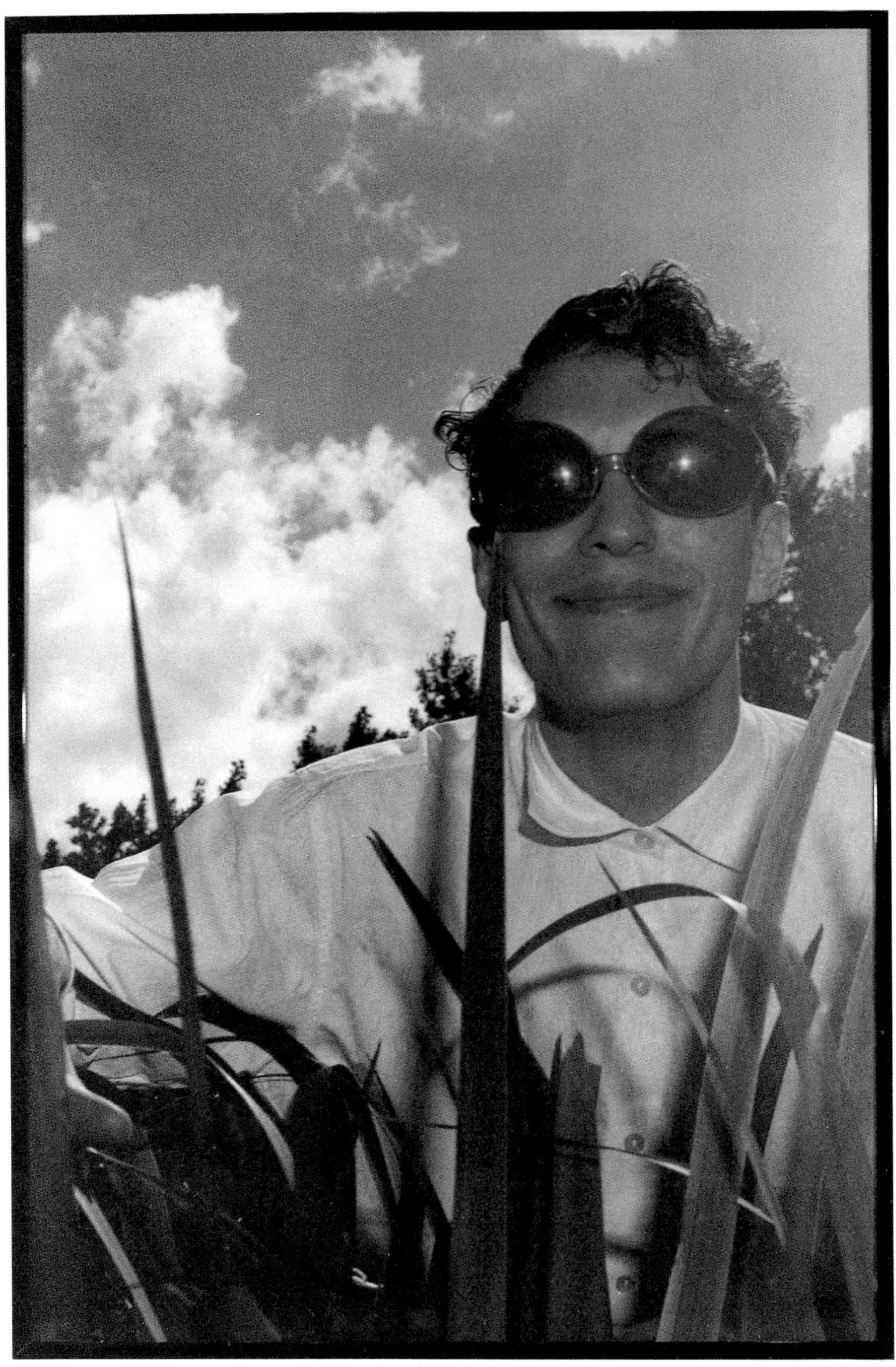

9 *Dragonfly (Libelle)*, 1994

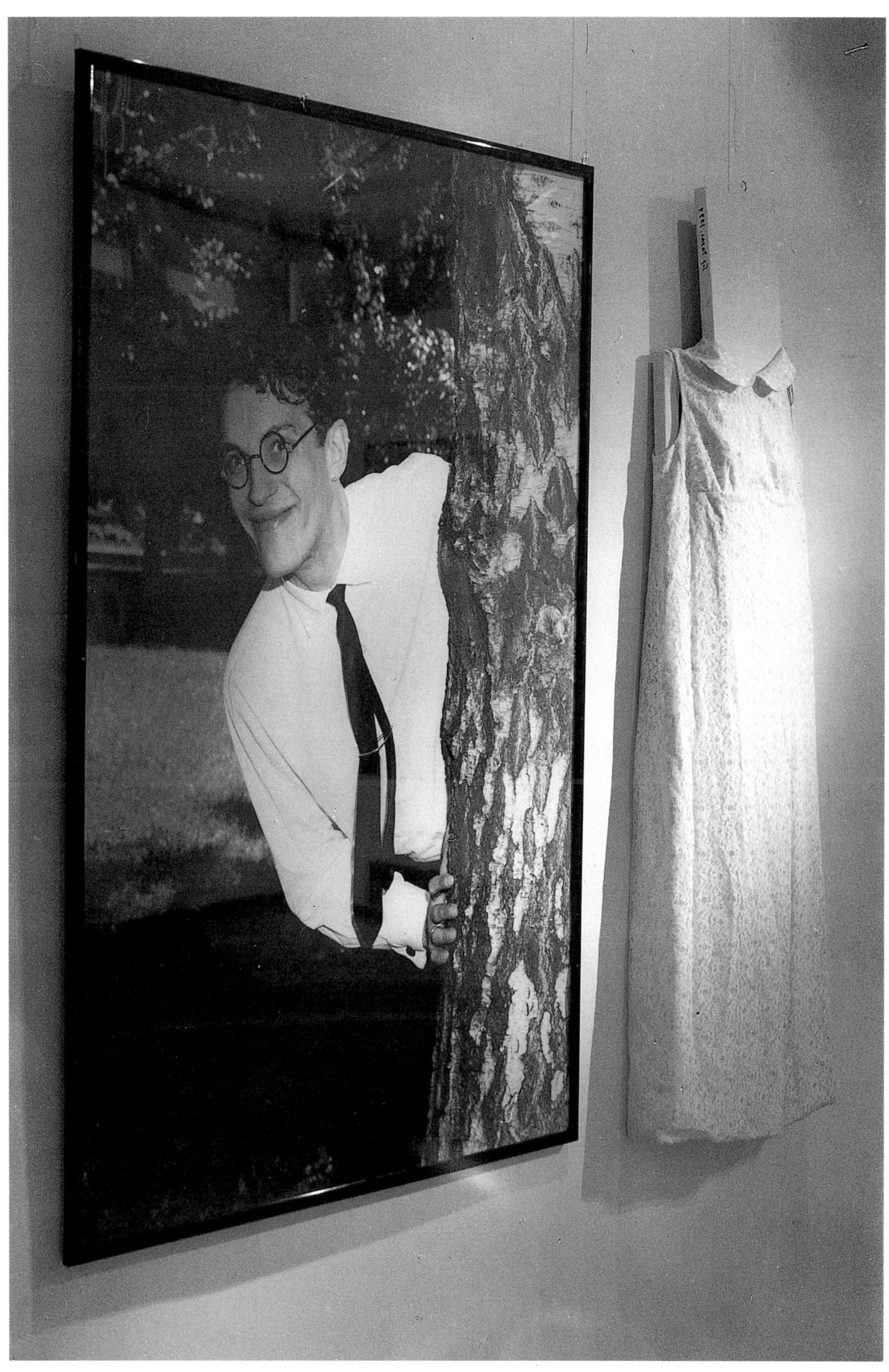

10 Untitled *(Ohne Titel)*, 1991–92

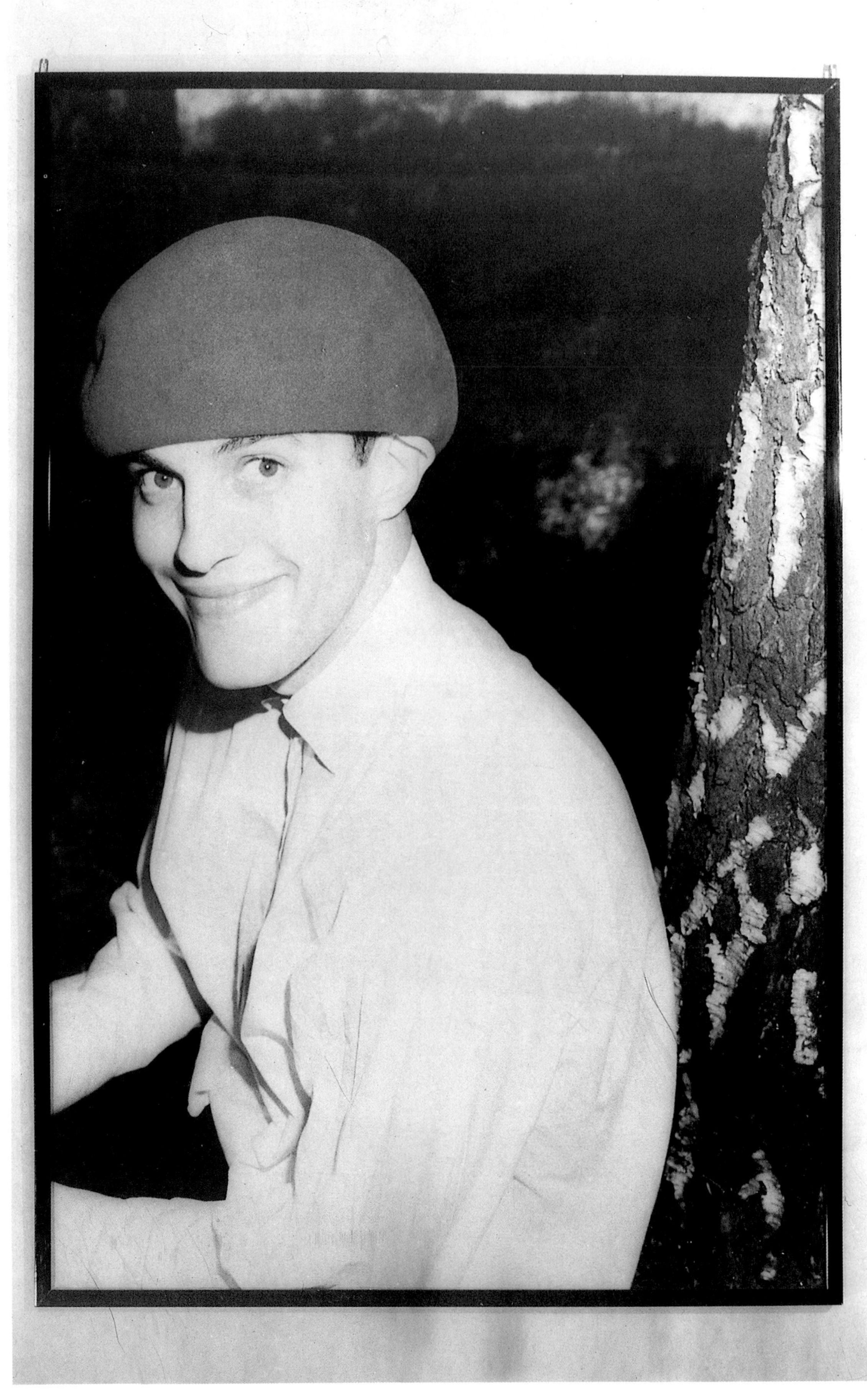

11 *Mushroom (Pilz)*, 1991

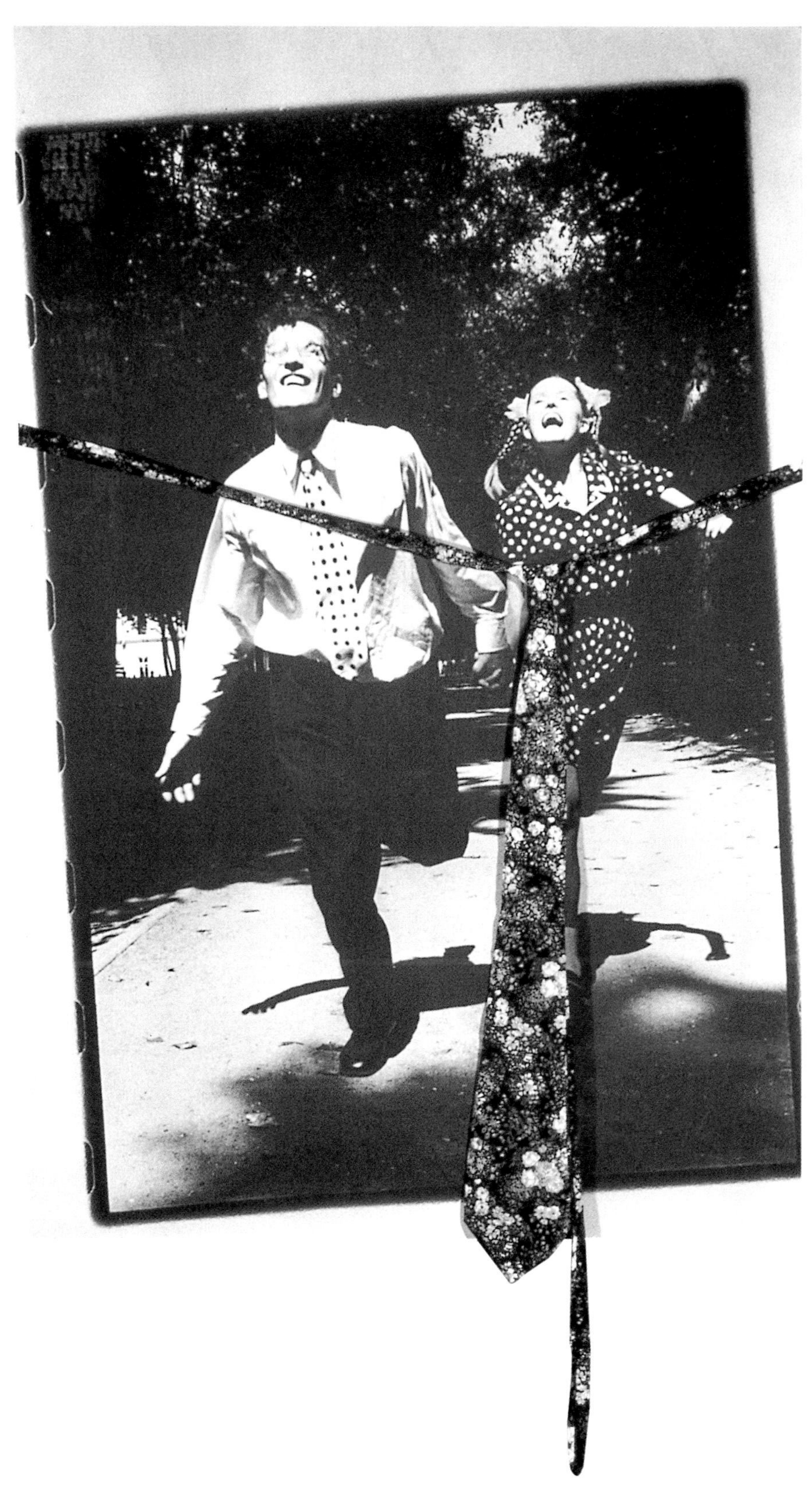

12 Untitled *(Ohne Titel)*, 1990

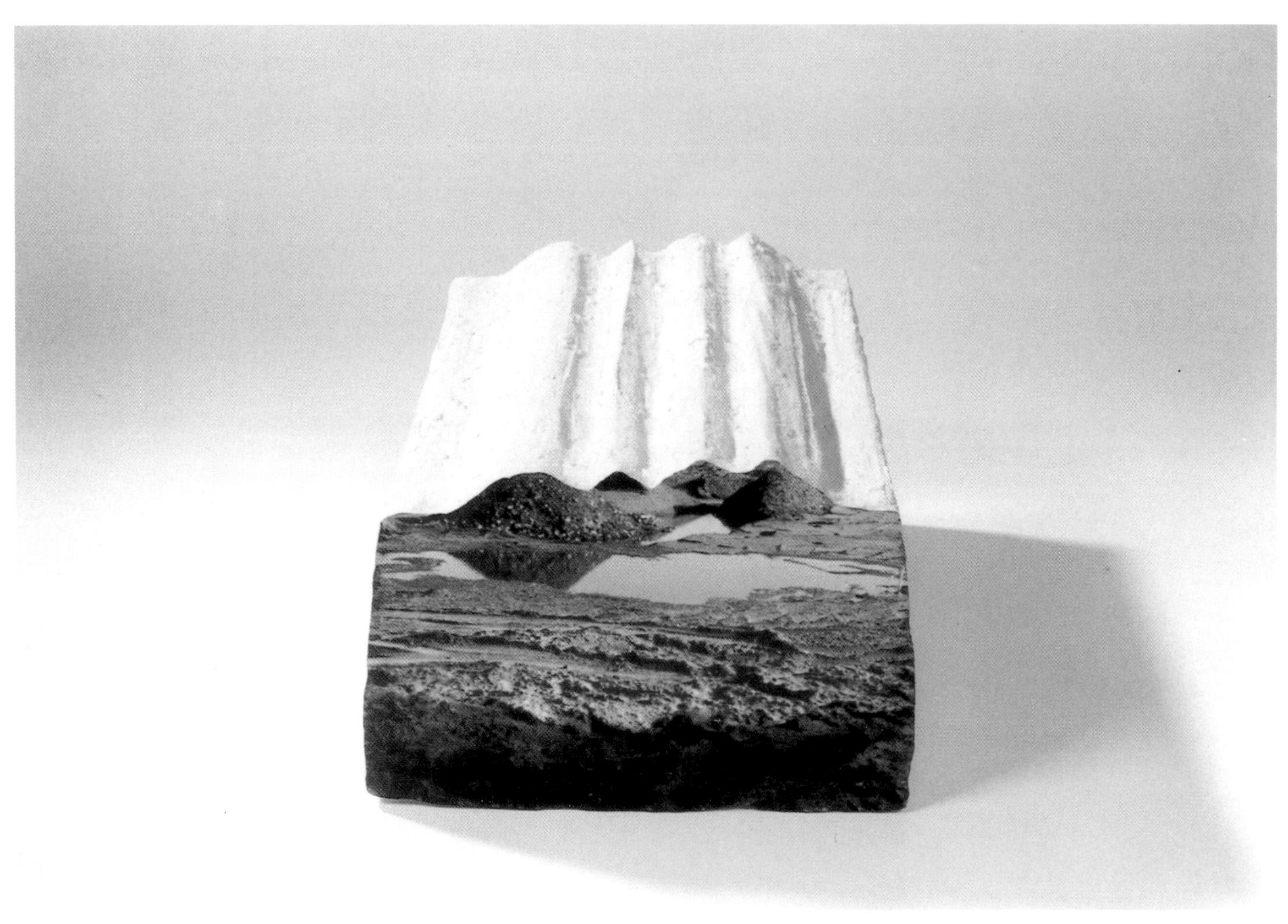

13 Untitled *(Ohne Titel)*, 1994

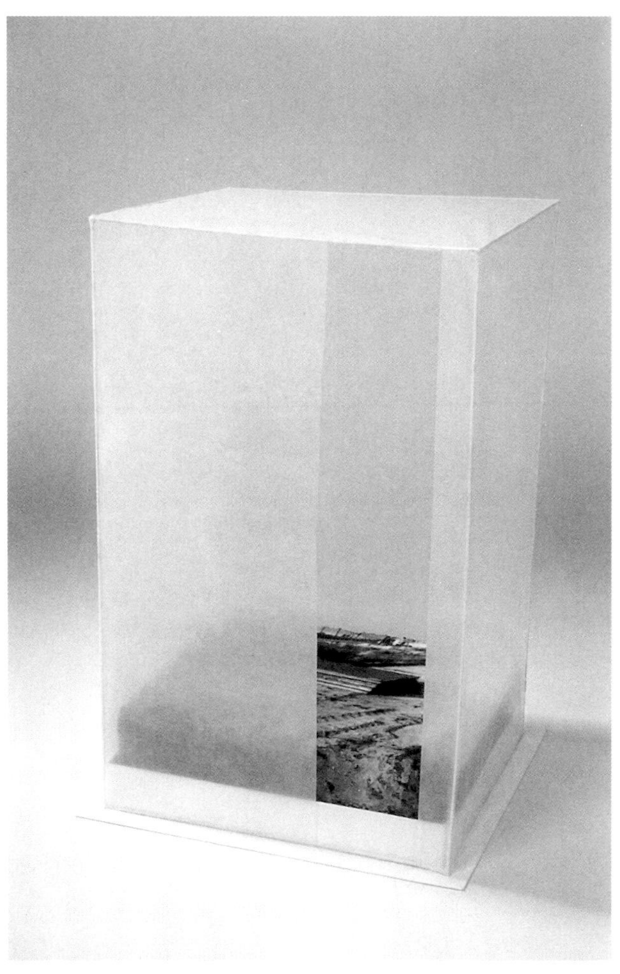

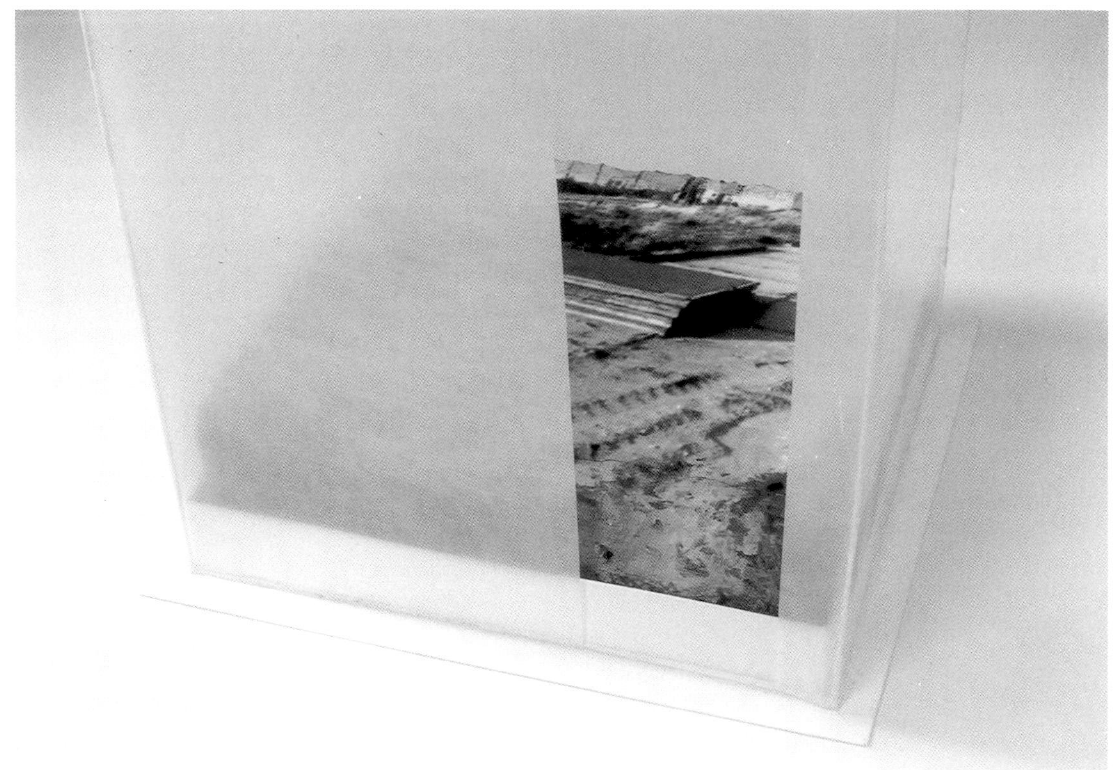

14 Untitled *(Ohne Titel),* 1994

15 Untitled *(Ohne Titel),* 1994 (detail)

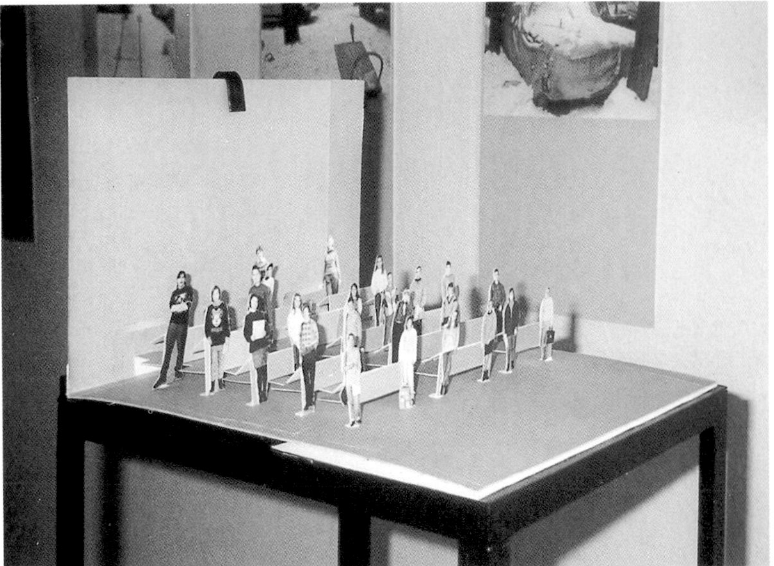

16 *School Installation (Schul-Installation)*, 1993

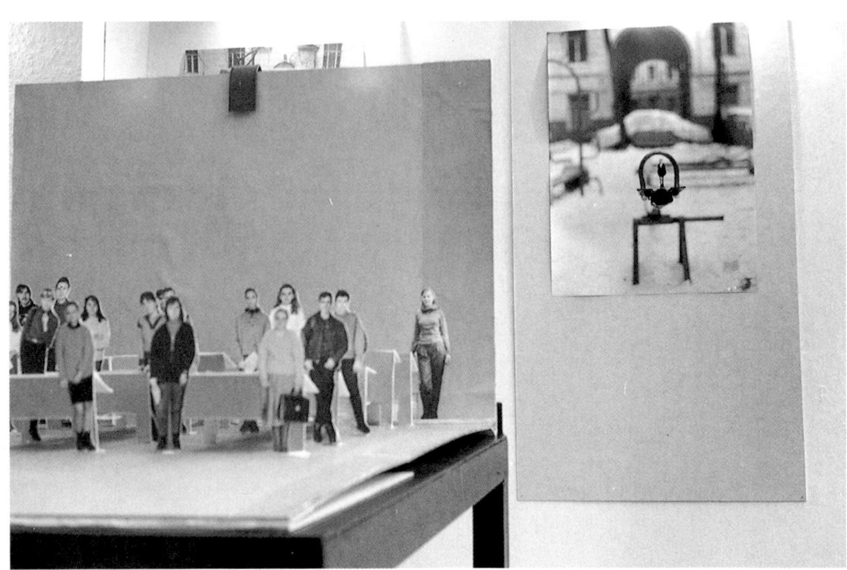

17 *School Installation (Schul-Installation)*, 1993

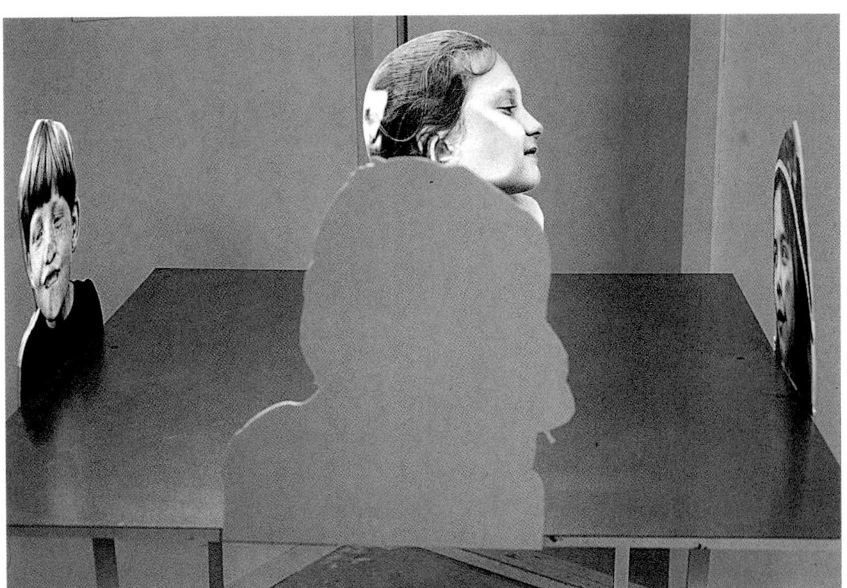

18 Untitled *(Ohne Titel)*, 1994

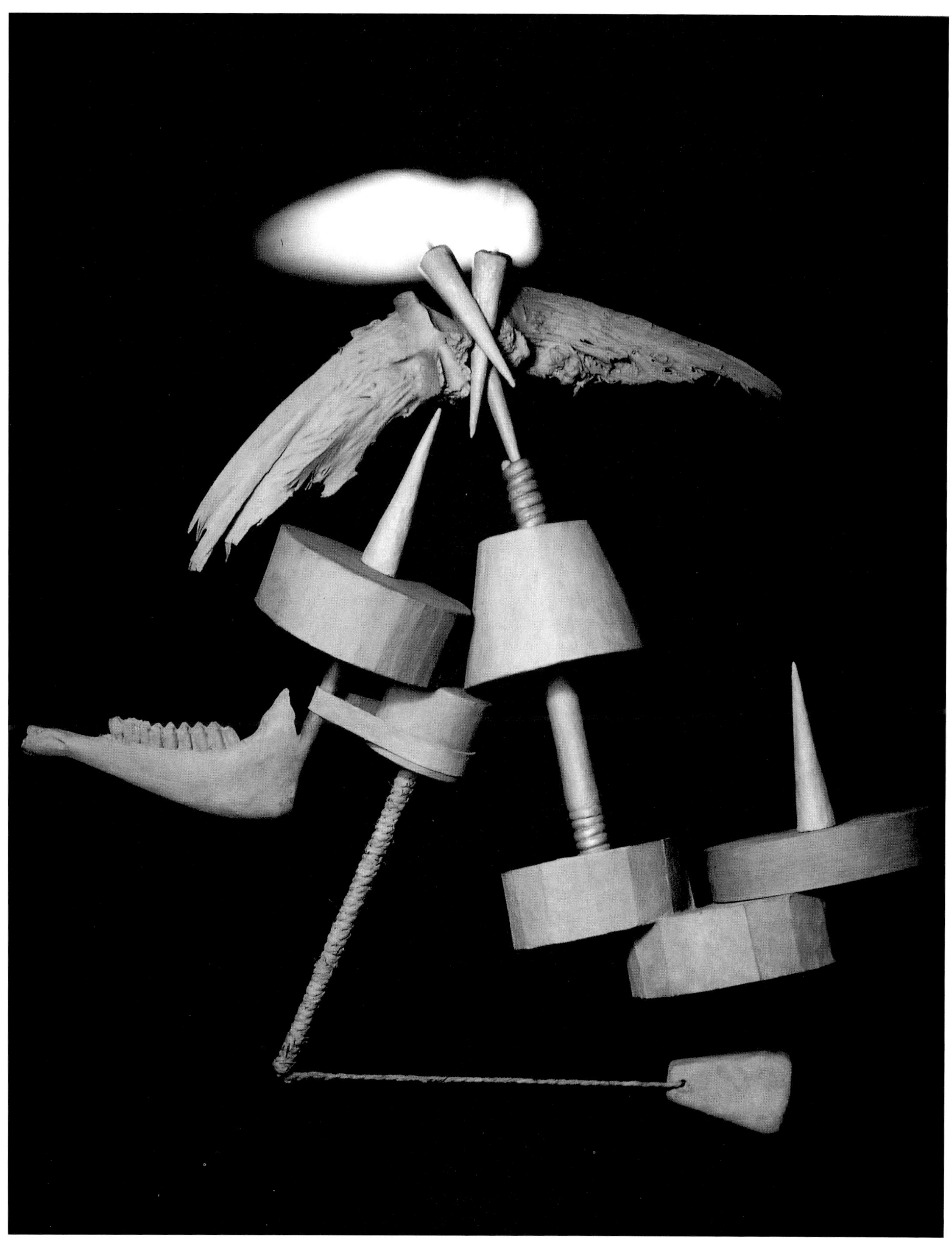

19 Untitled *(Ohne Titel)*, 1994

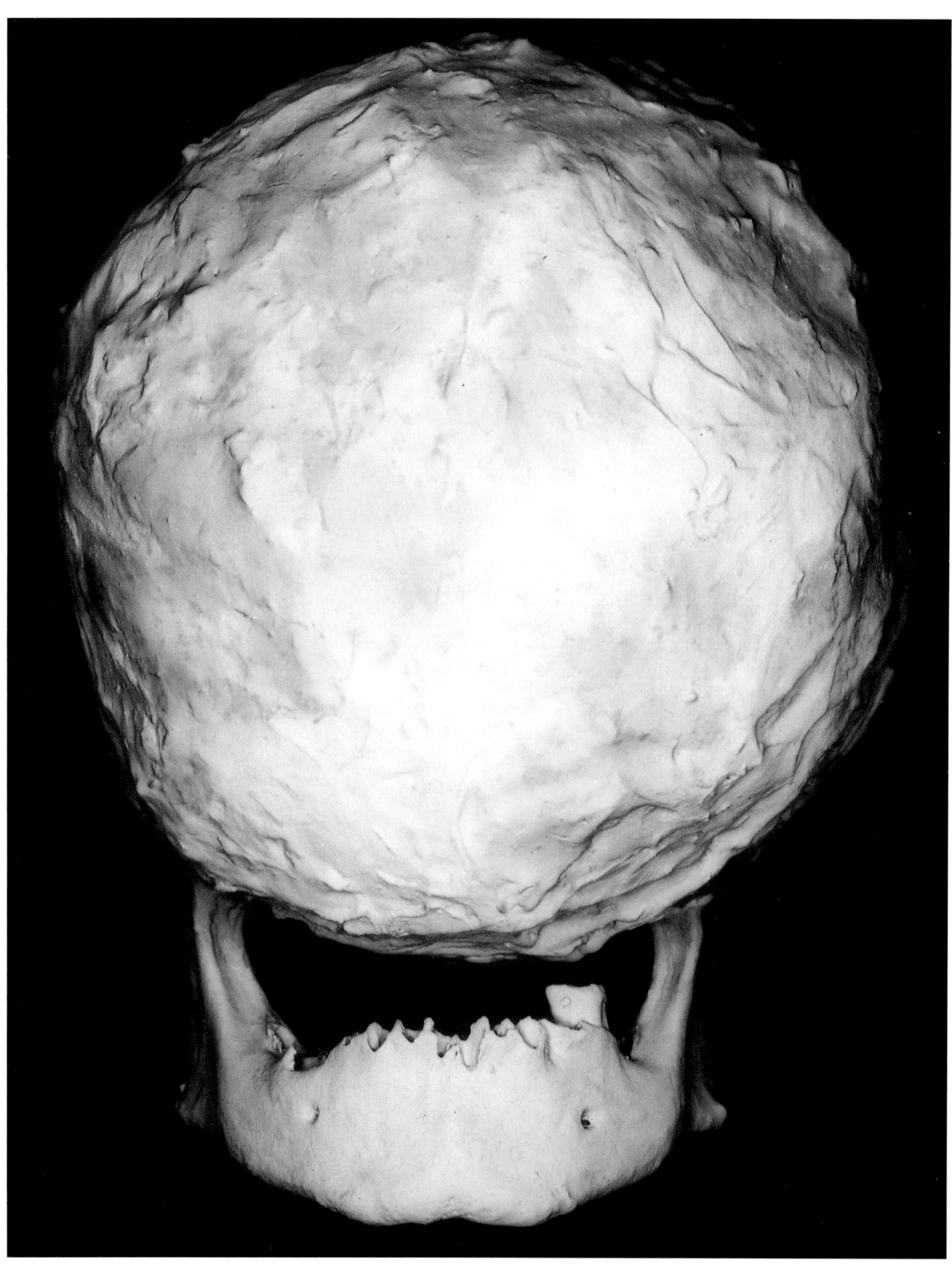

20 Untitled, n. d. *(Ohne Titel, o. J.)*

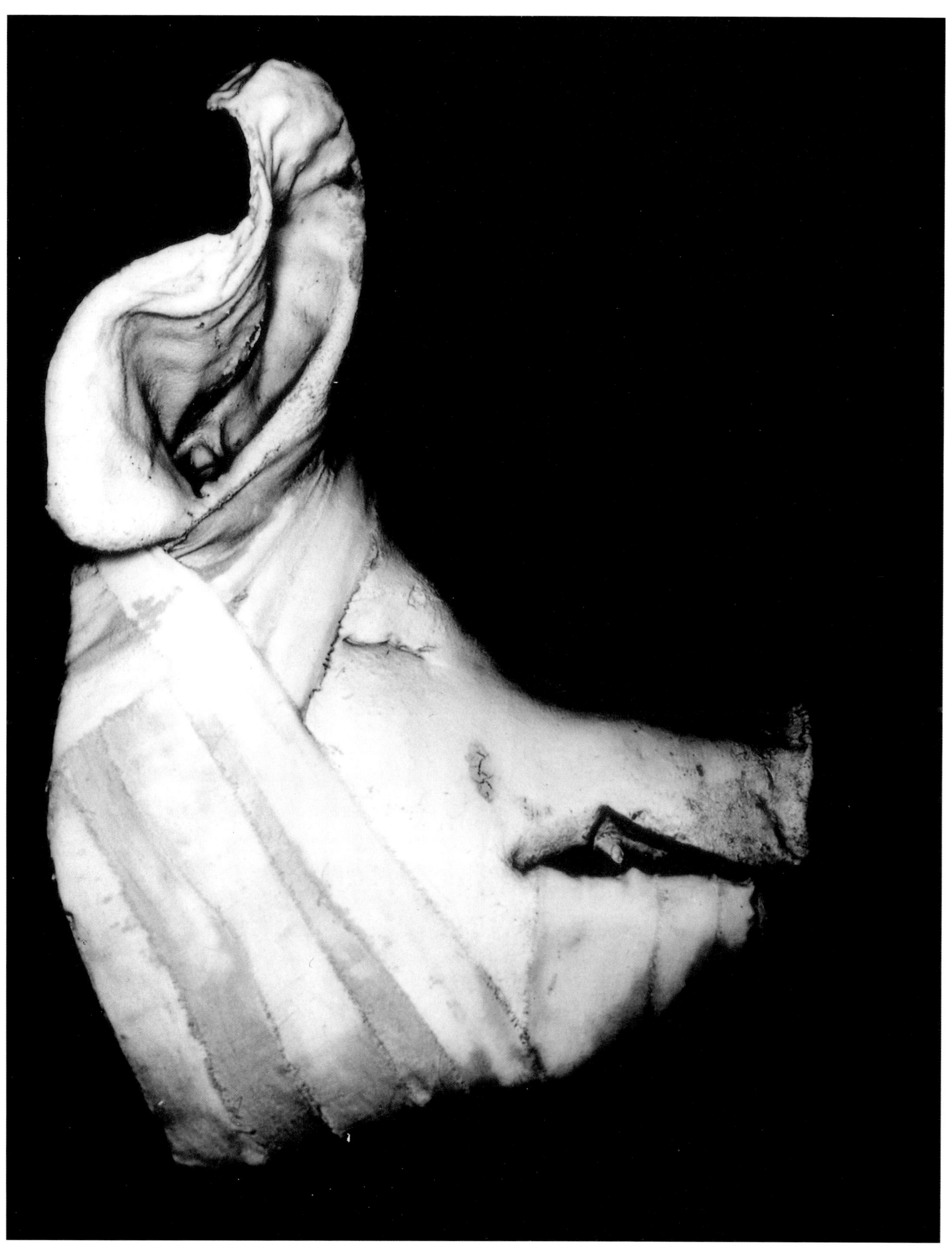

21 Untitled, n. d. *(Ohne Titel, o. J.)*

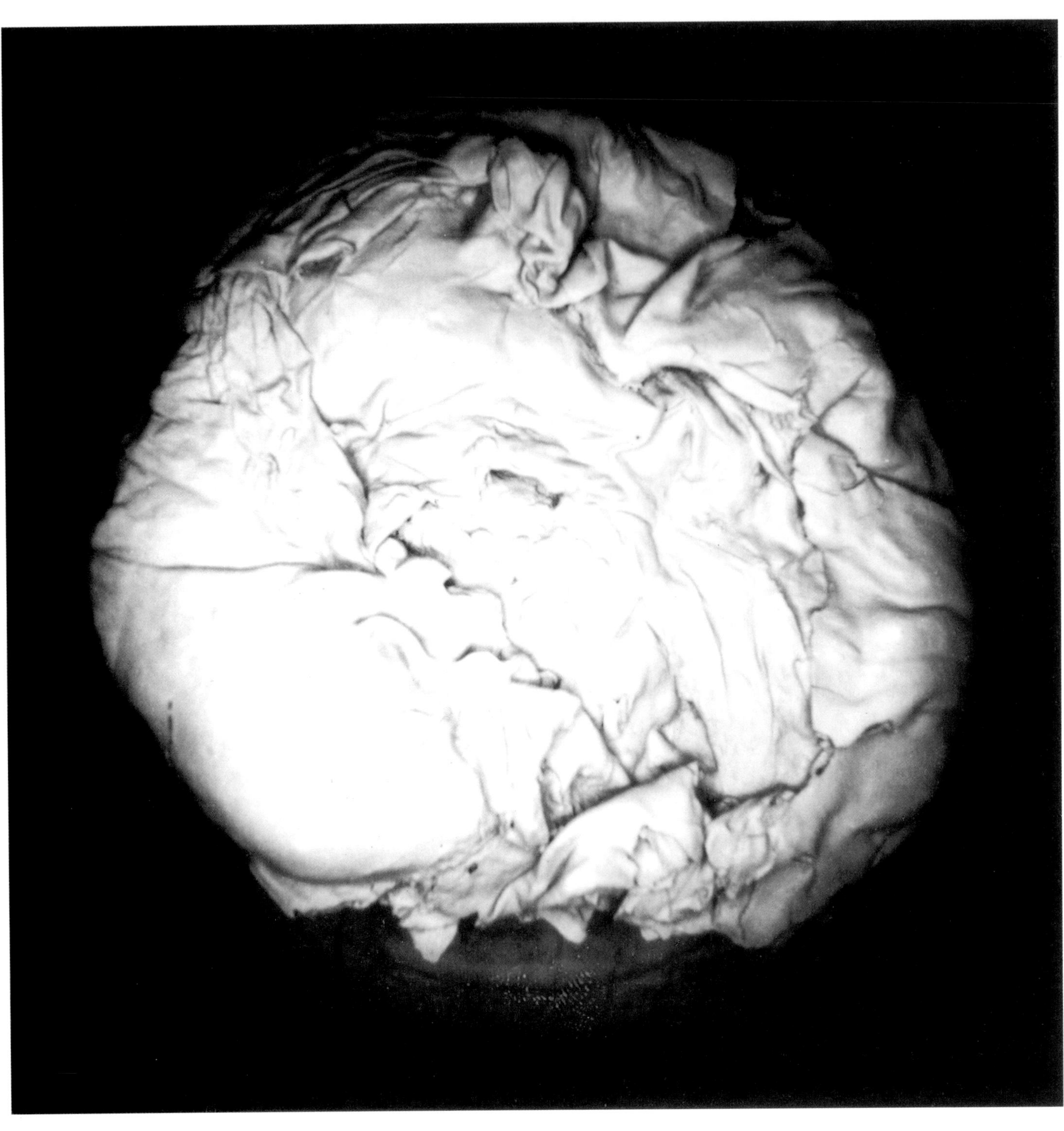

22 Untitled, n. d. *(Ohne Titel, o. J.)*

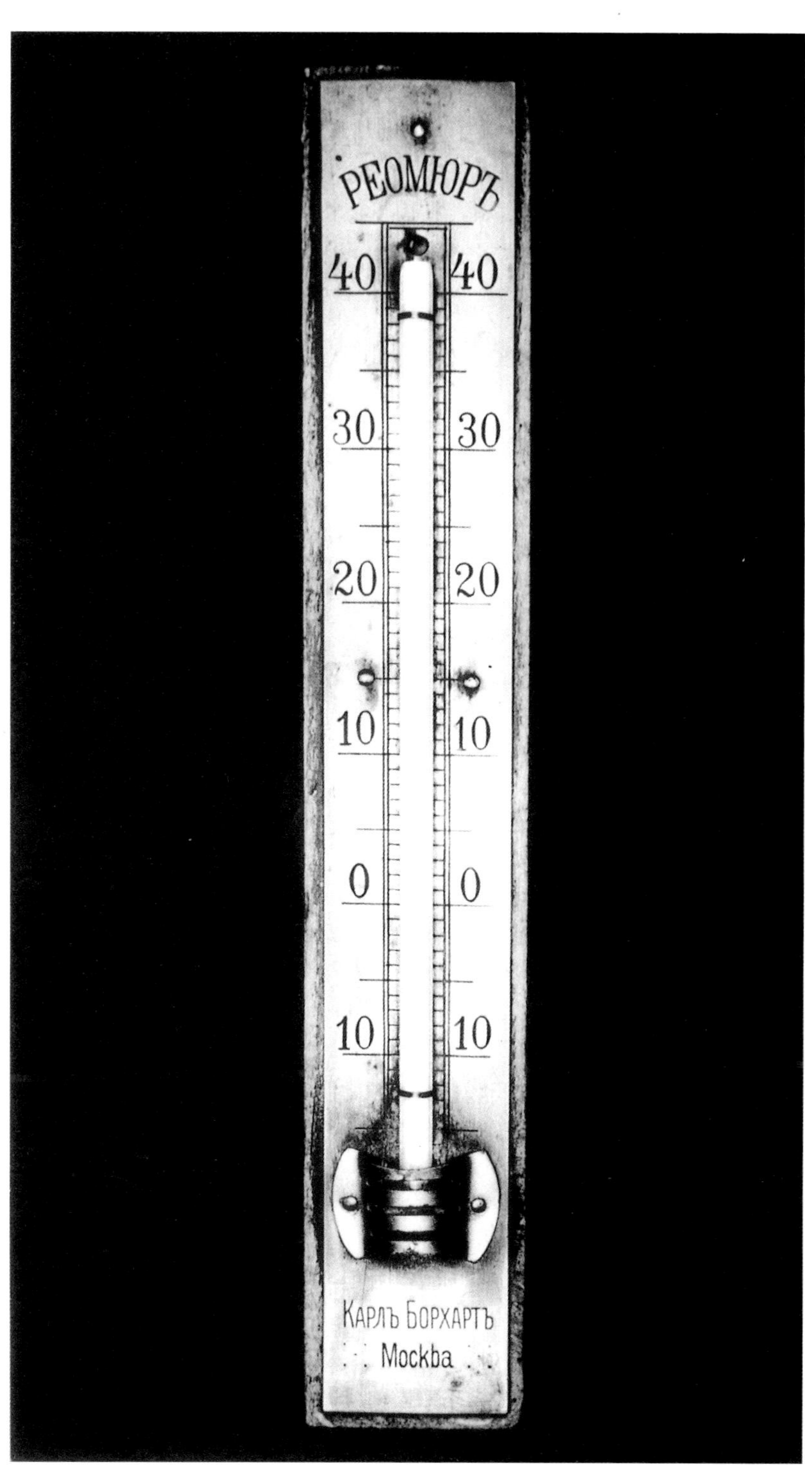

23 Untitled, n. d. *(Ohne Titel, o. J.)*

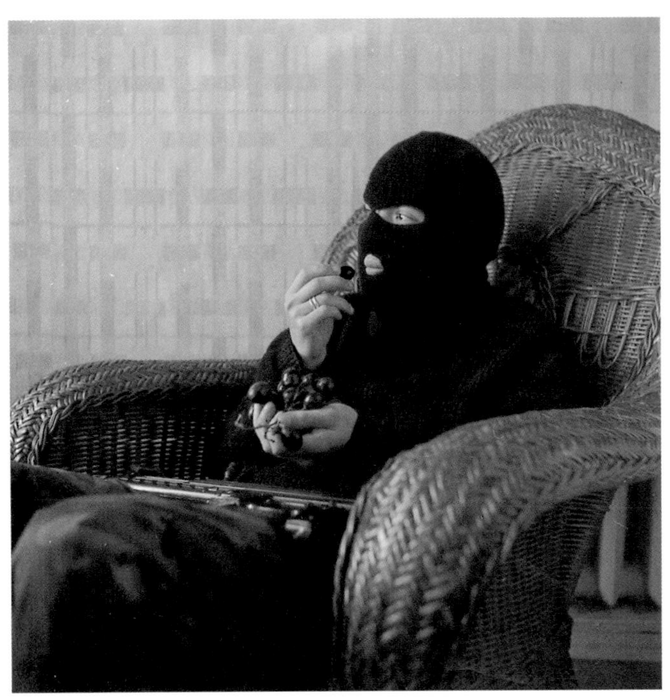

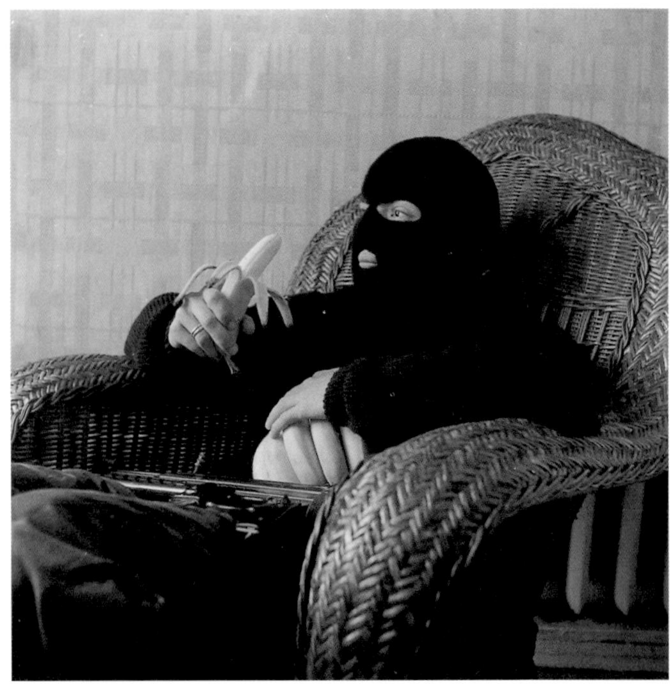

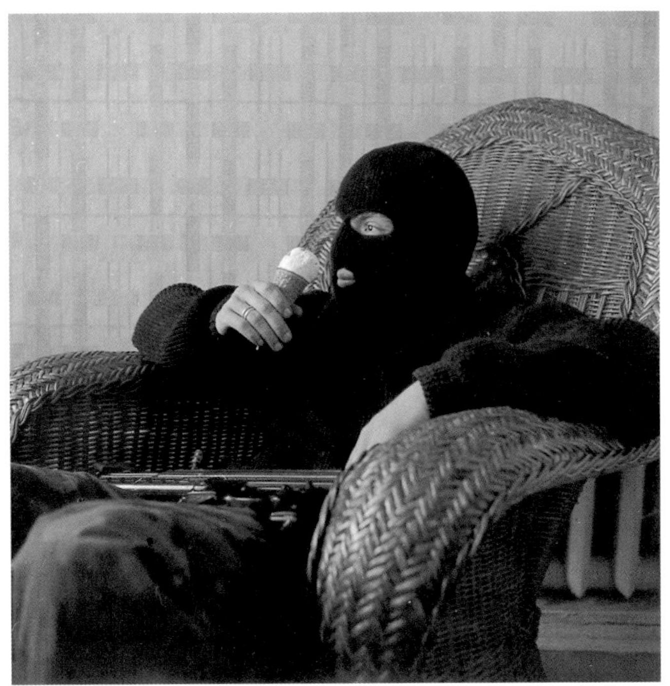

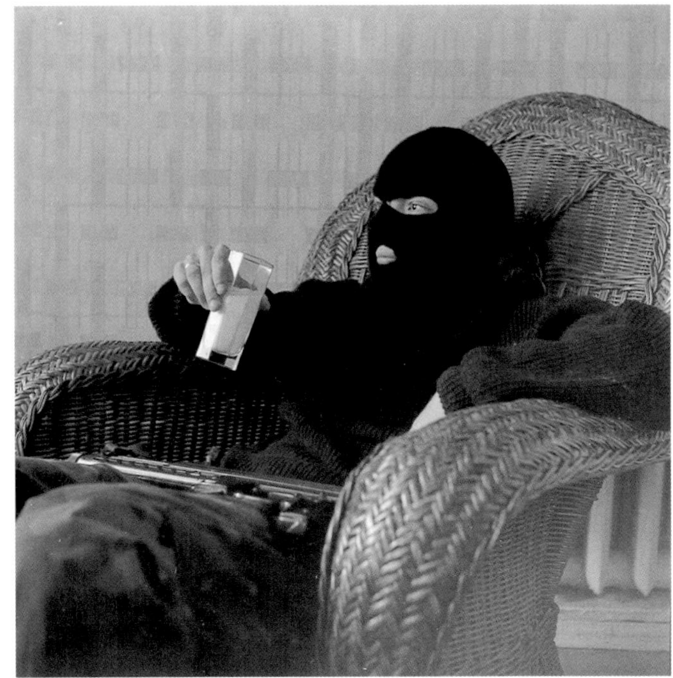

24 'Munchies', 1994

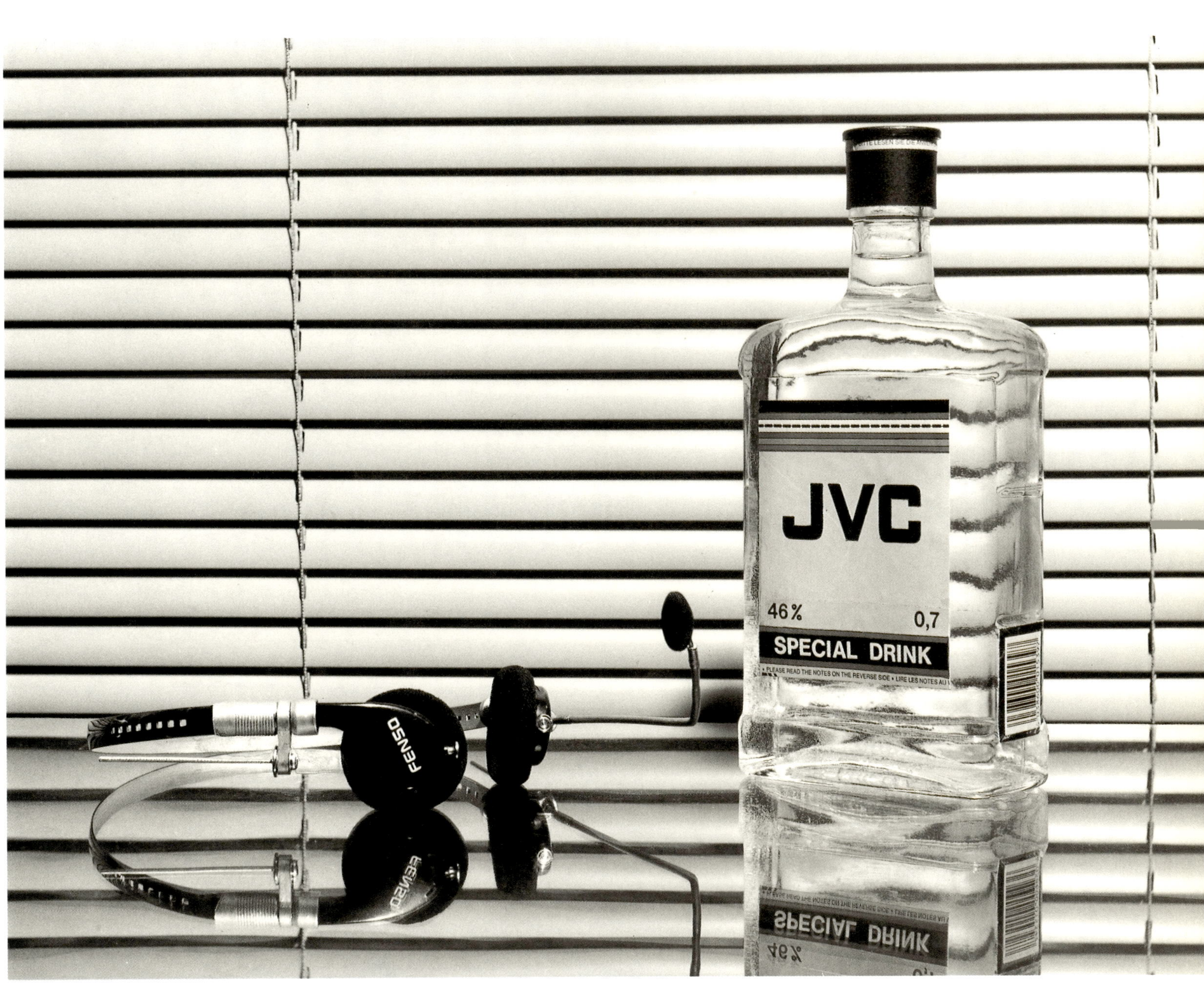

25 'Fenso and JVC' project *(Projekt „Fenso und JVC"),* 1994

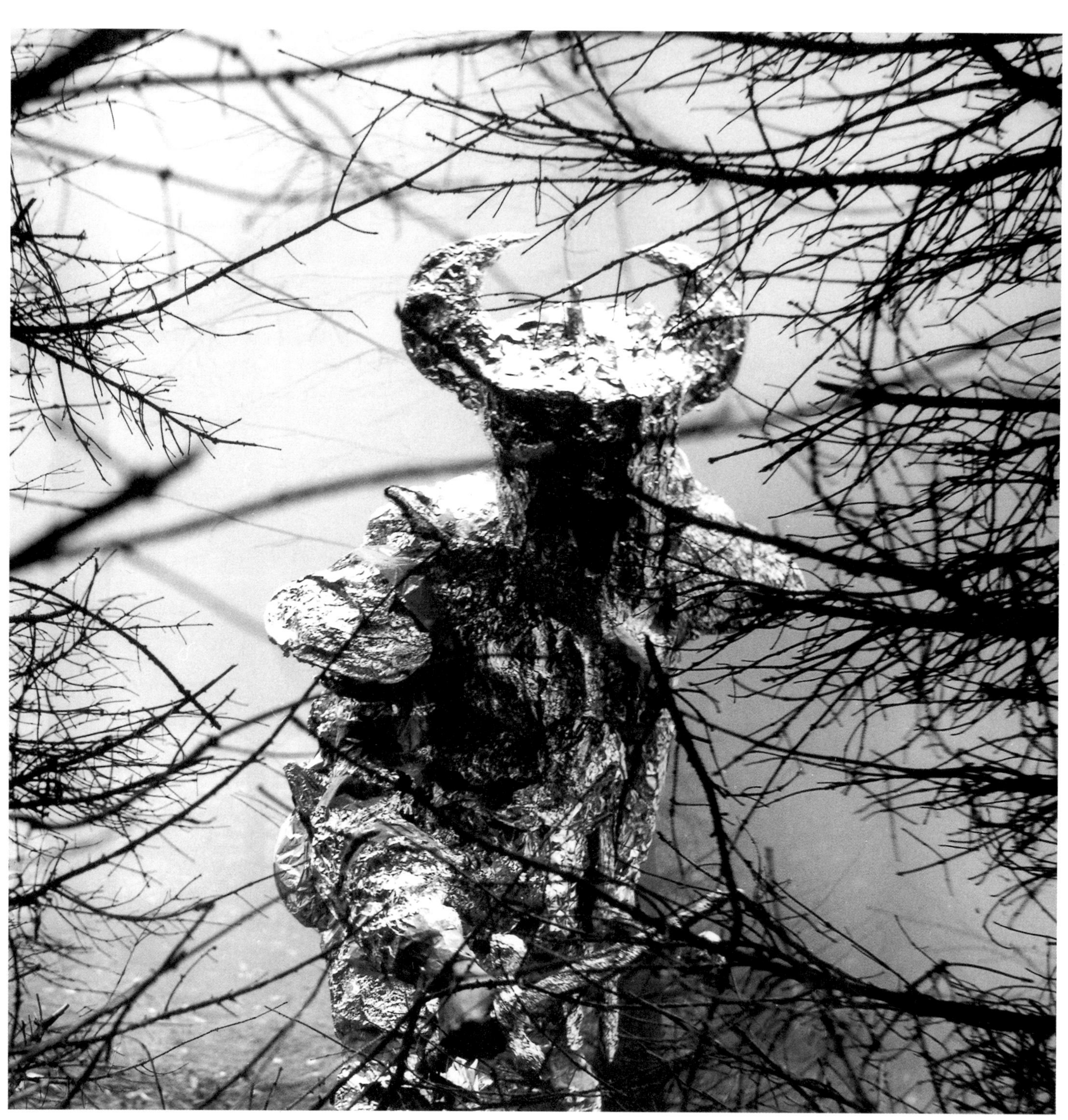

26 From the series 'Fenso Lights' *(Aus der Serie „Fenso Lights")*, 1993

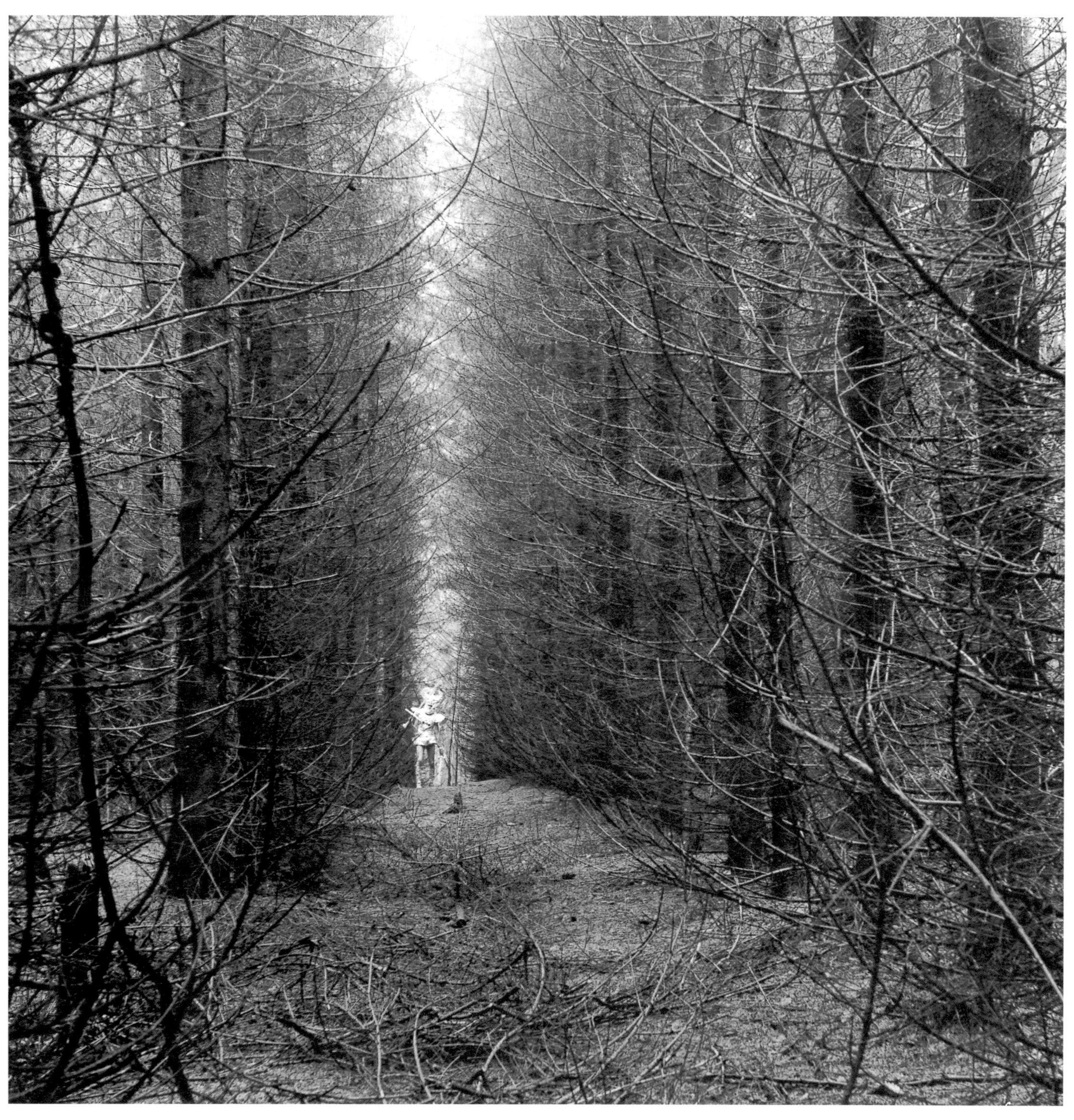

27 From the series 'Fenso Lights' *(Aus der Serie „Fenso Lights“)*, 1993

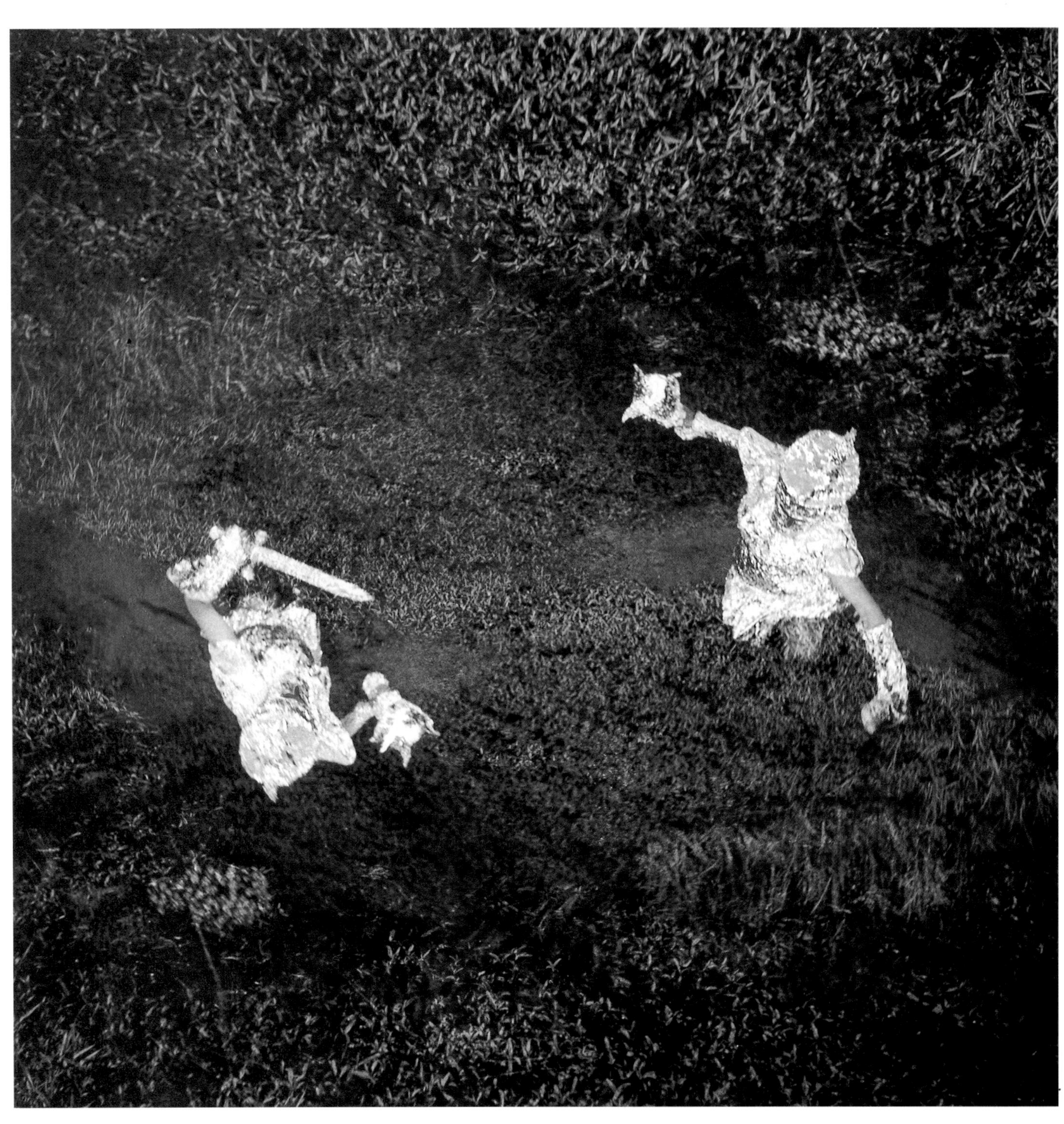

28 From the series 'Fenso Lights' *(Aus der Serie „Fenso Lights")*, 1993

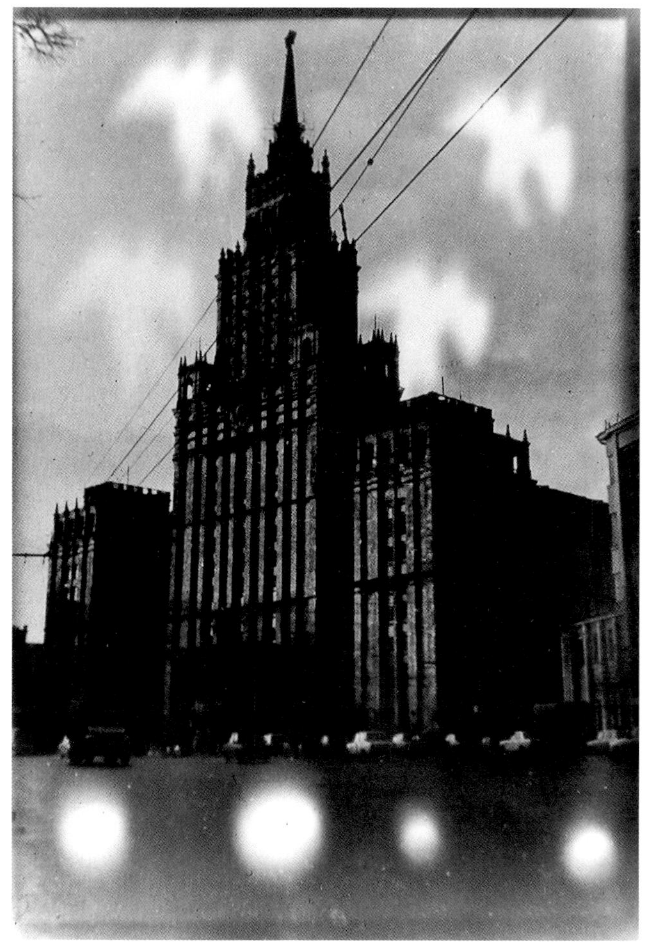

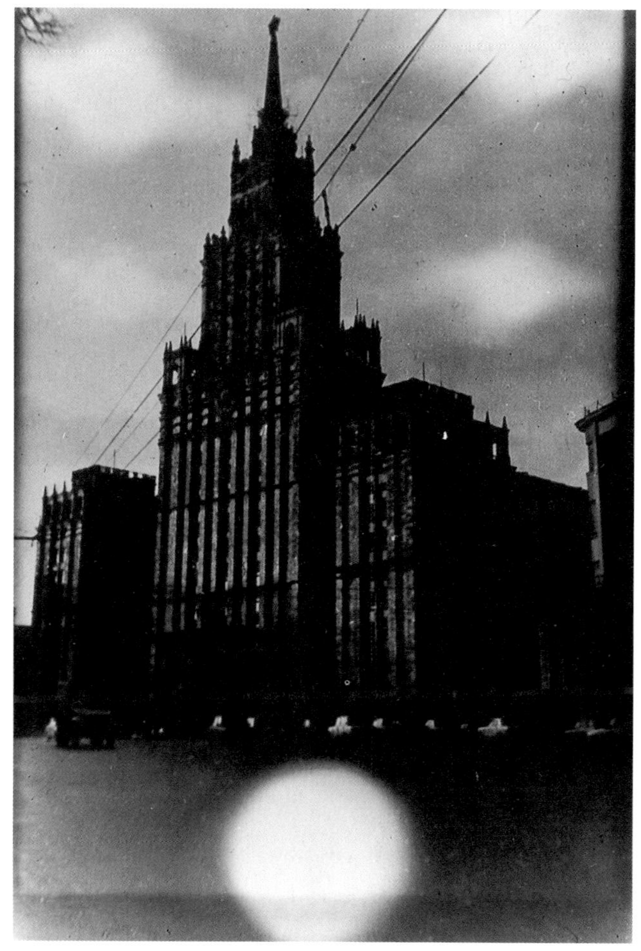

29 From the series 'Orbit 2' *(Aus der Serie „Umlaufbahn 2“)*, 1993

30 From the series 'Orbit 2' *(Aus der Serie „Umlaufbahn 2“)*, 1993

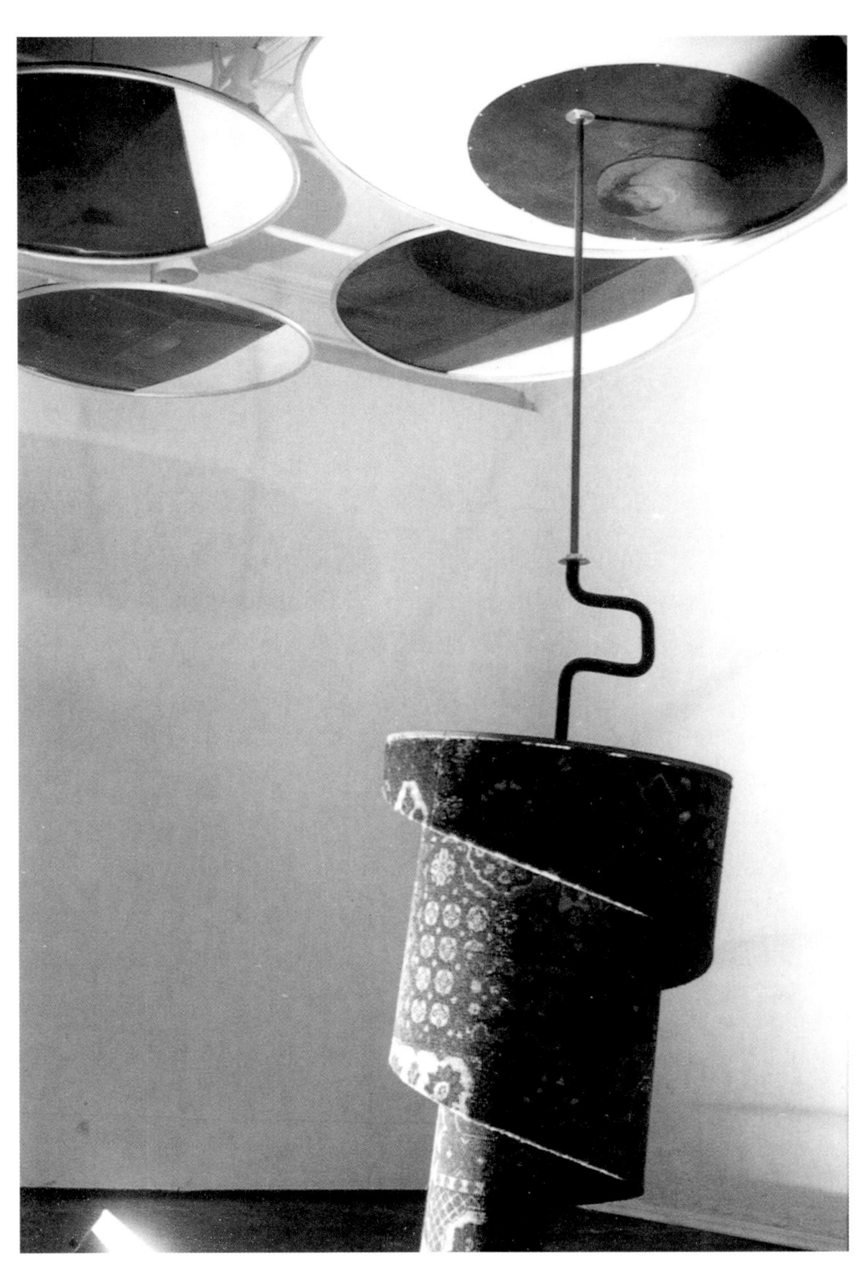

31 *Orbit S (Umlaufbahn S)*, 1994

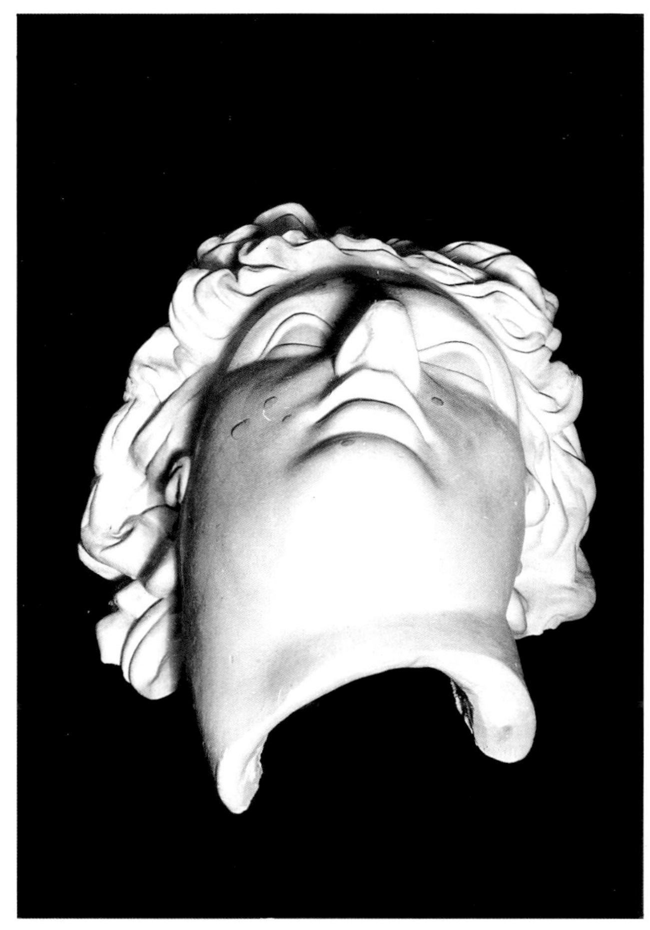

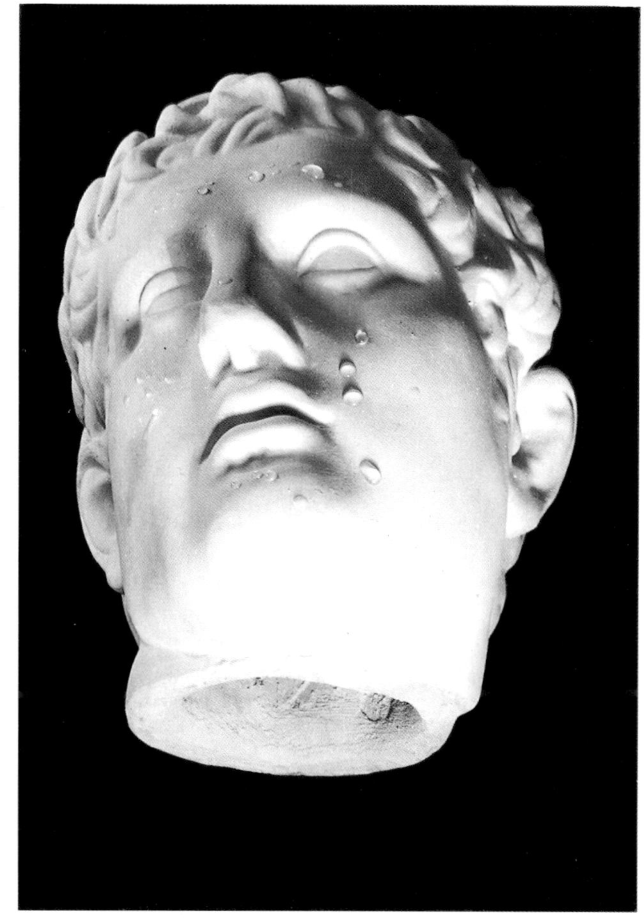

32 Untitled *(Ohne Titel)*, 1991

33 Untitled *(Ohne Titel)*, 1991

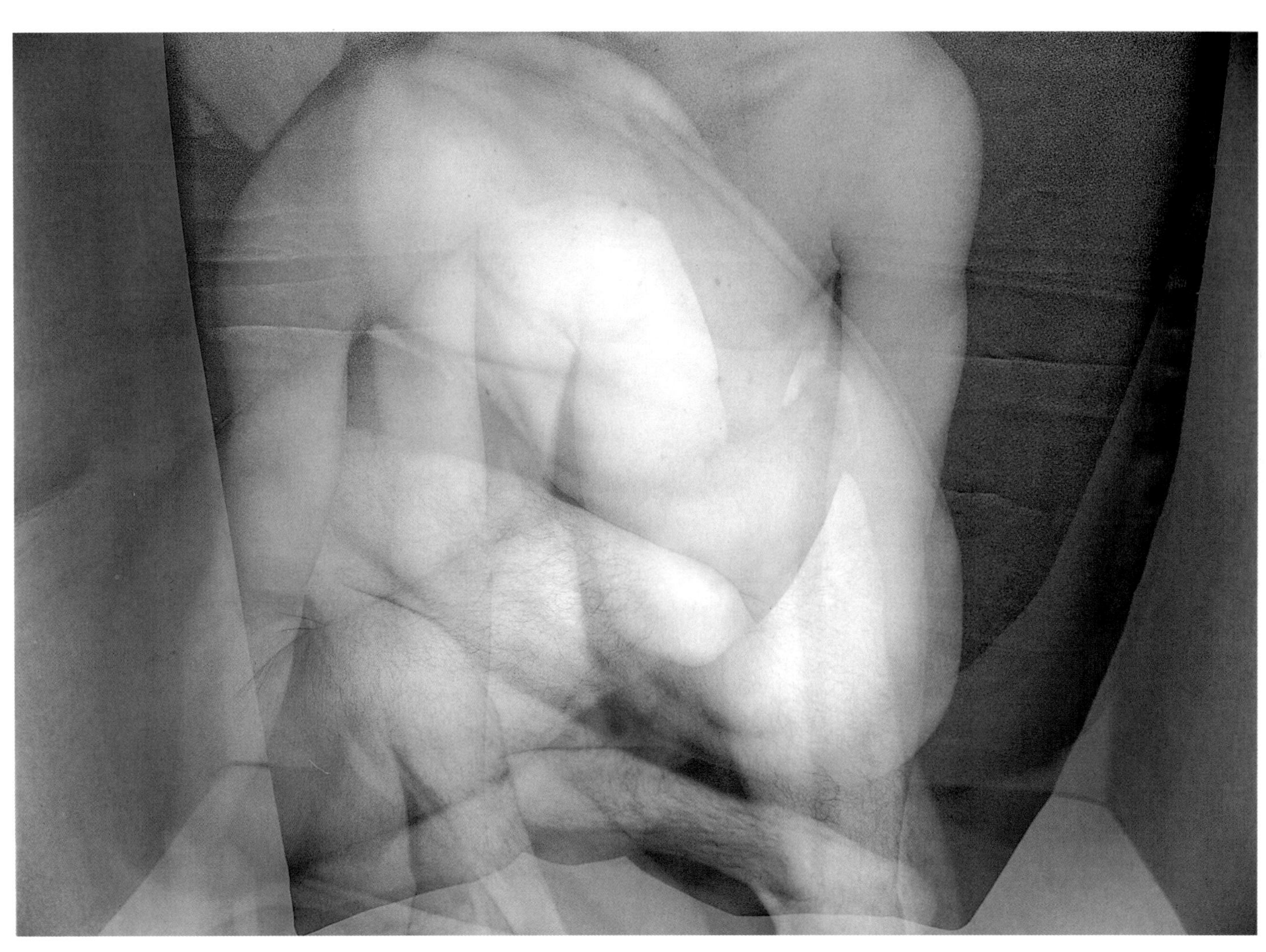

34 *Self-Portrait (Selbstportrait)*, 1993

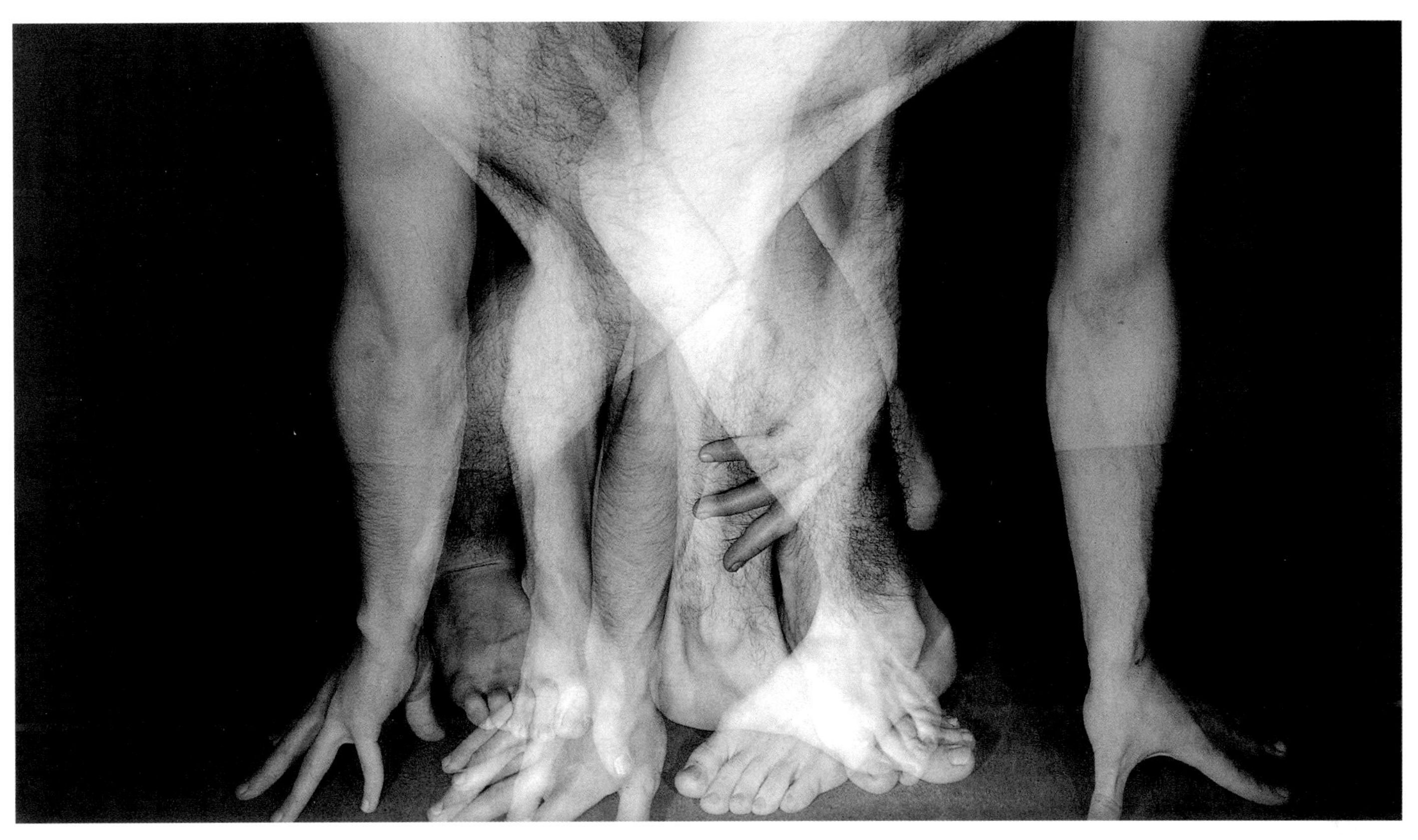

35 *Self-Portrait (Selbstportrait),* 1993

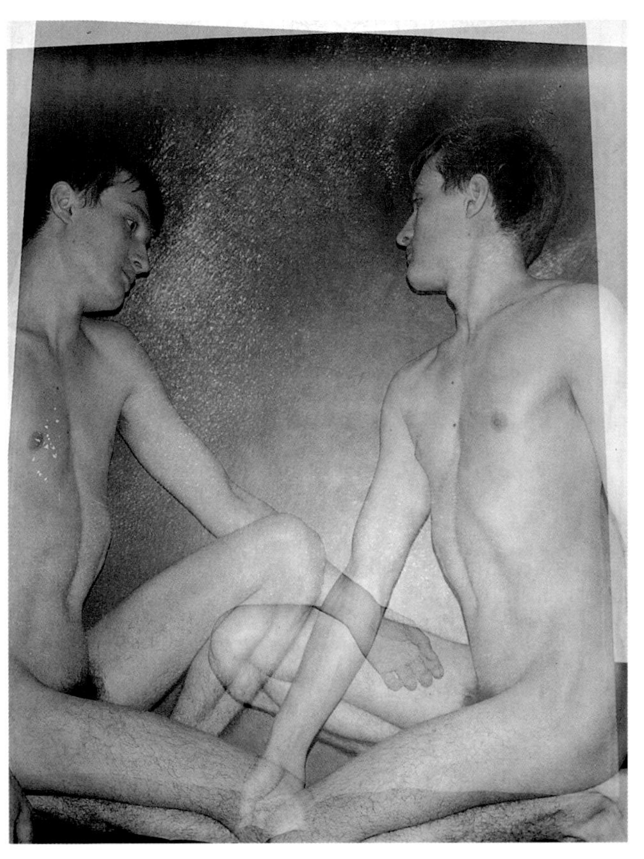

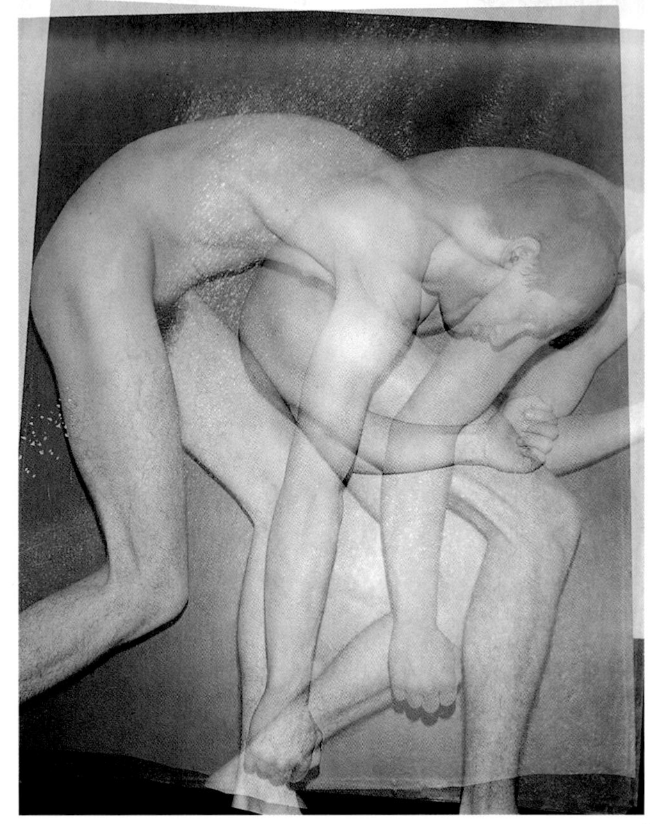

36 Untitled *(Ohne Titel)*, 1994

37 Untitled *(Ohne Titel)*, 1994

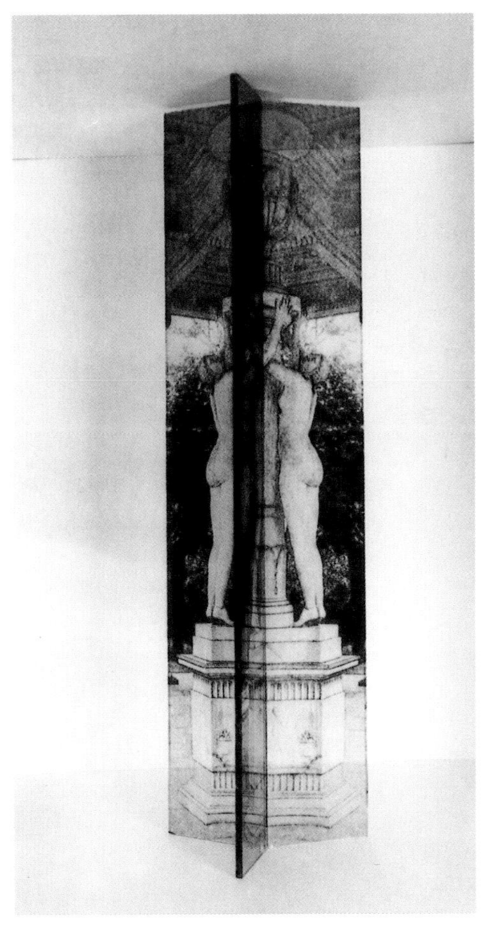

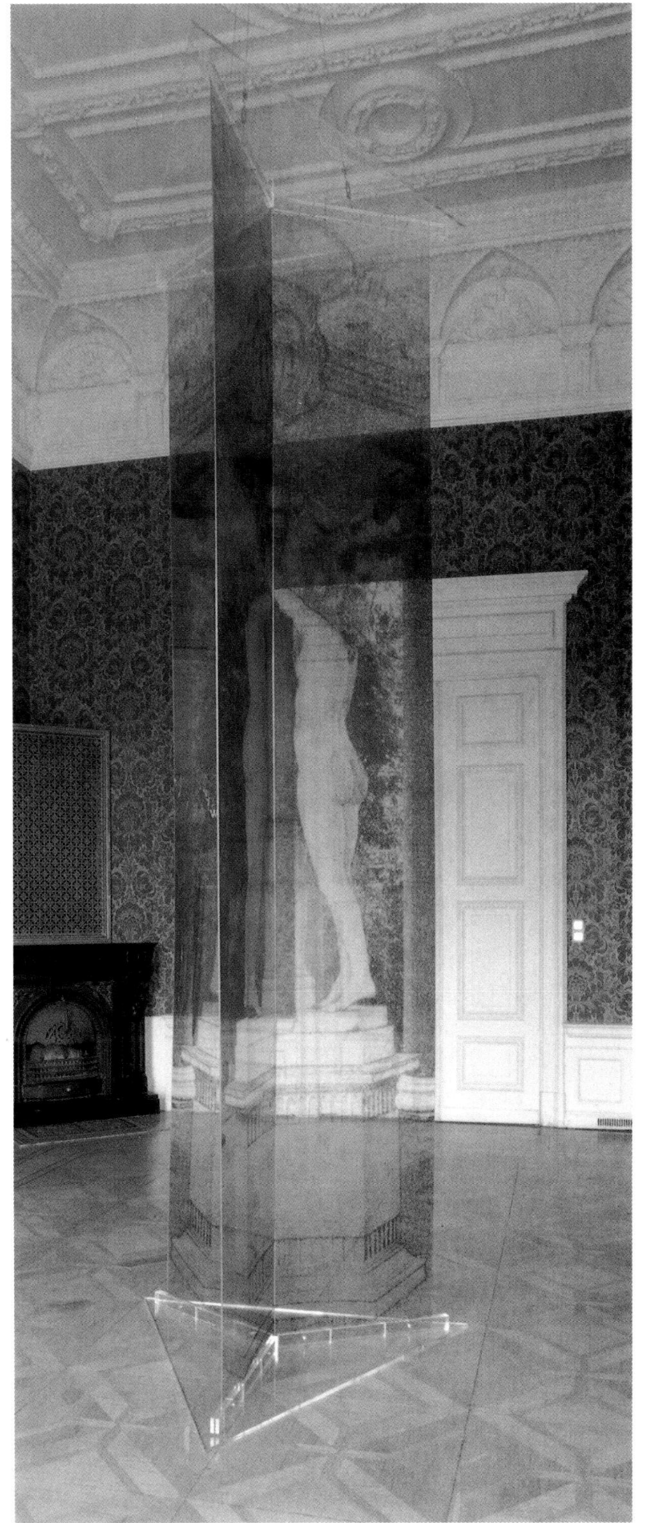

38 'The Three Graces' *(„Die drei Grazien")*, 1993–95

39 'The Three Graces' *(„Die drei Grazien")*, 1993–95

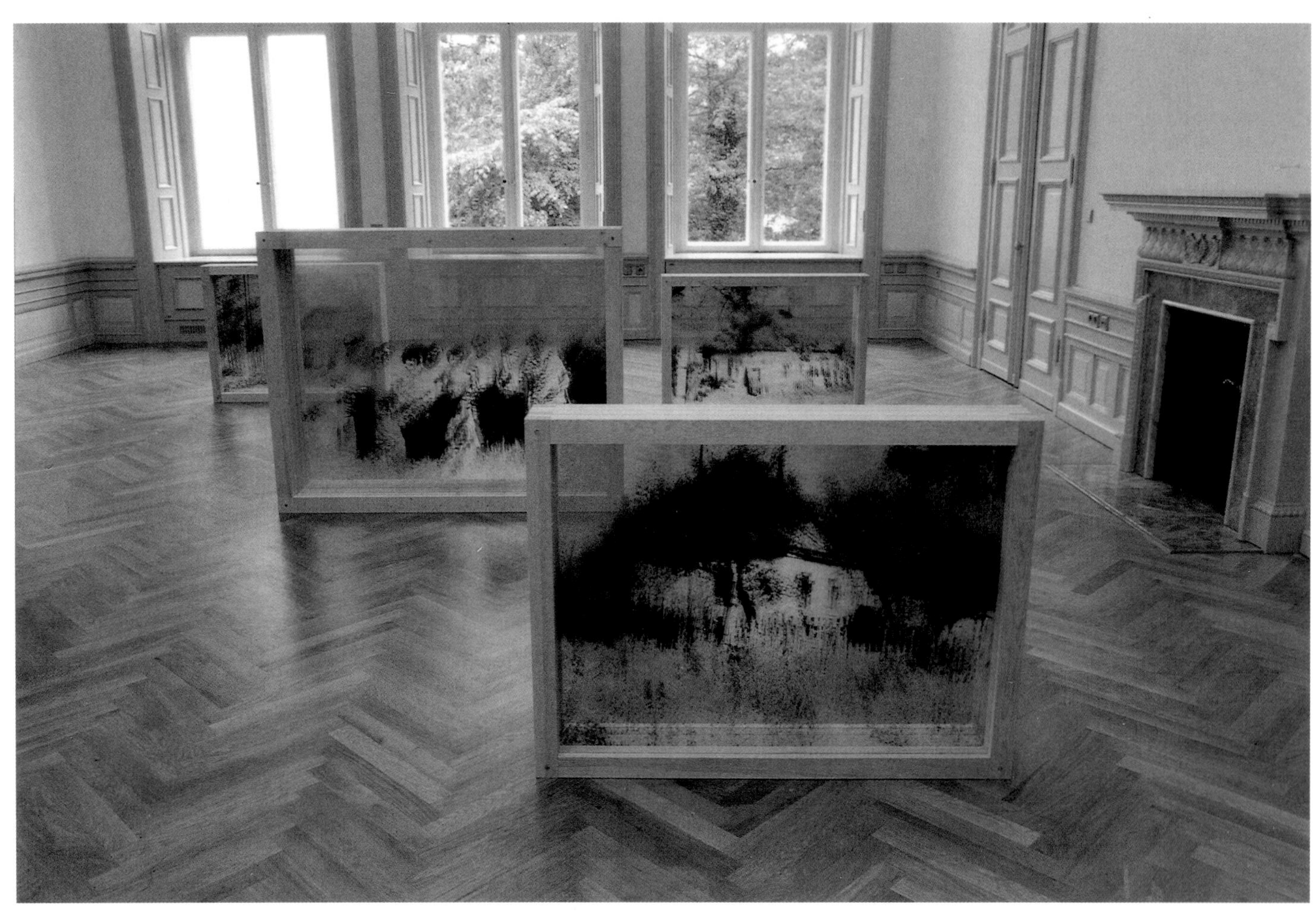

40 From the series 'The Hamlet' *(Aus der Serie „Das Dorf"),* 1992–95

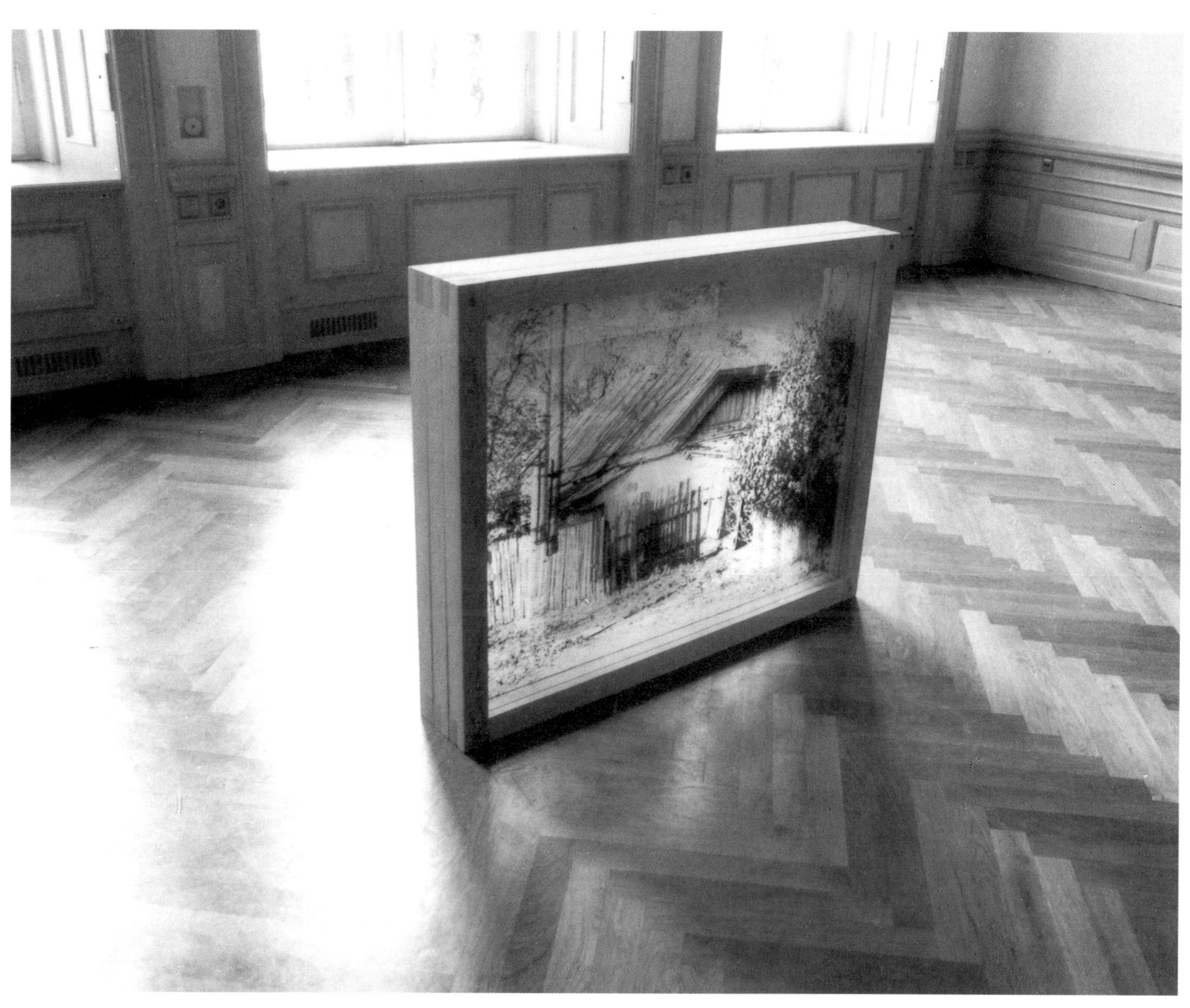

41 From the series 'The Hamlet' *(Aus der Serie „Das Dorf")*, 1992–95

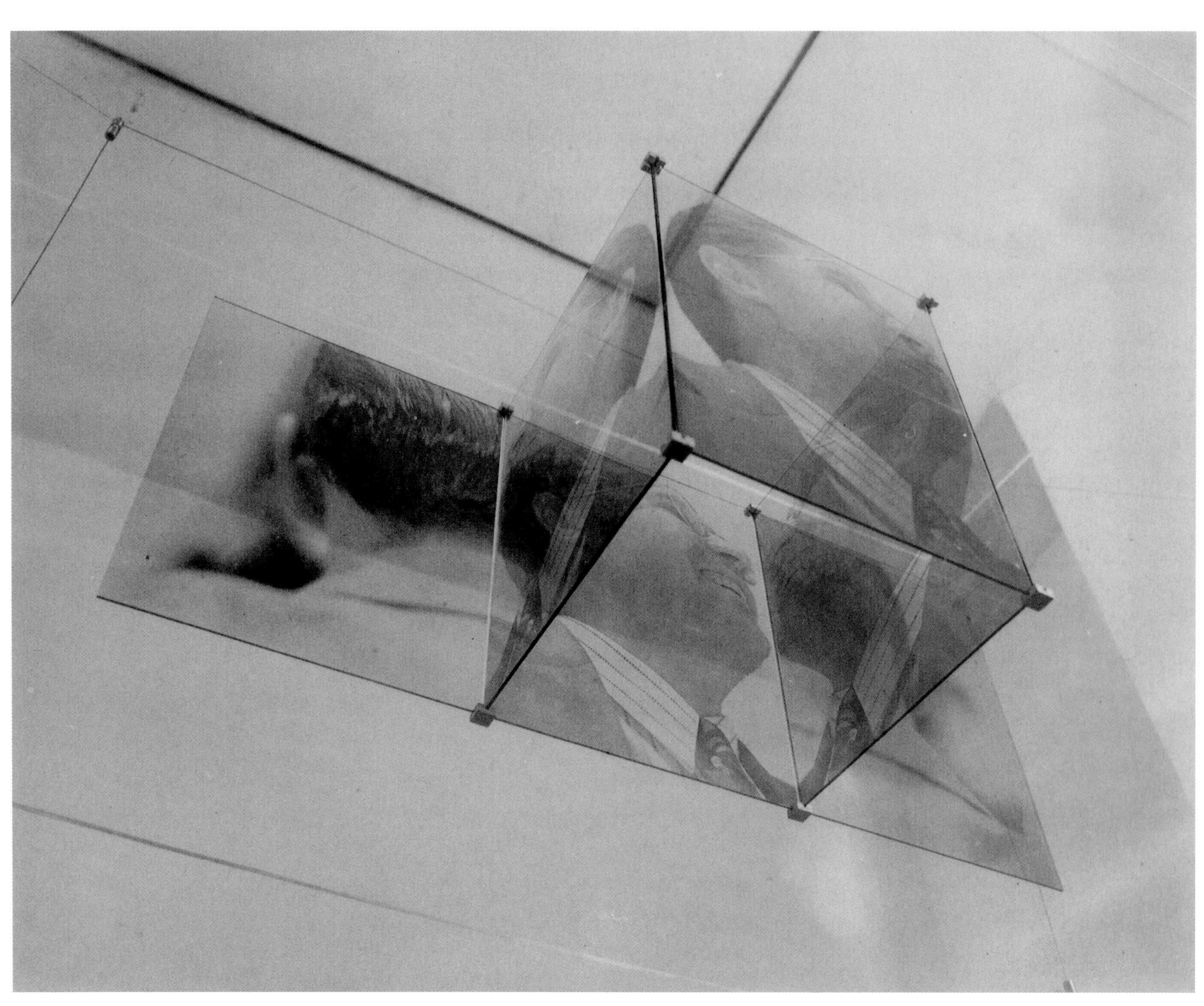

42 'On the Phantasmagorical' *(„Über das Phantasmagorische"),* 1994

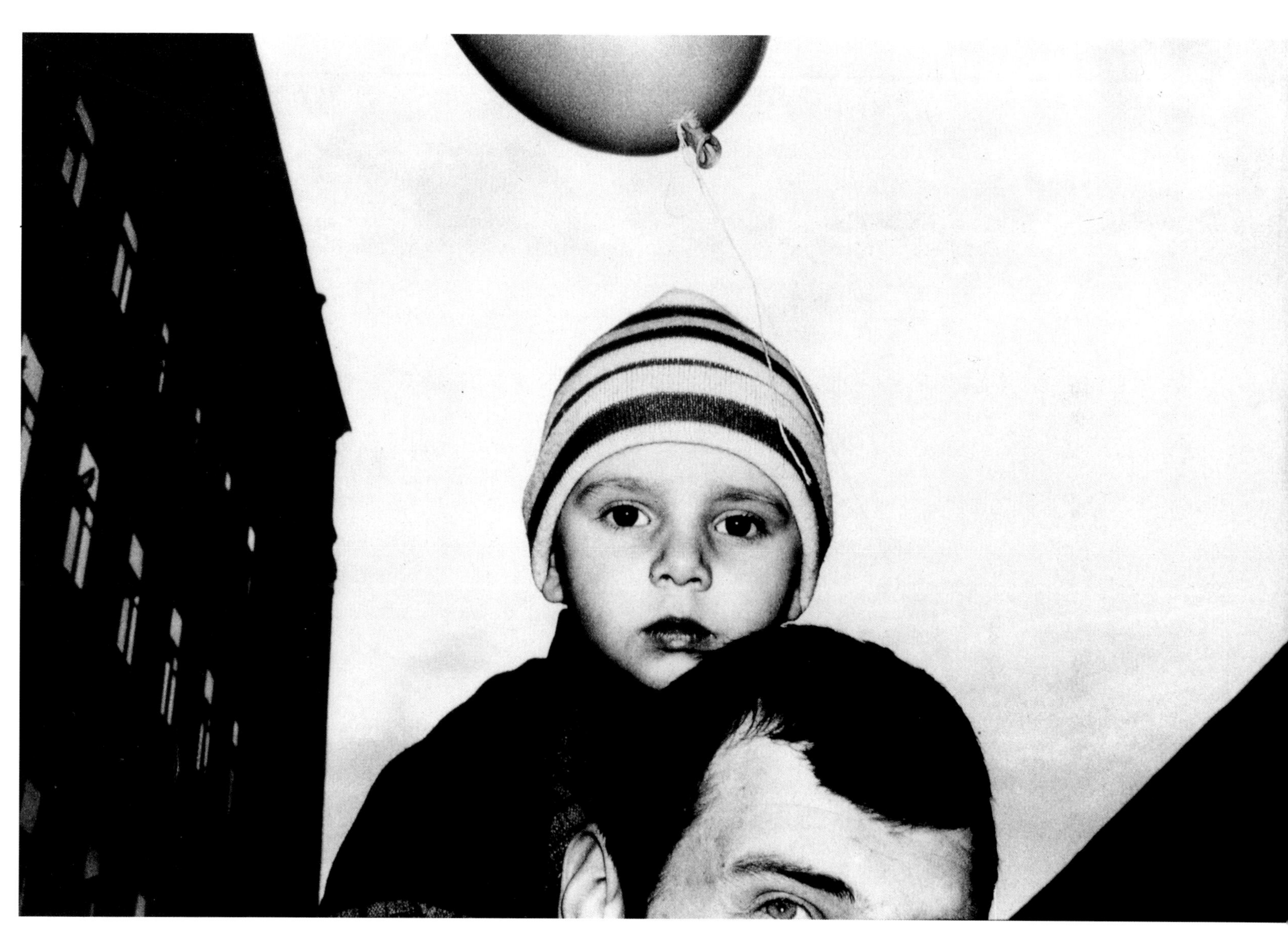

43 From the series 'Study in Hard Photography' *(Aus der Serie „Versuche in harter Fotografie")*, 1990–91

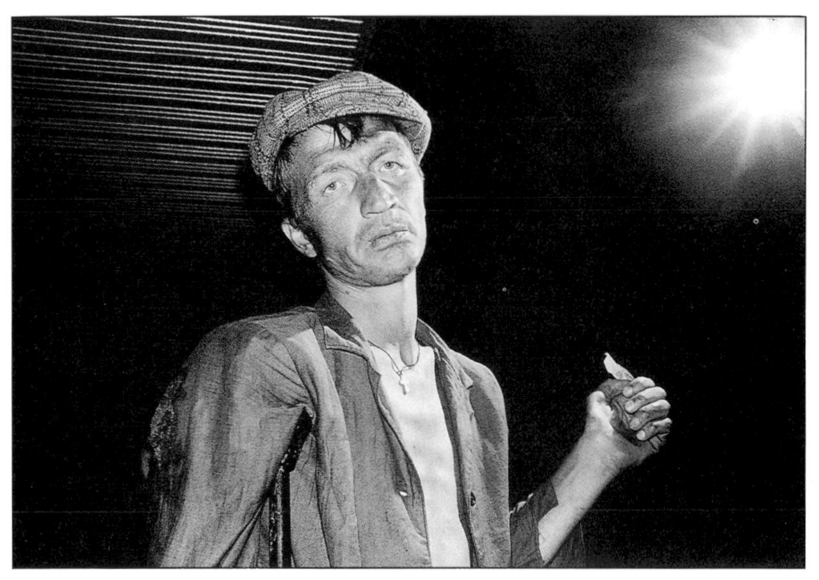

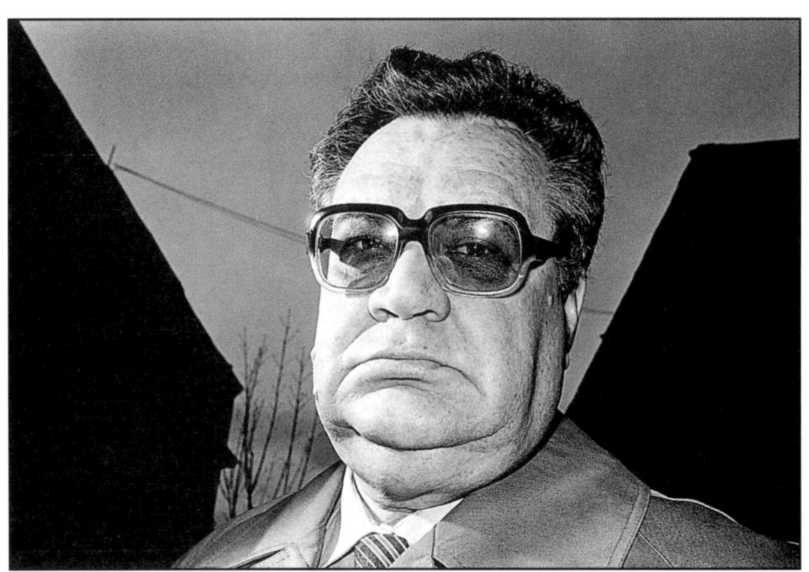

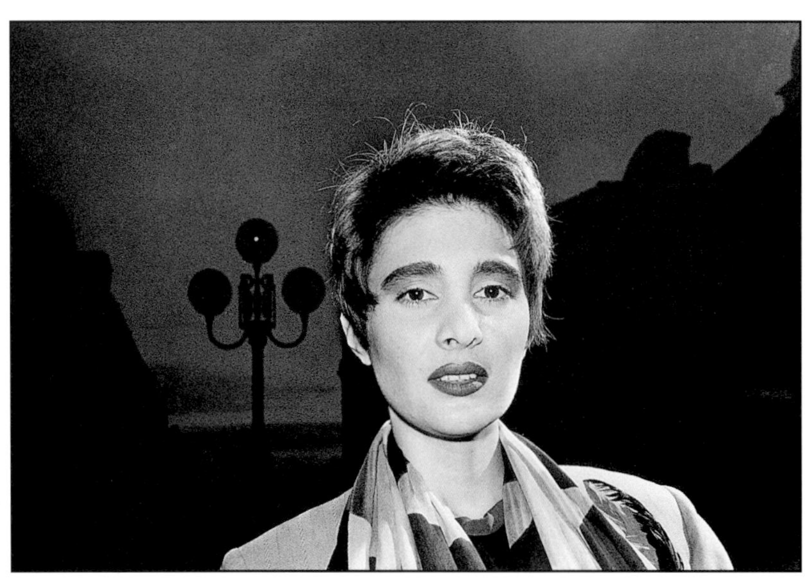

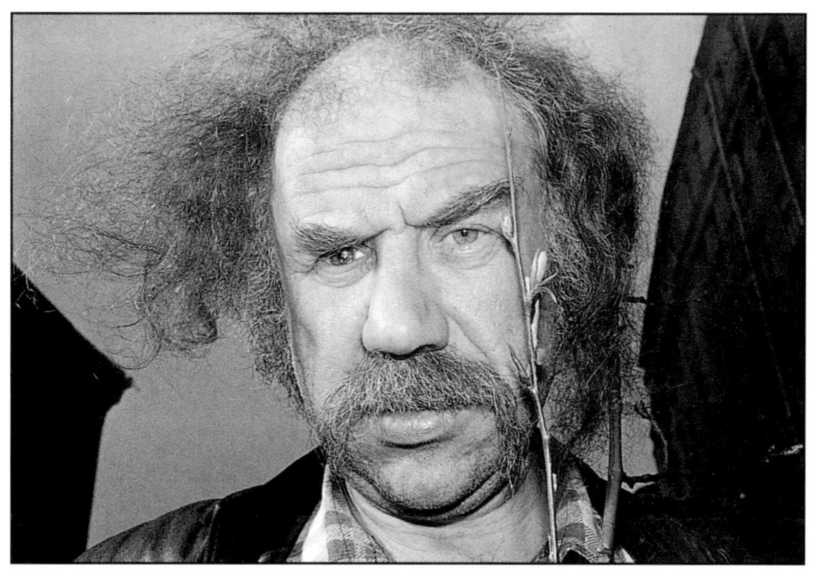

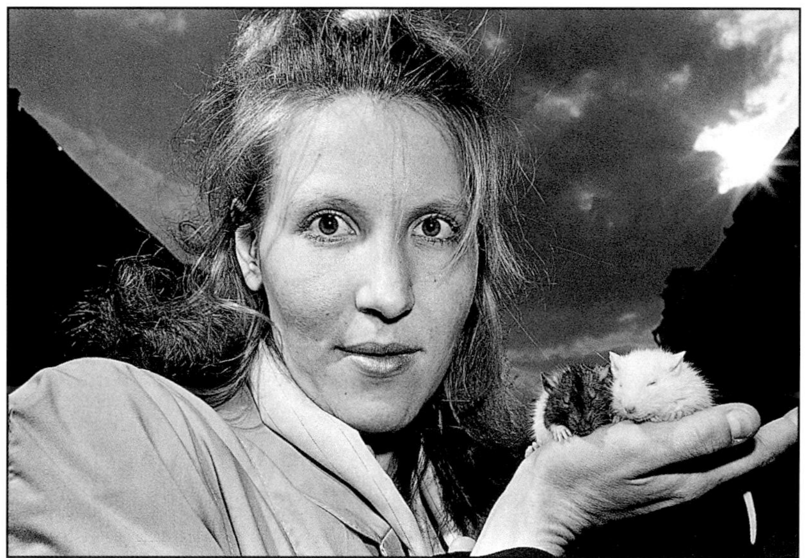

44–48 From the series 'Study in Hard Photography' *(Aus der Serie „Versuche in harter Fotografie")*, 1990–91

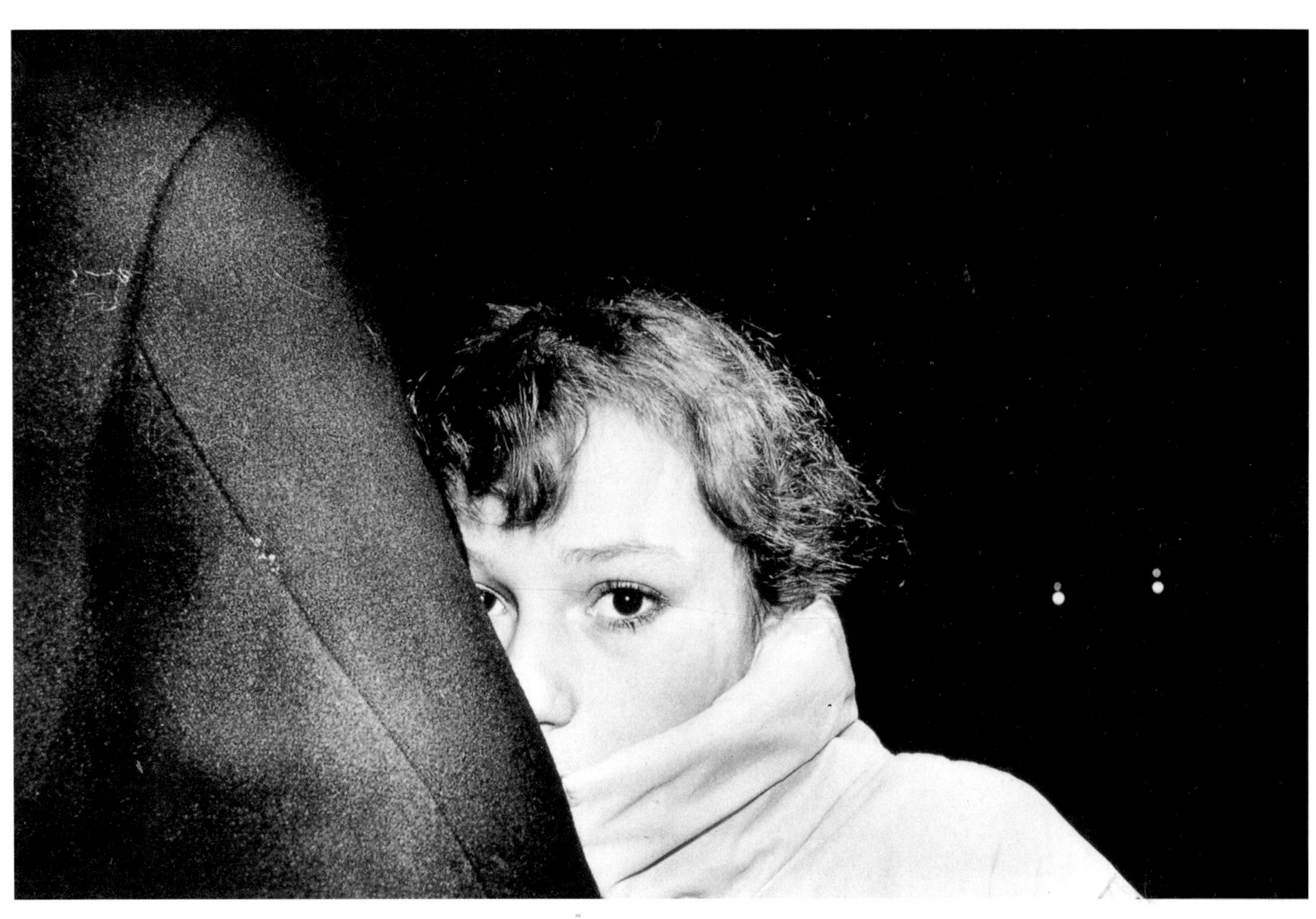

49 From the series 'Study in Hard Photography' *(Aus der Serie „Versuche in harter Fotografie")*, 1990–91

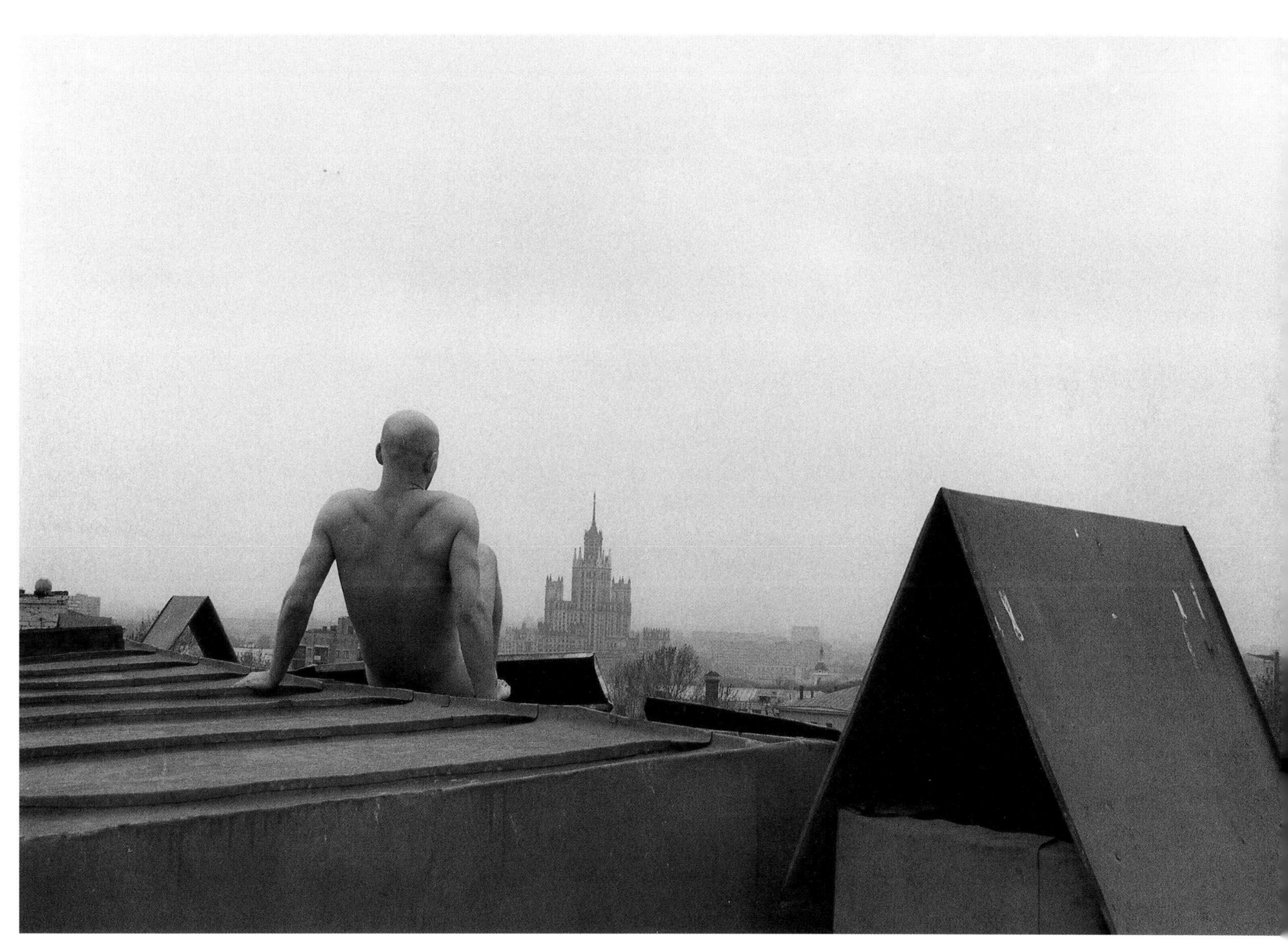

50 From the series 'Living Monument' *(Aus der Serie „Lebendes Monument"),* 1993

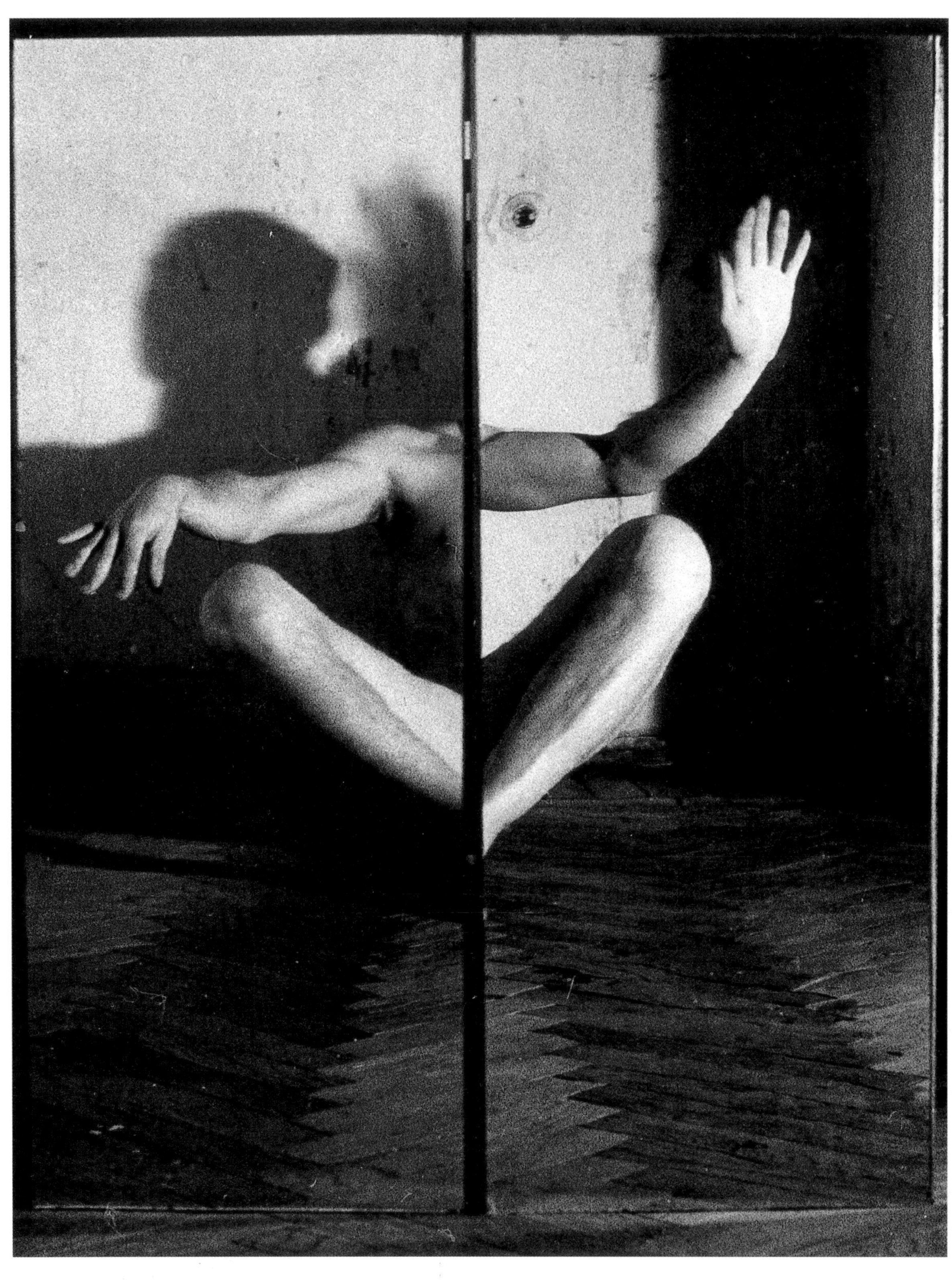

51 From the series 'Man and Mirror' (with G. Vinogradov) *(Aus der Serie „Mensch und Spiegel" [zus. mit G. Vinogradov]),* 1993

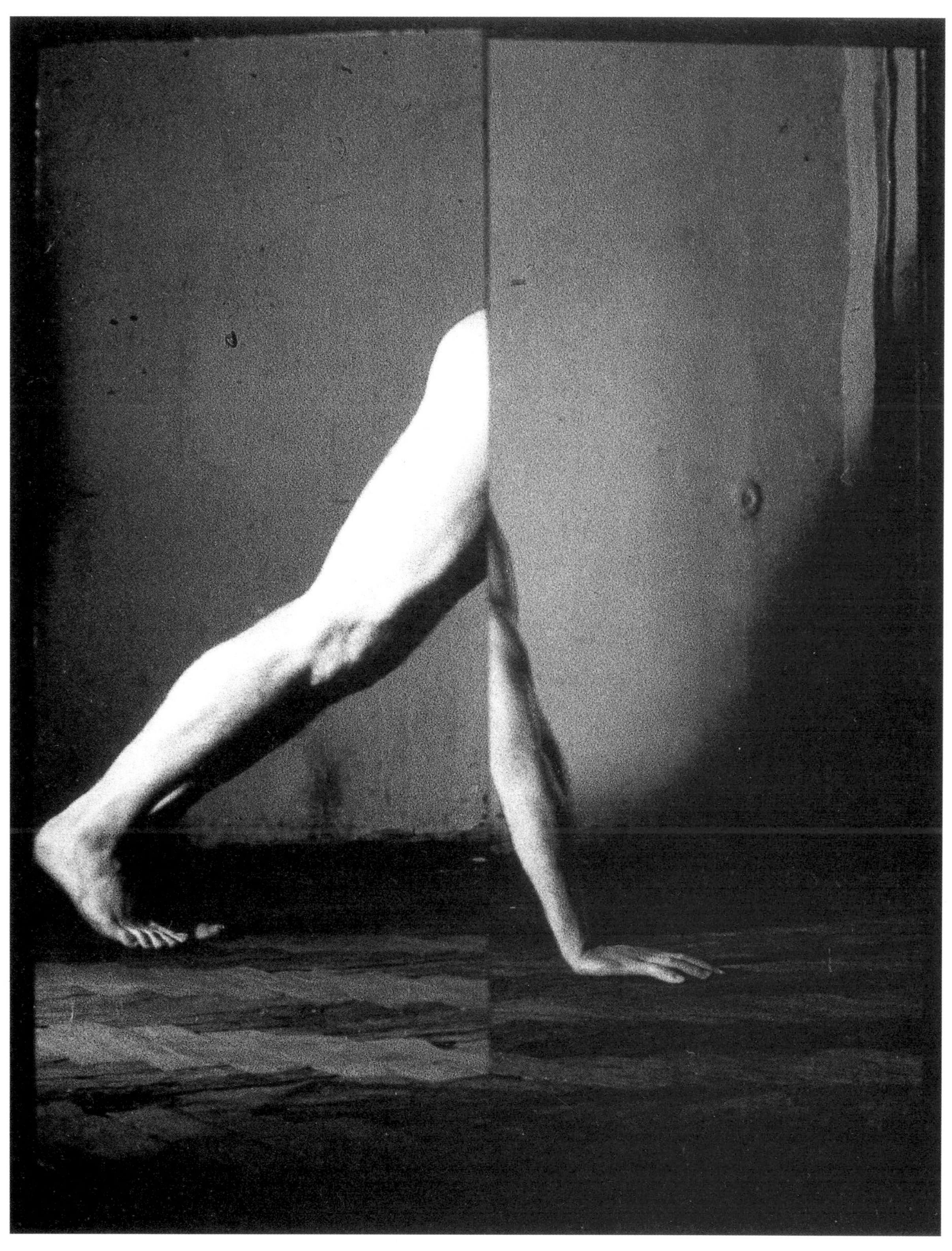

52 From the series 'Man and Mirror' (with G. Vinogradov) *(Aus der Serie „Mensch und Spiegel" [zus. mit G. Vinogradov]),* 1993

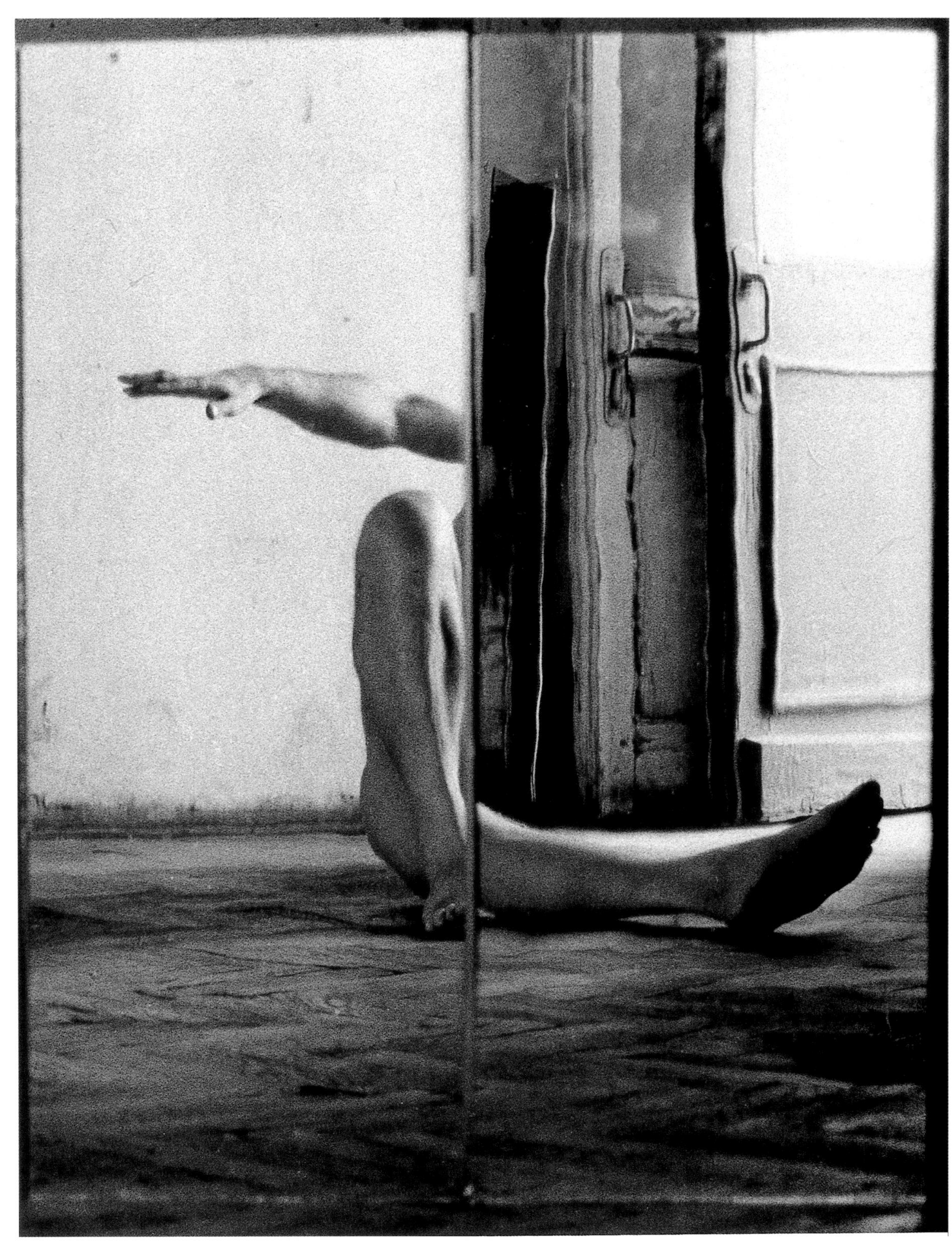

53 From the series 'Man and Mirror' (with G. Vinogradov) *(Aus der Serie „Mensch und Spiegel" [zus. mit G. Vinogradov]),* 1993

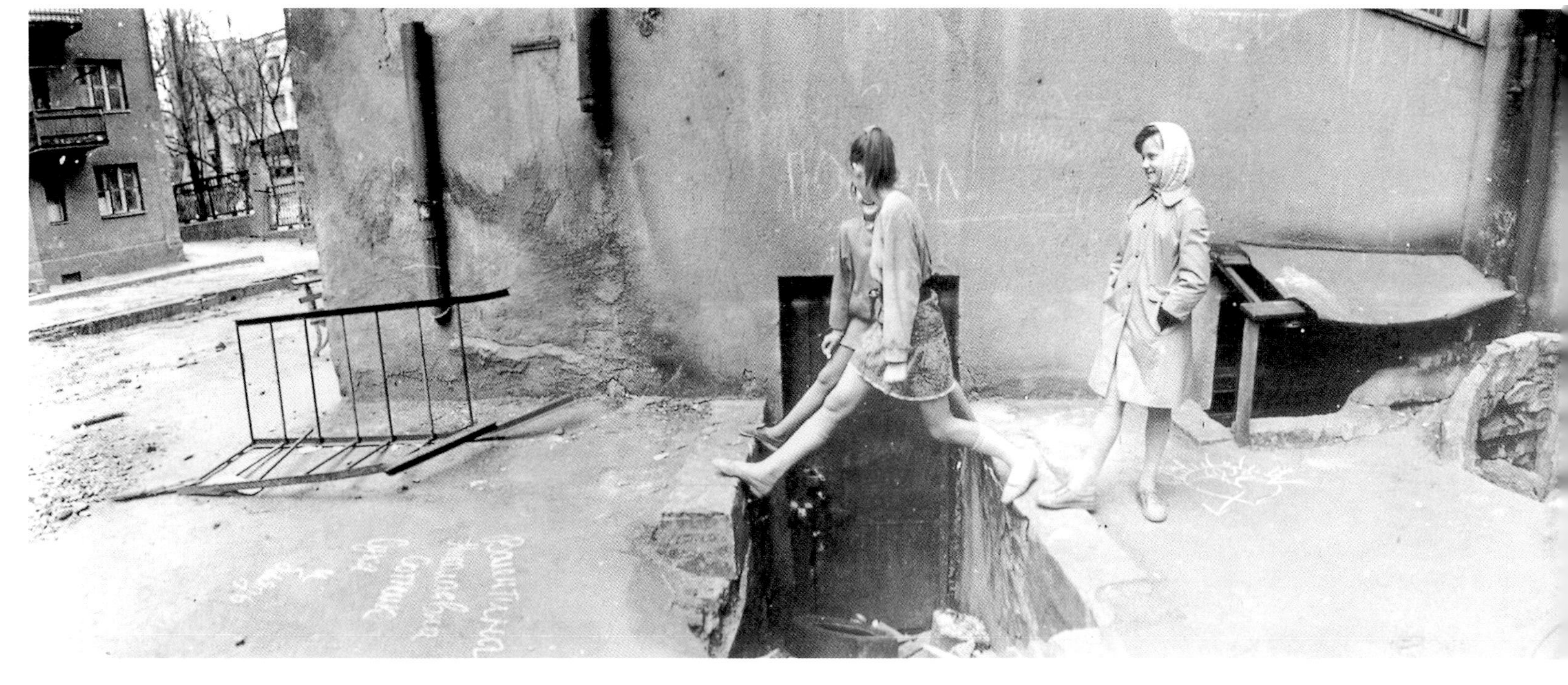

54 From the series 'Ground Bound' *(Aus der Serie „Bodenständig"),* 1991

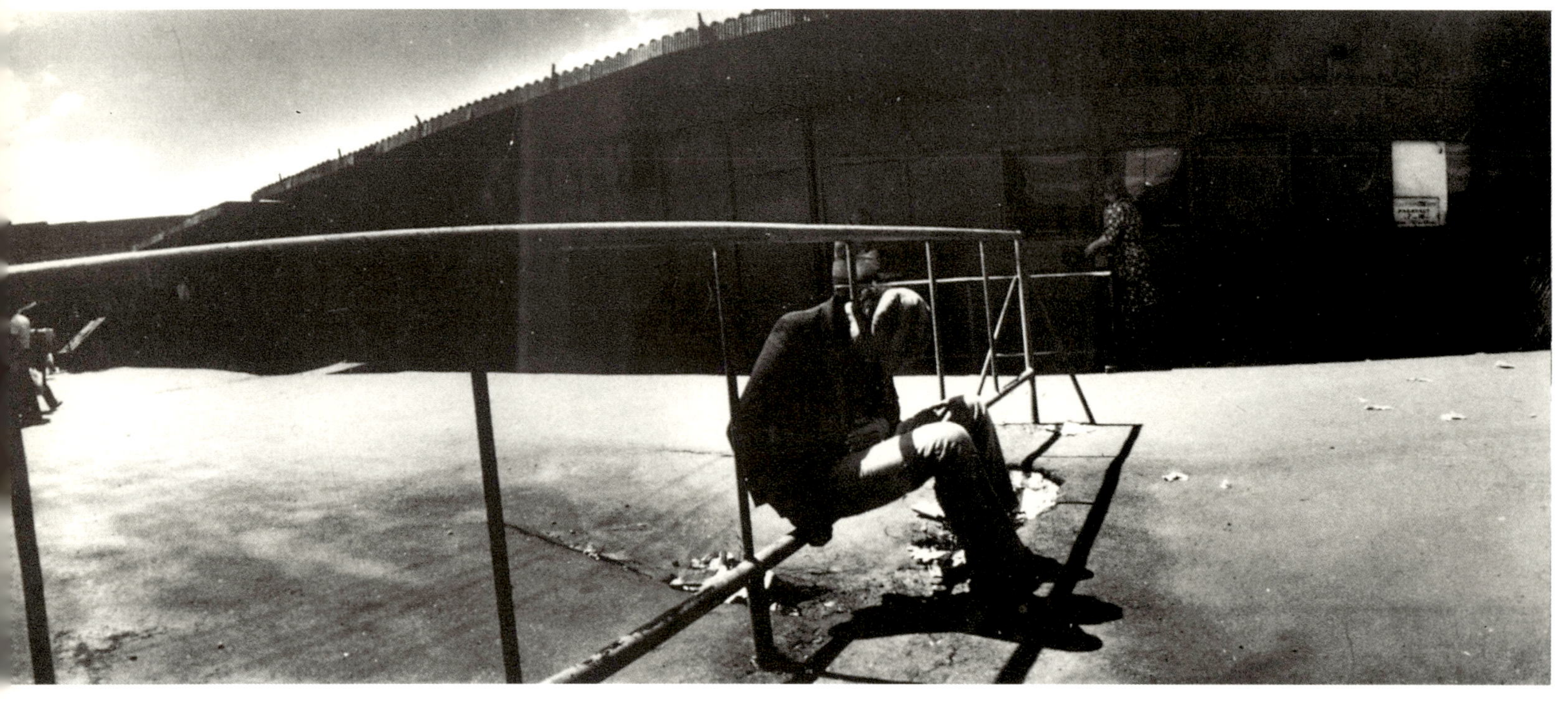

55 From the series 'Ground Bound' *(Aus der Serie „Bodenständig")*, 1991

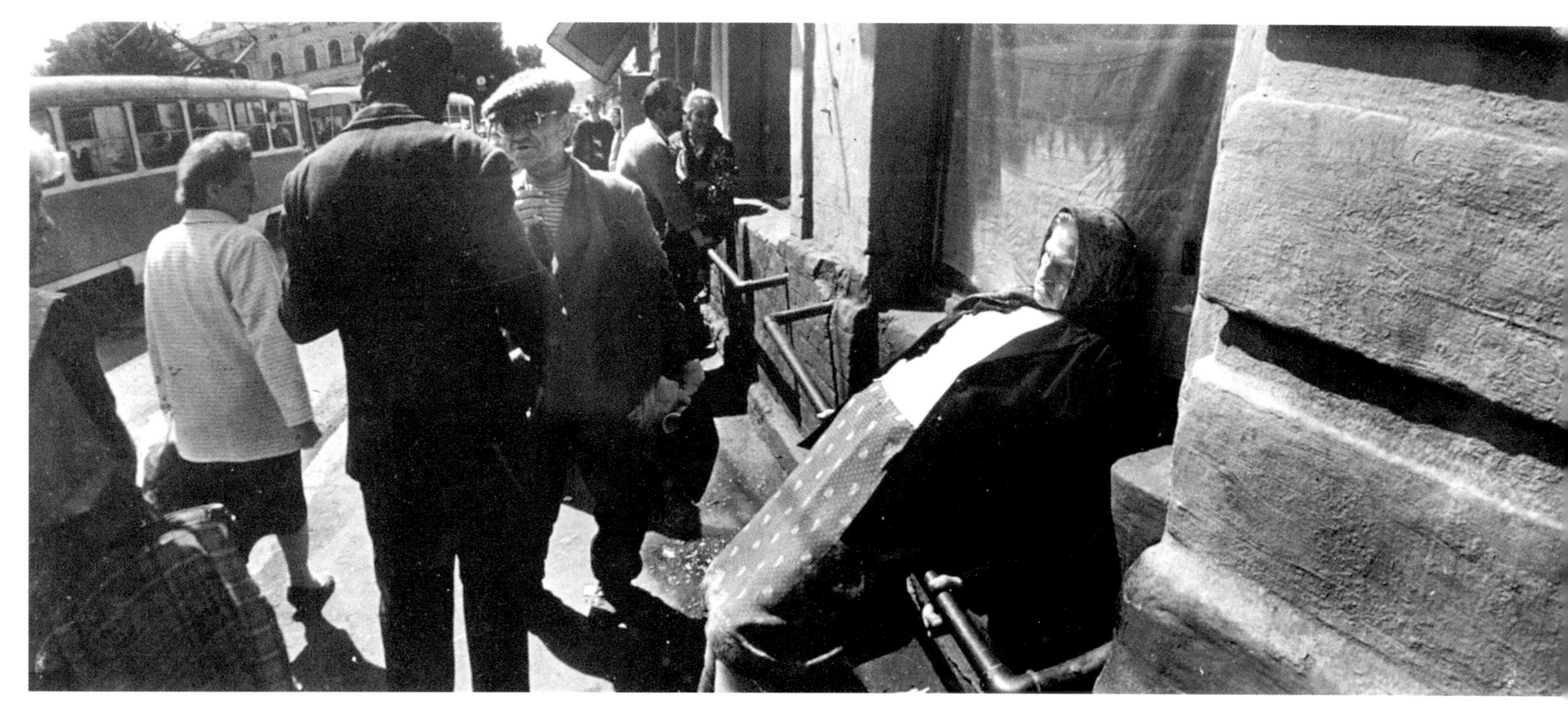

56 From the series 'Ground Bound' *(Aus der Serie „Bodenständig")*, 1991

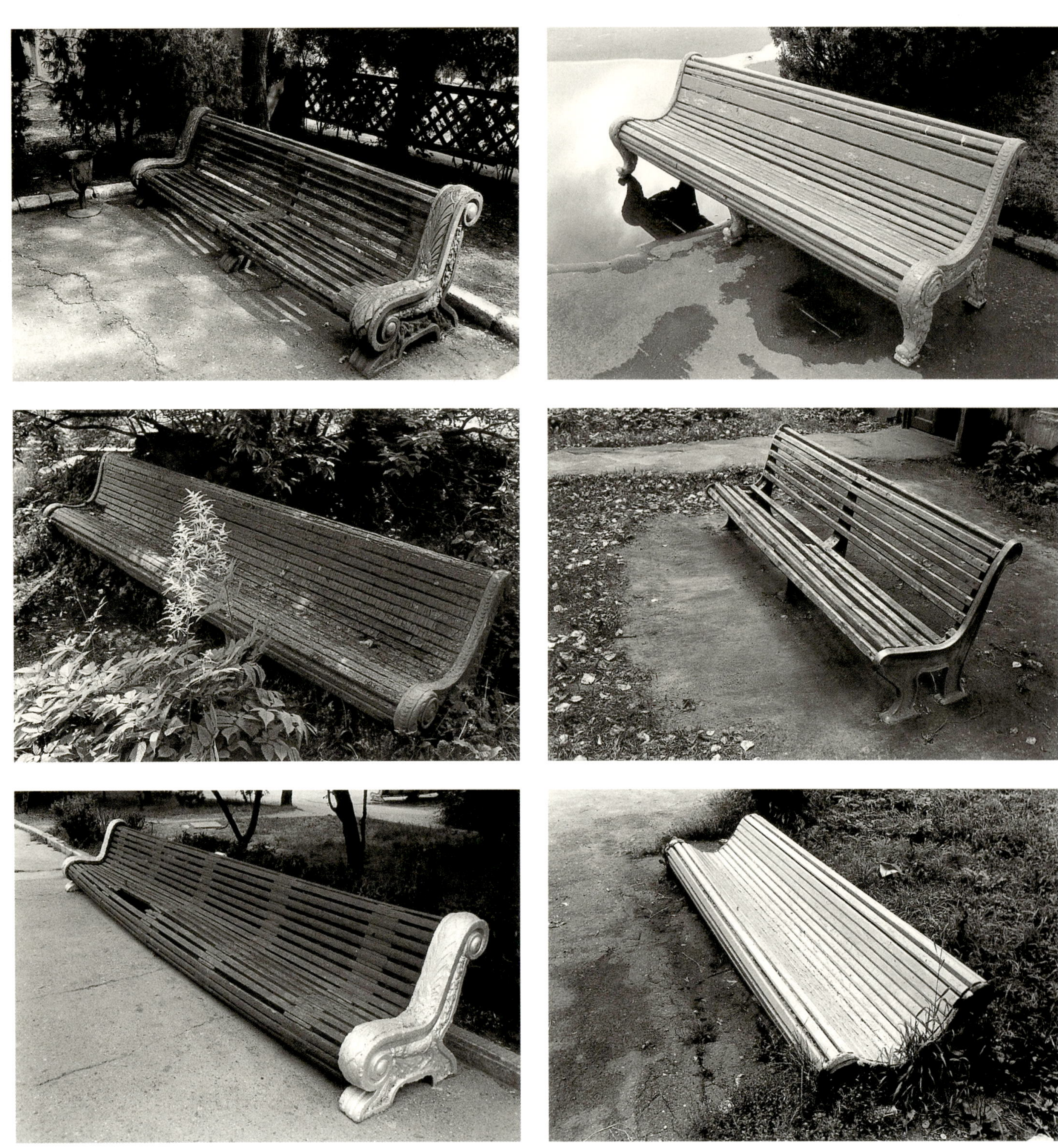

57 'Examination of a Soviet Bench' *(„Erforschung einer sowjetischen Parkbank")*, 1993–95

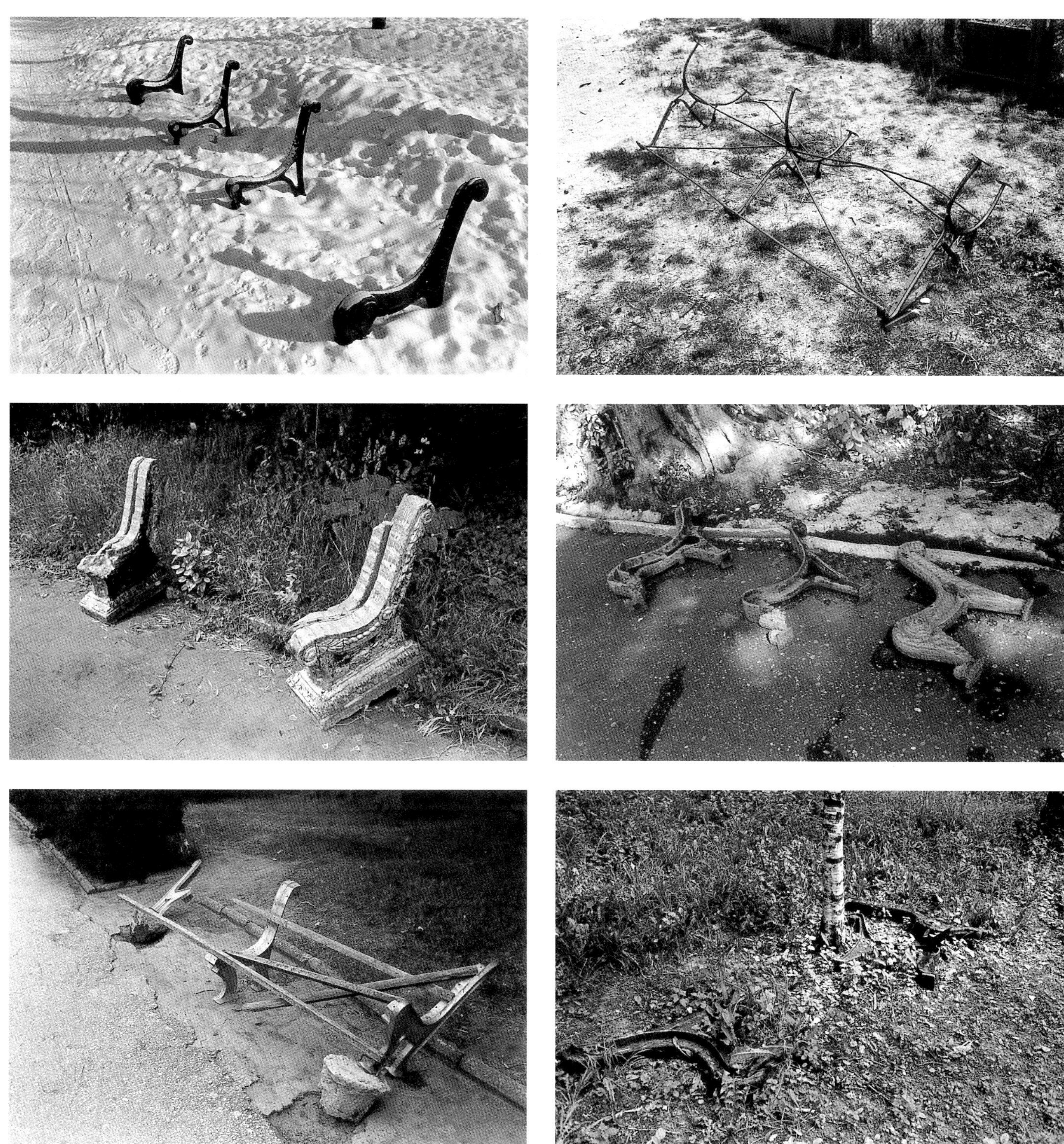

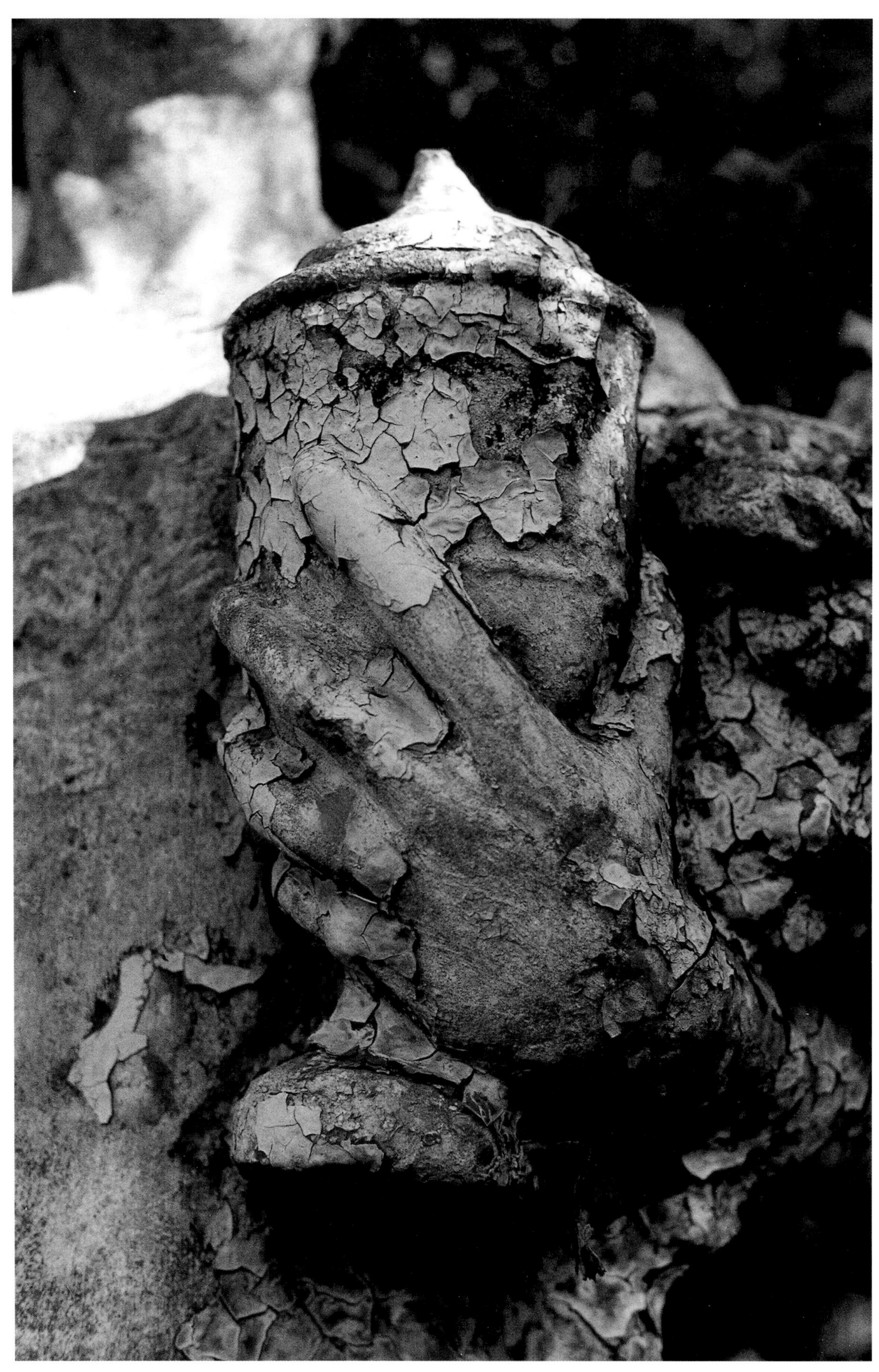

58 From the series 'Last Soviet Monumental Art': *Hand, Moscow (Aus der Serie „Letzte sowjetische Monumentalkunst": Hand, Moskau),* 1988–95

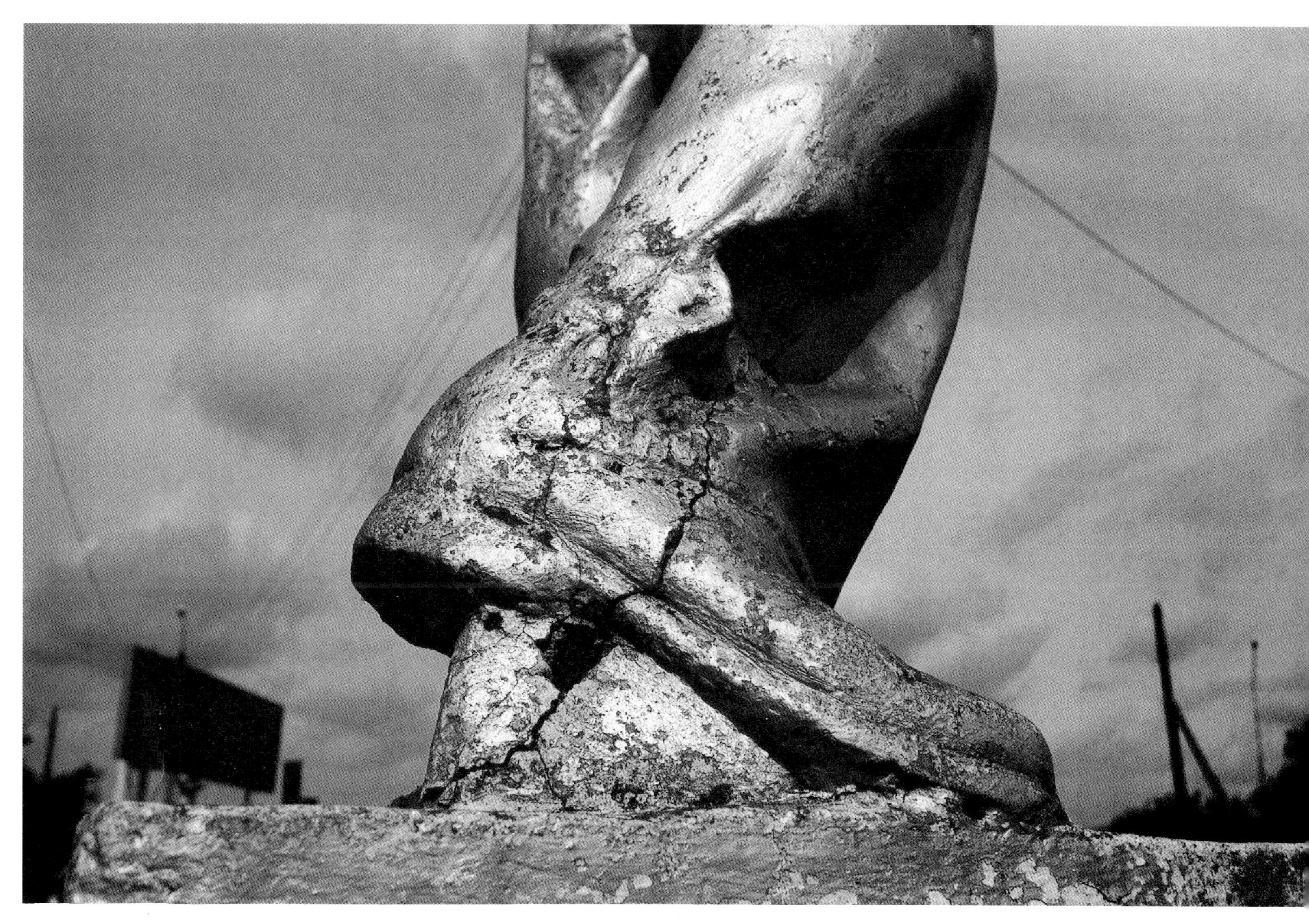

59 From the series 'Last Soviet Monumental Art': *Tractor Driver, Shukov*
(Aus der Serie „Letzte sowjetische Monumentalkunst": Traktorist, Shukov), 1988–95

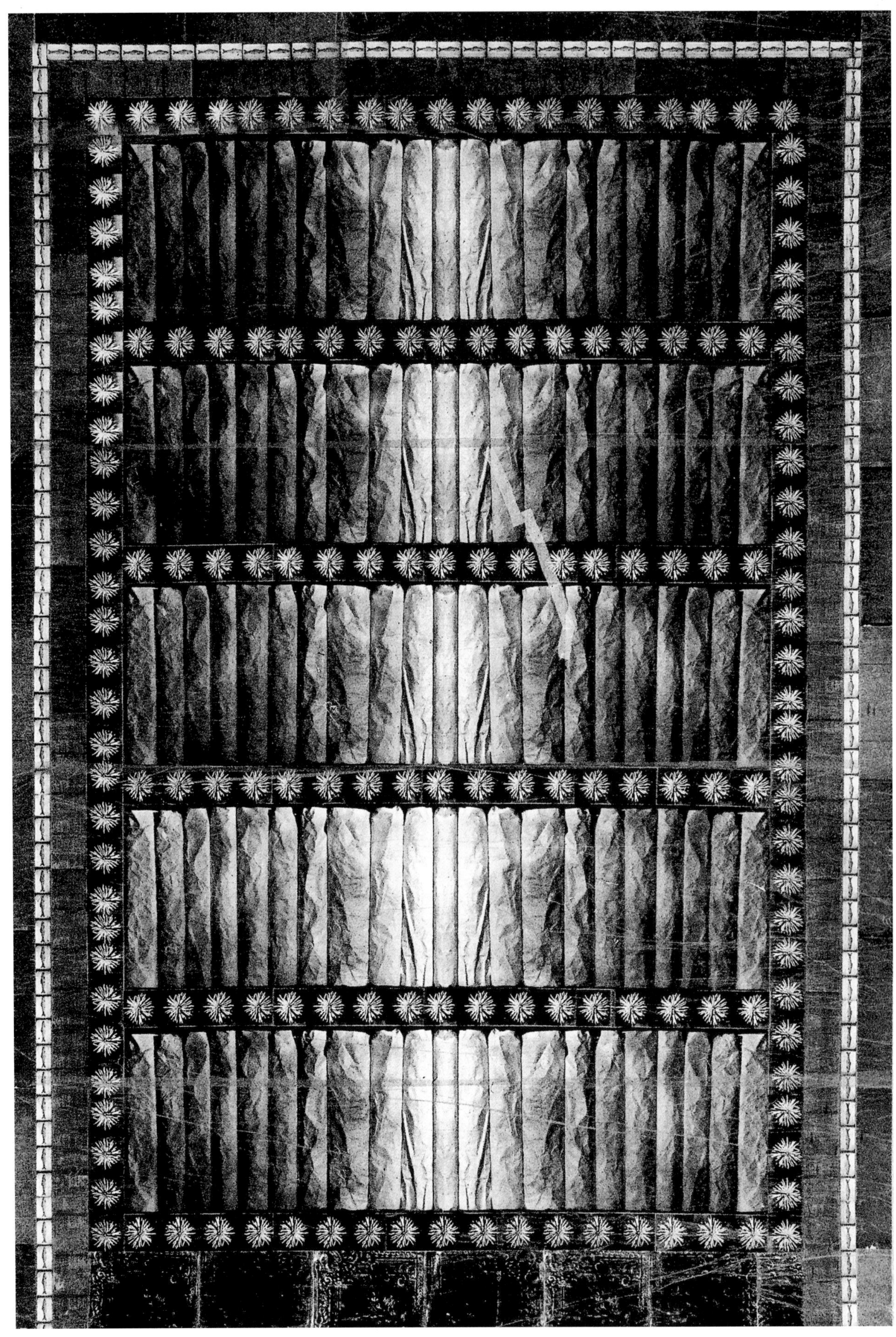

60 Untitled *(Ohne Titel)*, 1994

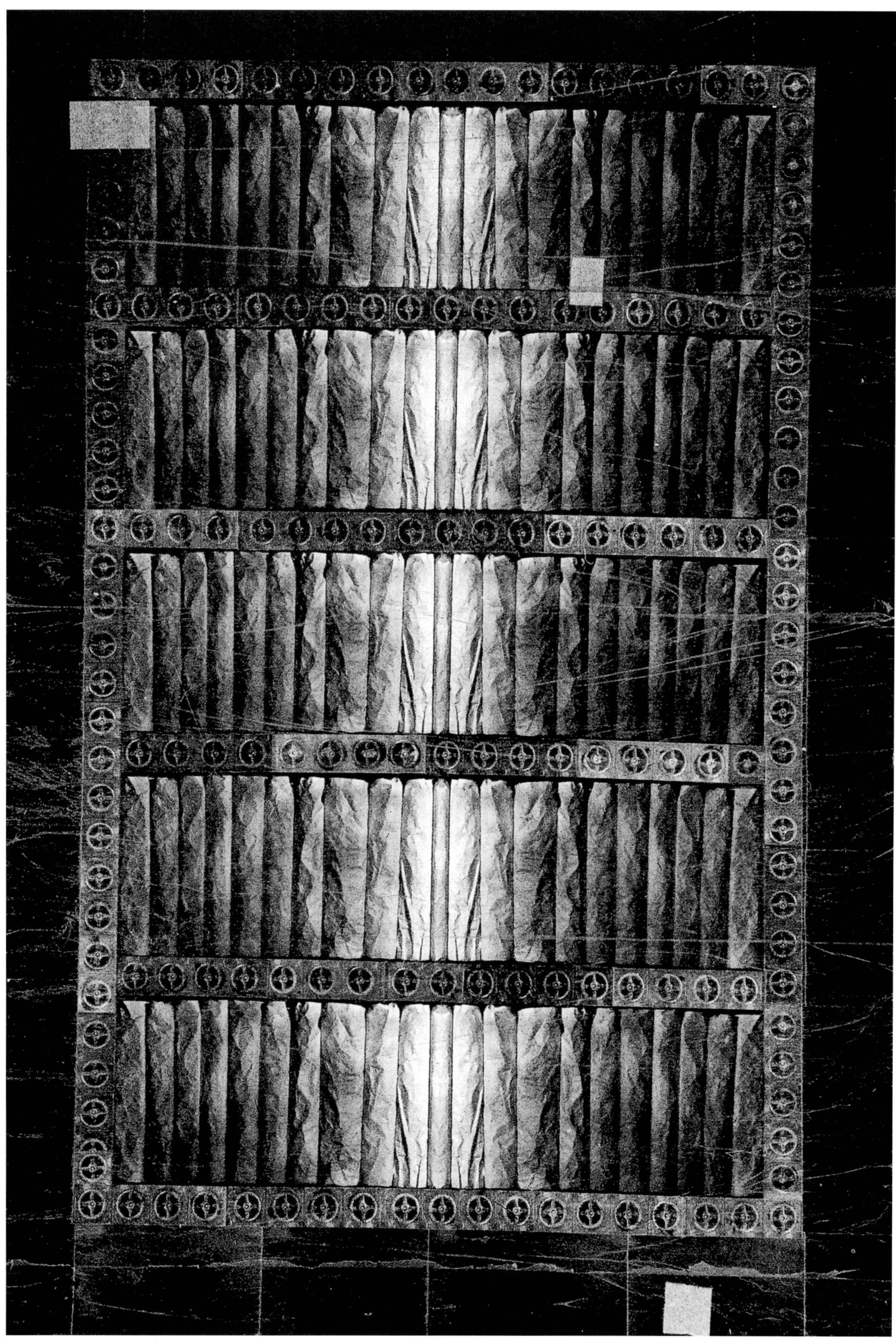

61 Untitled *(Ohne Titel)*, 1994

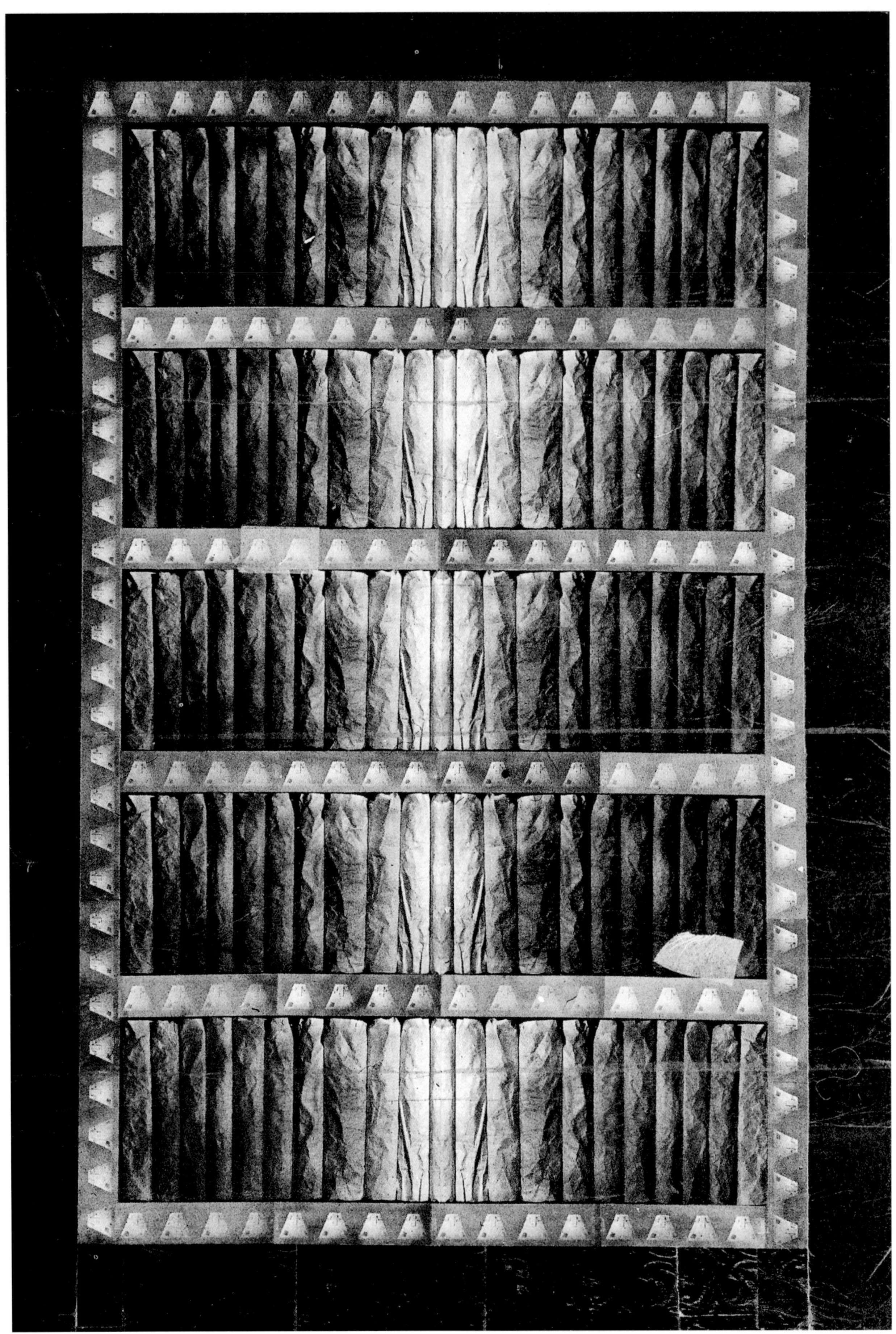

62 Untitled *(Ohne Titel)*, 1994

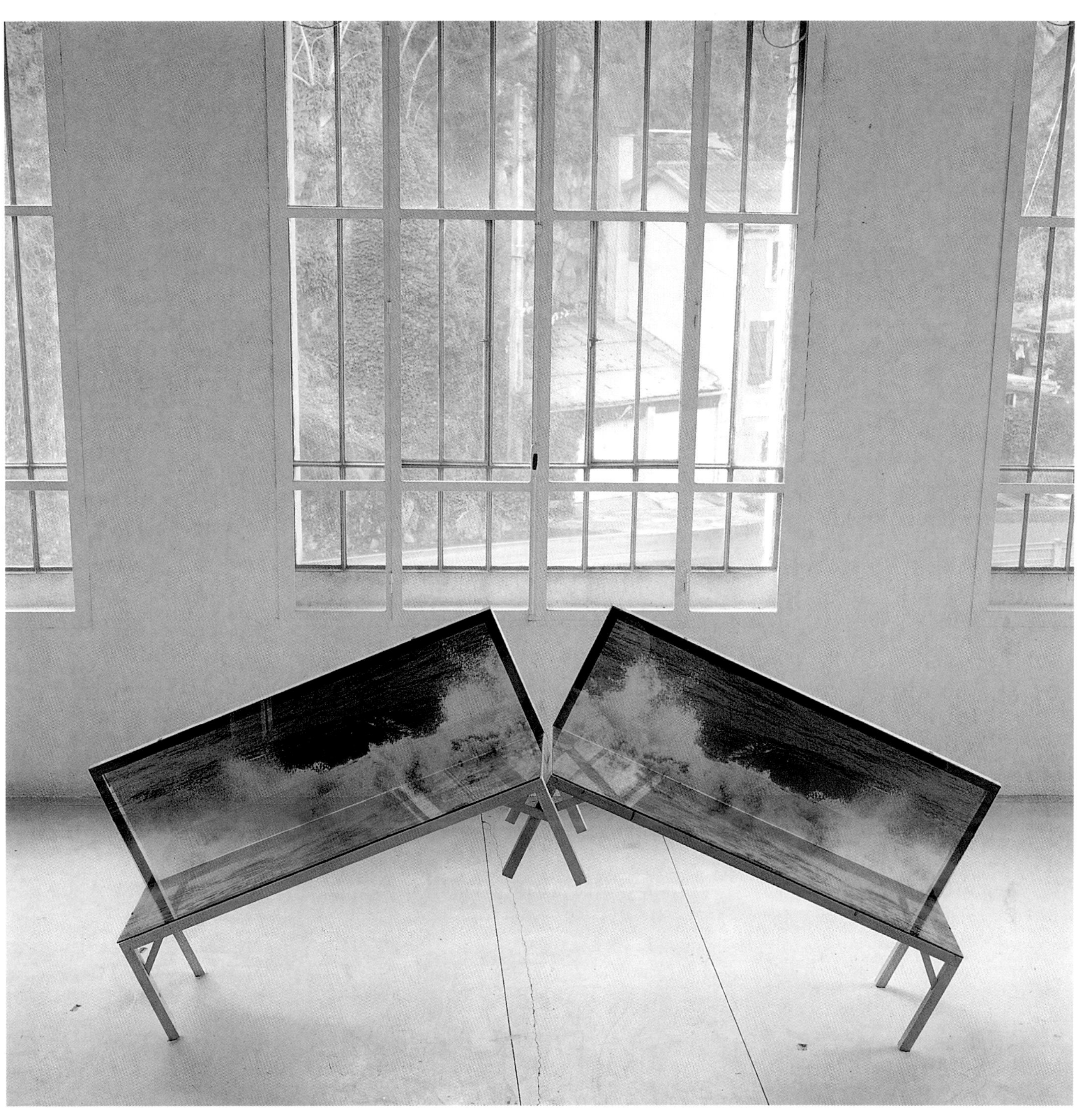

63 Untitled *(Ohne Titel)*, 1994

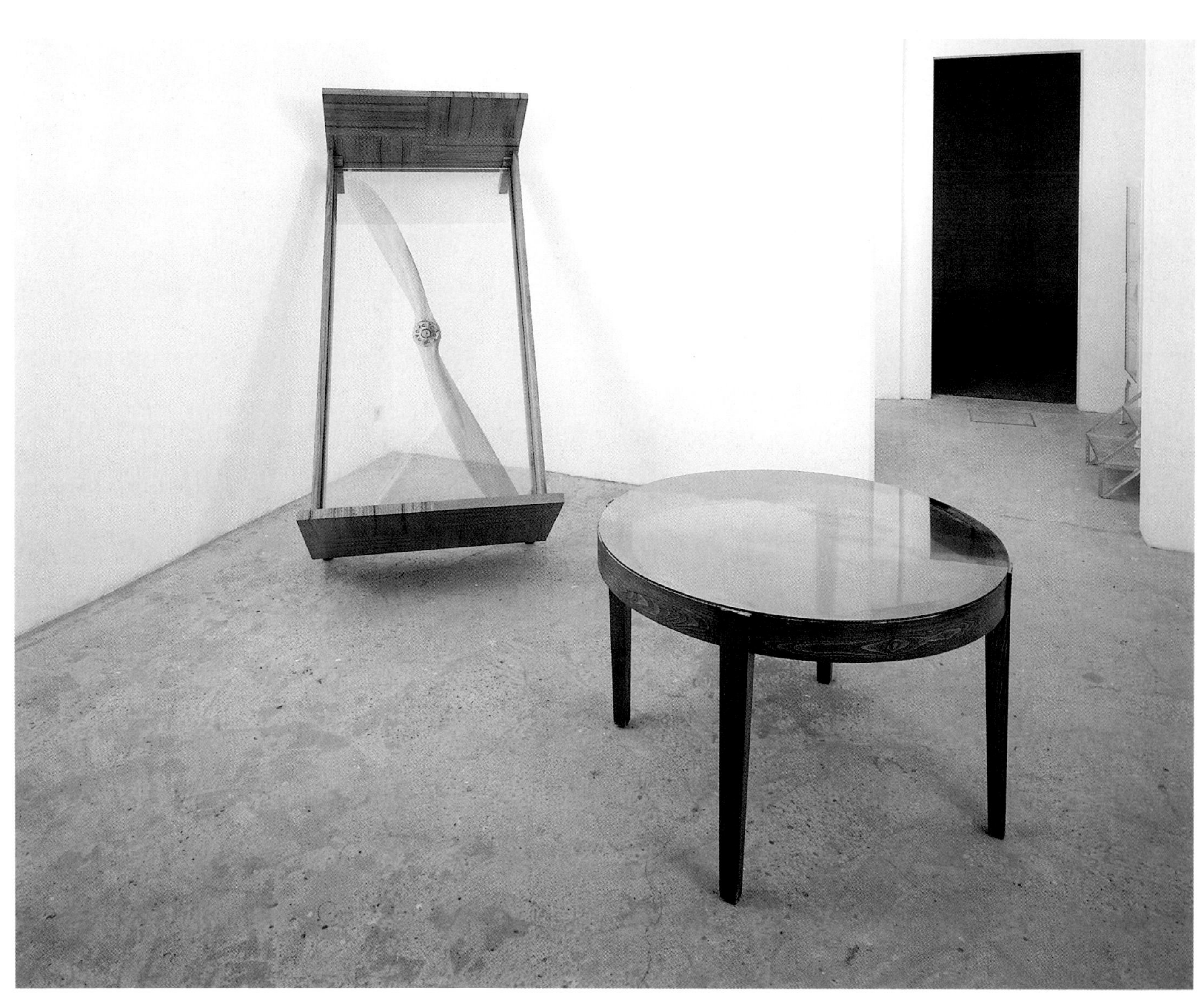

64 Untitled *(Ohne Titel)*, 1993

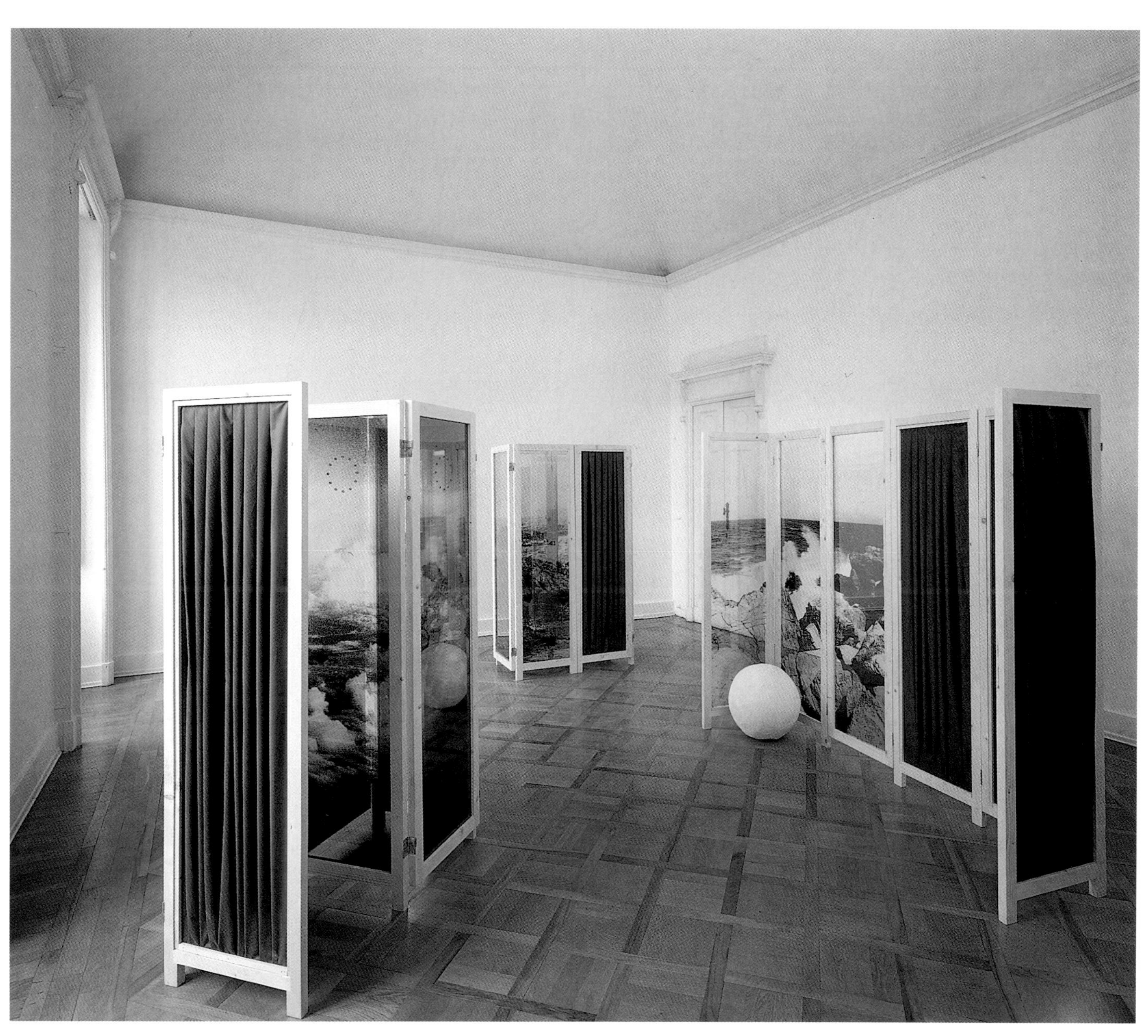

65 Untitled *(Ohne Titel)*, 1992

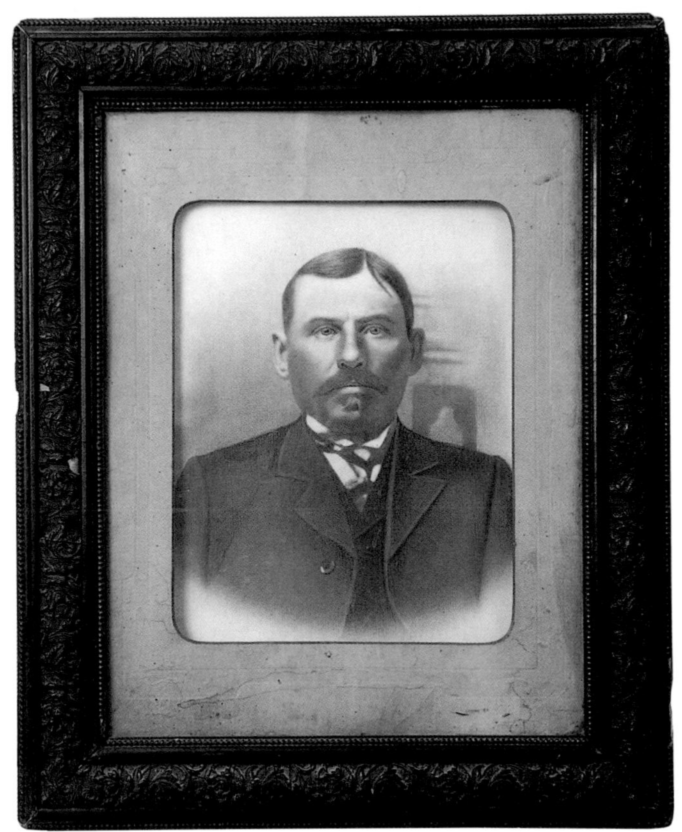

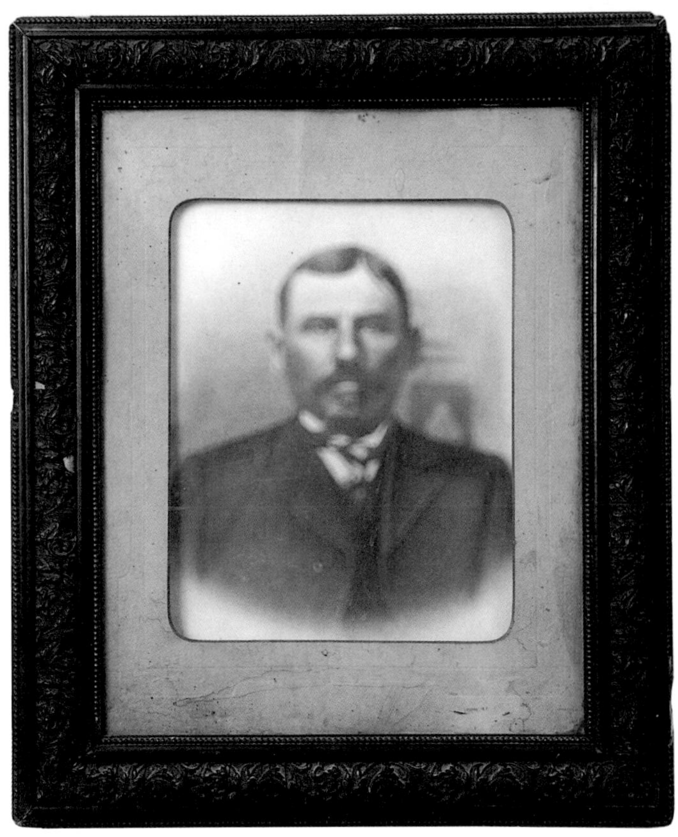

66 From the series 'Rotating Old Photographs' *(Aus der Serie „Rotierende alte Fotografien")*, 1992–95

67 From the series 'Rotating Old Photographs' *(Aus der Serie „Rotierende alte Fotografien")*, 1992–95

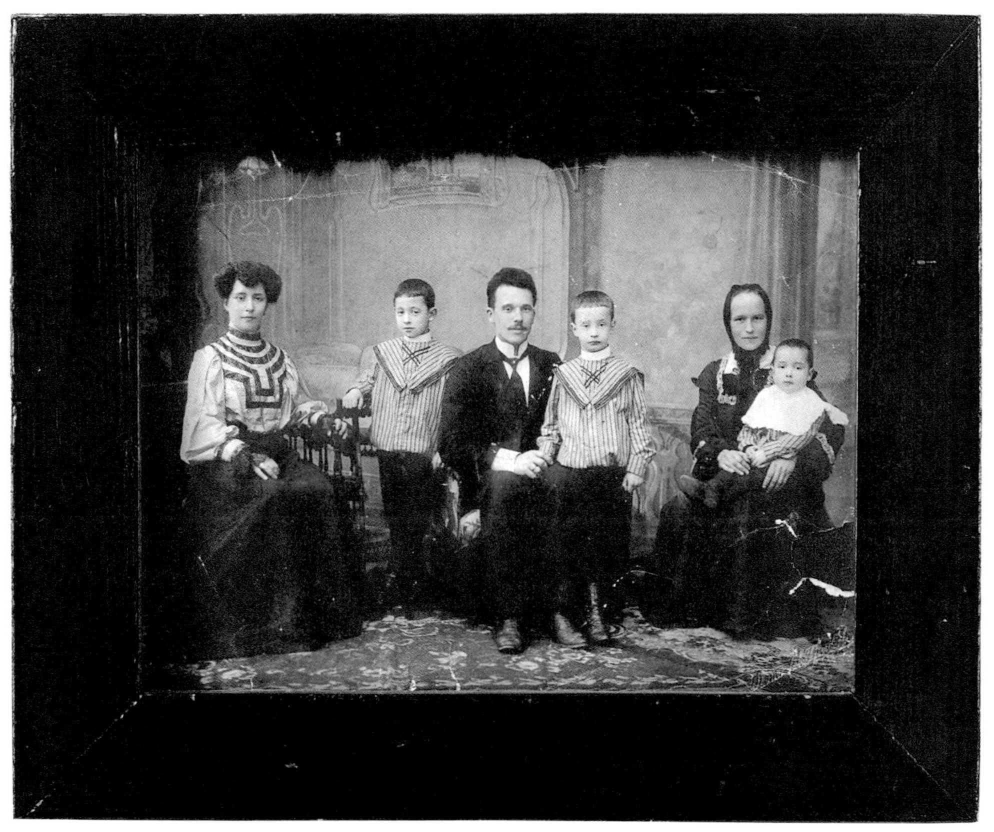

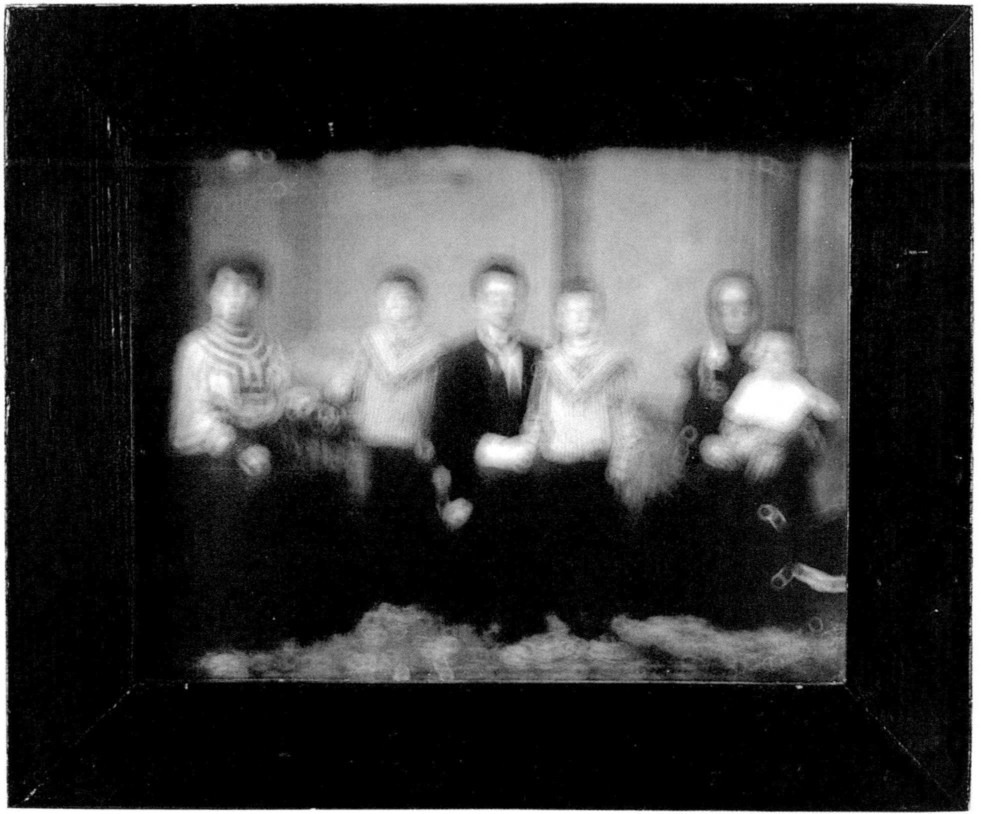

68 From the series 'Rotating Old Photographs' *(Aus der Serie „Rotierende alte Fotografien")*, 1992–95

69 From the series 'Rotating Old Photographs' *(Aus der Serie „Rotierende alte Fotografien")*, 1992–95

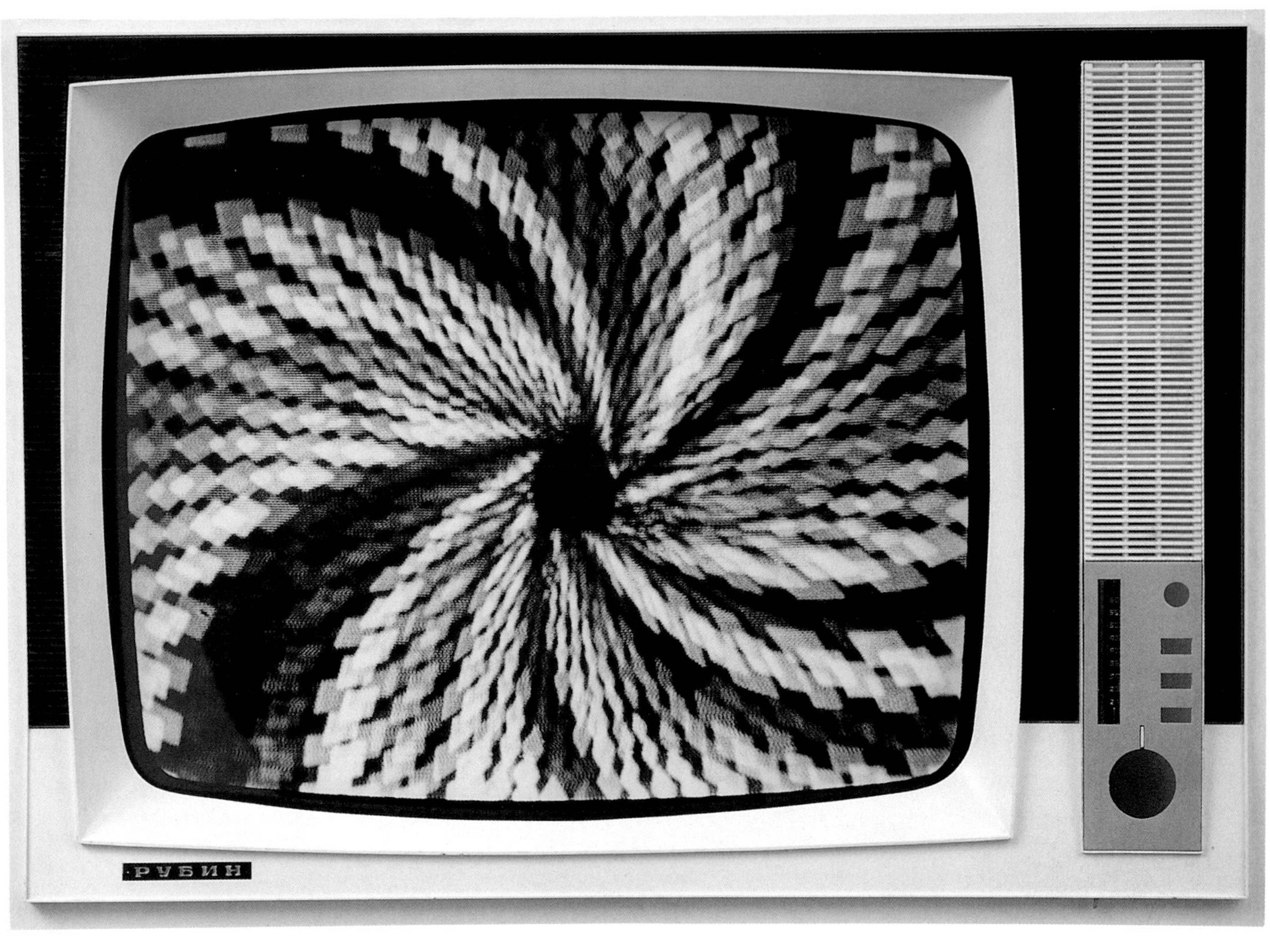

70 From the series 'Televisions' *(Aus der Serie „Fernseher"), 1989–93*

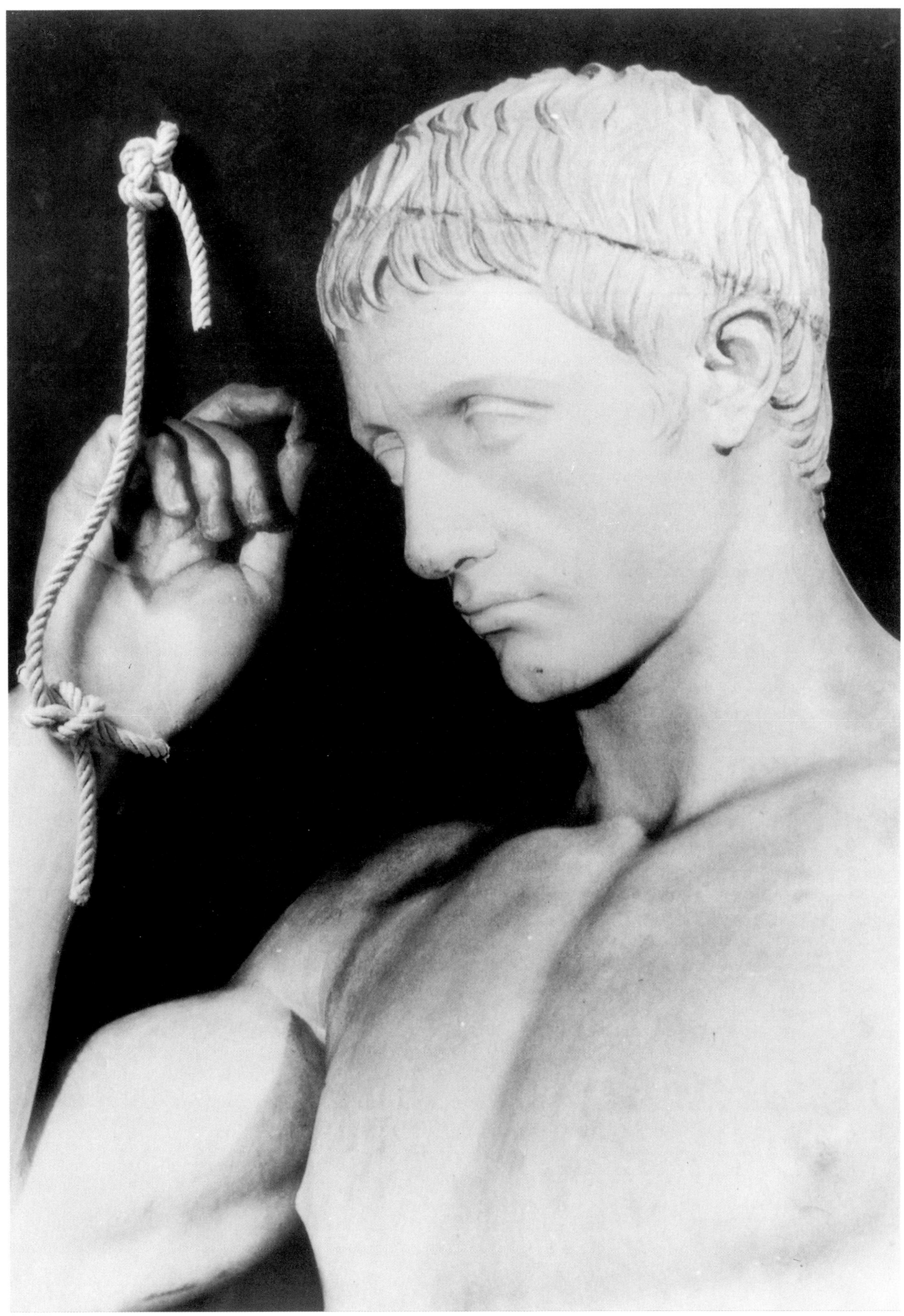

71 Untitled *(Ohne Titel)*, 1992

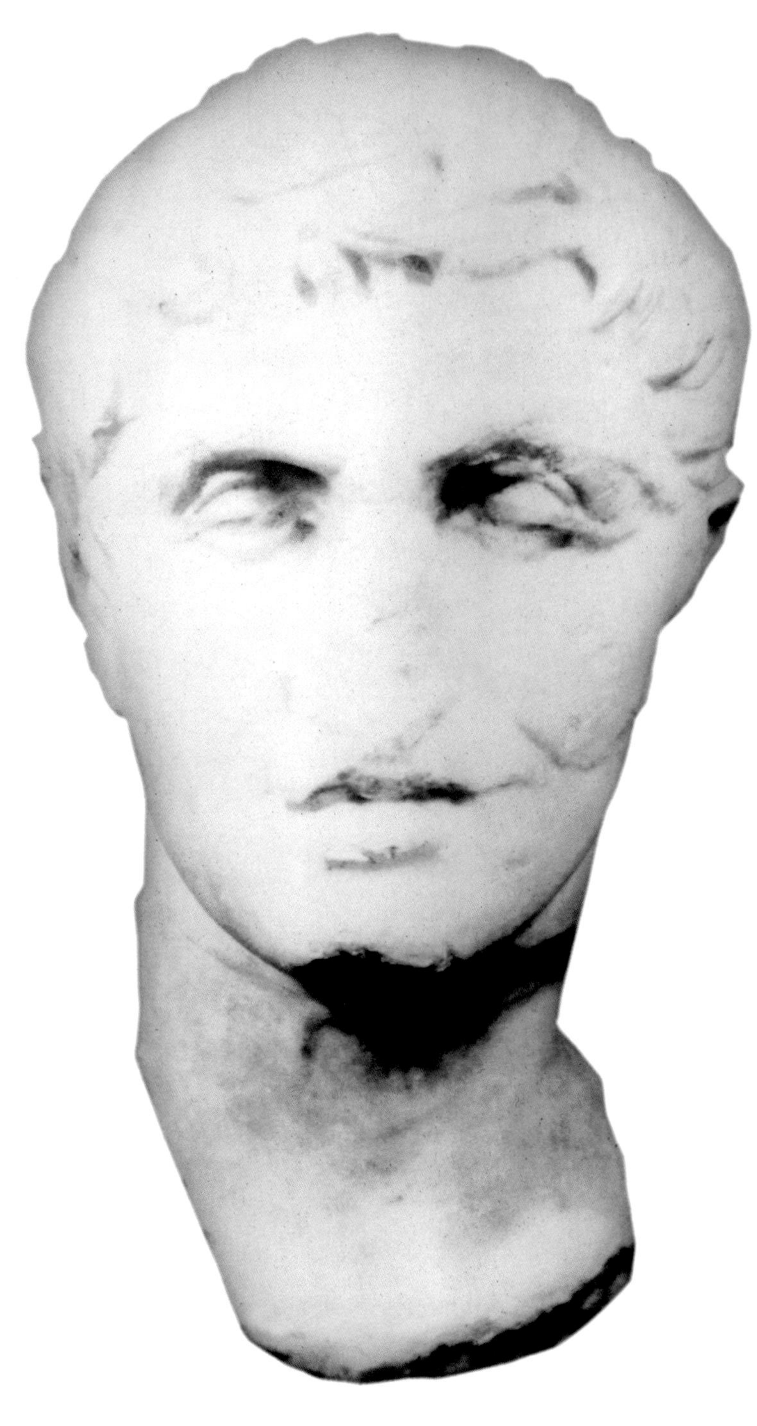

72 Untitled *(Ohne Titel)*, 1995

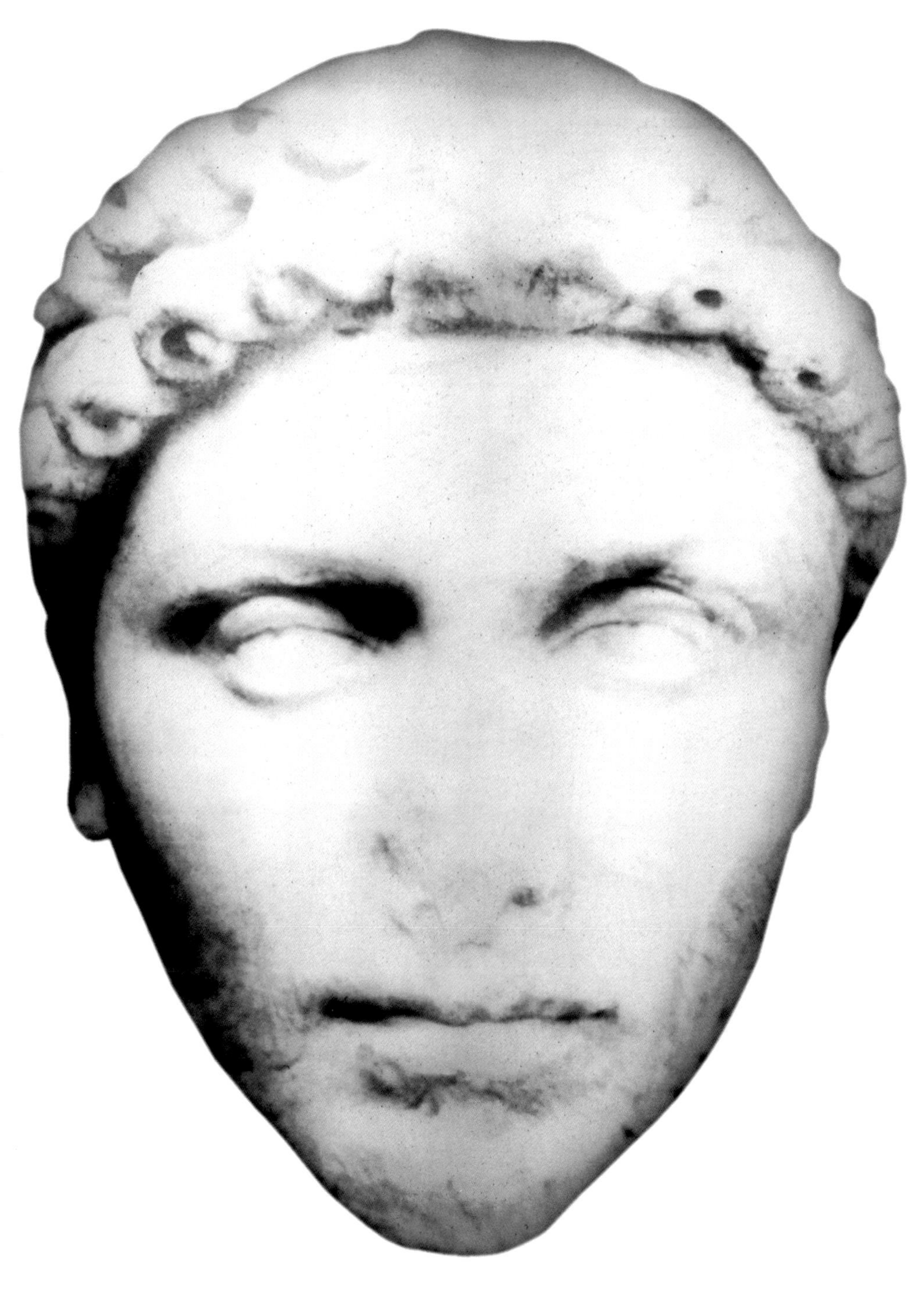

73 Untitled *(Ohne Titel)*, 1995

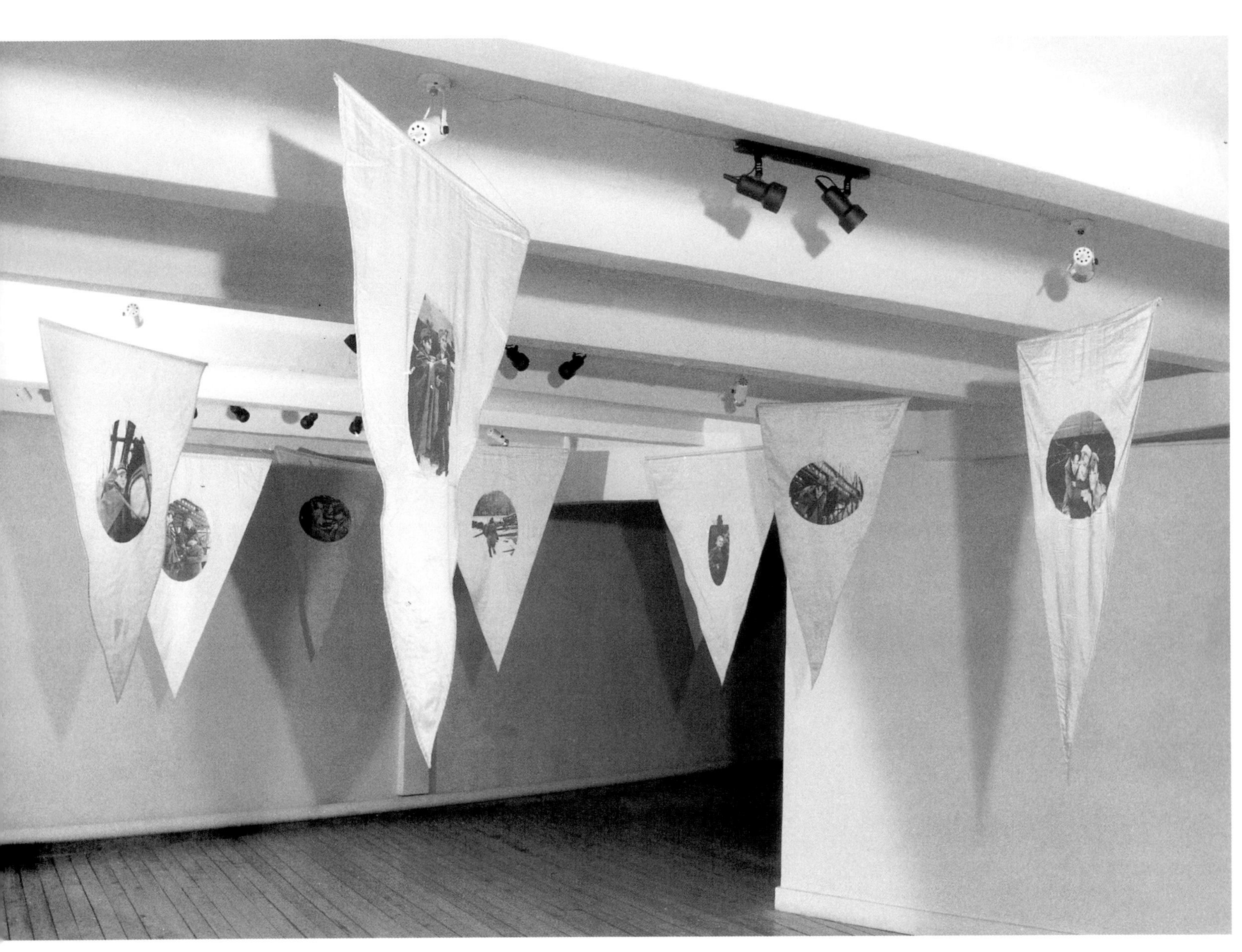

74 *Front Friends (Frontfreundinnen)*, 1995

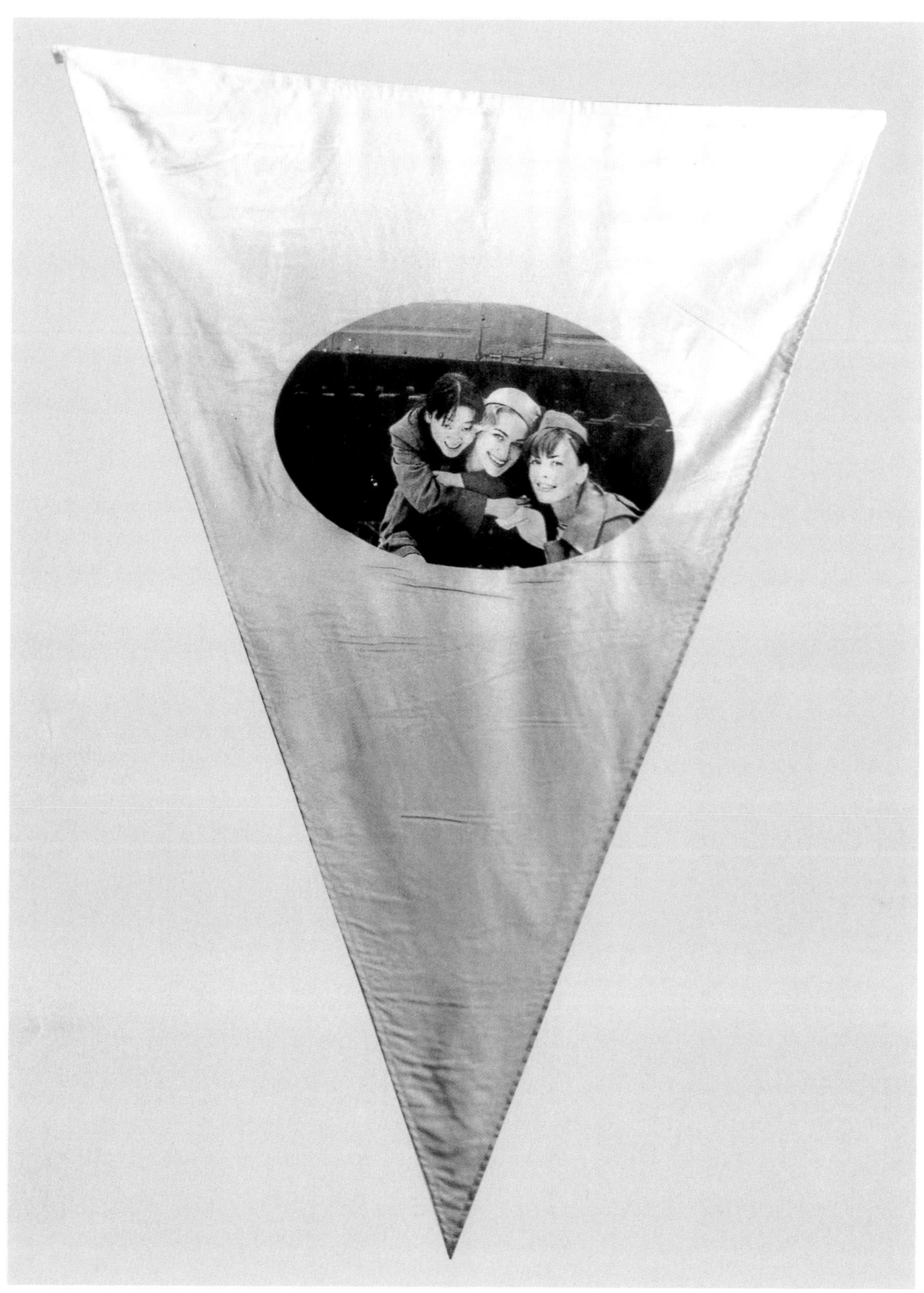

75 *Front Friends (Frontfreundinnen)*, 1995

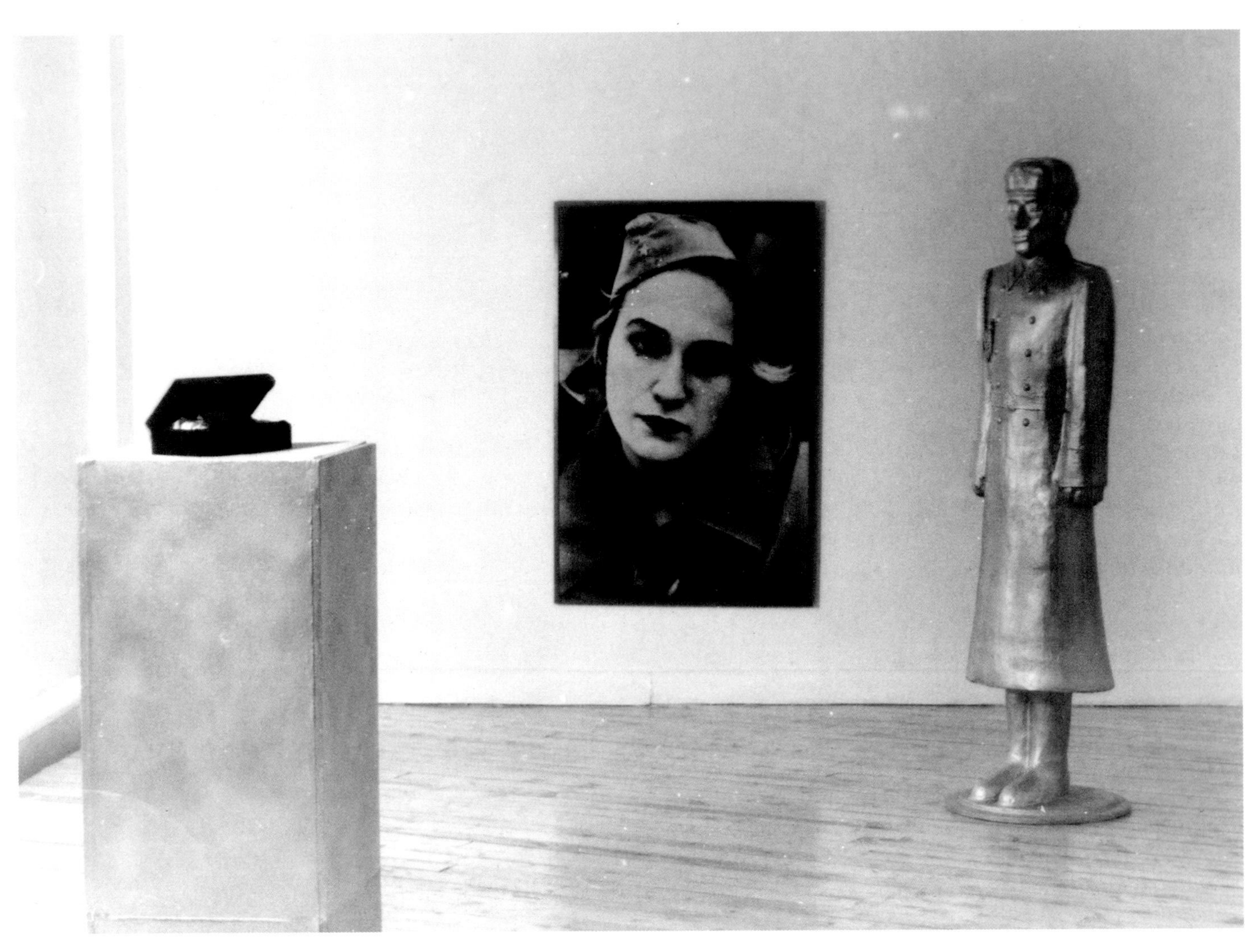

76 'Strategy, Tactics' project *(Projekt „Strategie, Taktik"),* 1995

BARBARA BARSCH

On Aspects of Cultural Change in Russia

Einige Aspekte des kulturellen Wandels in Rußland

Die gewaltigen politischen, territorialen und sozialen Umwälzungen in Osteuropa sind ursächlich bedingt durch den Zerfall der Sowjetunion und des gesamten Ostblocks. Nunmehr brechen die durch das sowjetische Imperium jahrzehntelang unterdrückten nationalen Konflikte vehement auf und finden in kriegerischen Auseinandersetzungen ihren weltweit sichtbaren Ausdruck. Das Schwinden der Vormachtstellung geht einher mit einer katastrophalen ökonomischen Lage in Rußland, einem Verfall des sozialen Systems und gleichzeitig dem Schwinden des Selbstwertgefühls des russischen Volkes. Die Macht ist dahin. Rußland fällt auf sich selbst zurück. Moskau als das ehemalige Zentrum spielt auch heute noch eine wesentliche, wenn auch veränderte Rolle innerhalb dieses Prozesses, dessen politische und soziale Realität tiefgreifende Auswirkungen auf die kulturelle Entwicklung und das Bewußtsein der russischen Intellektuellen hat und gleichermaßen neue Positionierungen innerhalb der sich nun ausbildenden Bewußtseinsstrukturen erfordert. Sie sind nicht zuletzt dadurch geprägt, daß das russische Volk jahrzehntelang zugleich Unterdrücker als auch Unterdrückter war, daß der imperiale Gestus gegenüber anderen Völkern auch nach innen auf das eigene Volk gerichtet wurde. Die Befreiung aus dieser Situation bringt es zugleich mit sich, als Volk plötzlich „Verlierer" zu sein und den Bedeutungsverlust individuell verarbeiten zu müssen. Solche tiefgreifenden Realitäts- und Bewußtseinsveränderungen bleiben selbstverständlich nicht ohne Auswirkungen. Sie bewirken einen Wandel des kulturellen Selbstverständnisses und damit die Suche nach der nationalen Identität. Die Vergewisserung in der Vergangenheit und die Frage nach der Wahrheit wird zwangsläufig zum zentralen Thema und für jeden Künstler individuell bedeutsam.

Im kulturellen Bereich sind drei Tendenzen der Orientierungssuche zu bemerken: zum einen eine auf die russische Tradition im Sinne einer idealisierten Volkskultur zurückgehende Orientierung; zum zweiten eine aus dem inneren Zusammenhang der russisch-sowjetischen Kunstszene zwischen offizieller und nichtoffizieller Kunst agierende Richtung, in deren Mittelpunkt hauptsächlich die Moskauer Konzeptualisten stehen, und zum dritten eine sich an westlichen Kunstentwicklungen orientierende Kunst, die bei unbewußt getroffener gesellschaftlicher Übereinkunft der Bedeutsamkeit von Identitätssuche und Selbstvergewisserung als „Verwestlichung" und als „Tyrannei des westlichen

The vast political, territorial and social upheavals in Eastern Europe are the result of the collapse of the Soviet Union and of the Eastern Bloc system as a whole. Bitter ethnic and national disagreements suppressed during decades of Soviet rule now flare up violently, finding their expression in armed conflicts transmitted to television screens around the world. The waning of Soviet supremacy has been accompanied by a catastrophic economic situation in Russia itself, the collapse of an entire social system and the simultaneous dwindling of a sense of self-worth among the Russian people. The might of the former 'superpower' has disappeared, and so Russia is thrown back upon its own resources. Moscow, as the former centre, still plays a significant, albeit altered, role within this process of change. The political and social reality of which is having far-reaching effects on the cultural development and awareness of Russian intellectuals. It is also demanding the adoption of new positions within the structures of consciousness now being developed. These structures of consciousness are defined not least by the fact that the Russian people were for decades effectively both the oppressor and the oppressed; that Soviet 'imperialism' was a form of rule directed both outwards, towards other peoples, and inwards, towards Russia's own. For every Russian, freedom from this situation also brings with it the sudden awareness of being the 'loser'; and each individual is thus confronted with the necessity of coming to terms with this loss of significance. Such far-reaching changes in reality and in consciousness are bound to have repercussions. They are bringing about a transformation in cultural reflections of the consciousness of the self and thus a search for national identity. Anxious re-examination of the past and questioning of what is the truth automatically become central preoccupations, of significance for each and every artist.

In the cultural realm we can distinguish three tendencies emerging in the current search for new identities and directions: firstly a tendency to look back to Russian tradition in the form of an idealized folk culture; secondly the solution offered by playing on the inner connection that existed between official and unofficial art as formerly distinguished in the Soviet art scene in Russia (the Moscow Conceptualists being the leading representatives here); and thirdly a readiness, prompted by instances of unconscious assimilation of artistic developments in the West, to attack the search for identity and the eagerness for self-scrutiny as forms of 'Westernization' and examples of the 'tyranny of Western taste'. Yekaterina Dyogot describes the situation as follows:

> Whether contemporary Russian art should be 'Russian for the West' or 'Russian for itself' or 'Western for Russia' – this is now a matter for individual decision or collective strategies. These mostly traditional questions were provoked by the period of perestroika, when artists found themselves to be objects offered up for the selection of gallery owners and museum curators from the West... Their reaction to this is the frustration expressed in Russian art now, itself more immediately provoked by the contradiction between the struggle to retain its identity and the need to avoid equating this with an identity that presupposes a Western audience focusing on Russian art the 'gaze of the other'.[1]

This passage also articulates a fundamental and understandable rejection of Western influence on the inner process of self-discovery, a process the author defends within the context she has outlined.

The artists at work in Moscow today have to contend with the pressure of contradictory factors: awareness of Russian traditions and virtues; the simultaneous loss and gain of moral values; the need to steer clear of, or adapt to, Western artistic categories and the westernized international art world – and this in an age when the impact of social forces, ideas and doctrines can be hard to resist. Contemporary photography in Russia should not only be seen in a Russian (and ex-Soviet) context but also in an international context. Especially striking is the adoption and further development of Moscow Conceptualism as a distinct form of artistic expression, in which both a mentality and a national culture are reflected and on which art bestows its own accent. The inclination to look to the past, in most cases as an artistic means of addressing family history, is an attempt to establish one's own place relative to historic events of the age, and to find a sense of direction through searching for truth.

The youngest artists, in particular, combine Conceptualism with staged photography, often achieving a note of elegy or nostalgia. The necessary distance and scepticism is re-established in their work by countering the deep desire for a safe world located in the past with an irony that savagely violates that world. This preoccupation with the self, and the simultaneous attempt to come to terms with international developments and establish a foothold in the international art scene on one's own terms, bestows on the works of these artists a greater significance than is at first apparent. For, within the Russian art scene, it requires a breaking of aesthetic and, above all, of moral taboos to gain attention and prompt discussion; conventionally 'political'

Geschmacks" angegriffen wird. „Ob die zeitgenössische russische Kunst nun ‚russisch für den Westen' sein soll oder ‚russisch für sich selbst' oder ‚westlich für Rußland' – das ist Gegenstand individueller Entscheidungen oder kollektiver Strategien. Diese im Ganzen traditionellen Fragestellungen wurden von der Perestroika-Zeit hervorgerufen, als die Künstler sich als Auswahlobjekte westlicher Galeristen und Kuratoren fühlten... Die Reaktion darauf war eine Frustration der heutigen Kunst, hervorgerufen durch den Widerspruch zwischen dem Bestreben, seine Identität zu bewahren und dem Vermeiden, sich mit jener Identität der russischen Kunst gleichzusetzen, die die Funktion des westlichen Blicks voraussetzt – des ‚Blicks des Anderen'": So beschrieb Yekaterina Dyogot die Situation, wobei auch eine grundsätzliche und verständliche Ablehnung westlicher Einflußnahme auf den inneren Prozeß der Selbstfindung artikuliert wird, mit der sich die Autorin innerhalb des skizzierten Zusammenhangs positioniert.[1]

Im komplizierten Spannungsverhältnis der Besinnung auf russische Traditionen und Tugenden, dem Verlust und Gewinn moralischer Werte und dem Versuch, sich von den Kunstkategorien und von dem Kunstbetrieb des Westens fernzuhalten oder anzupassen und in einer Phase der Virulenz gesellschaftlicher Kräfte, Ideen und Doktrinen arbeiten die Künstler und Künstlerinnen Moskaus. Die heutige Fotokunst in Rußland ist nicht allein in einem nationalen und ehemals sowjetischen Zusammenhang zu sehen, sondern ebenso im internationalen Kontext. Auffällig ist die Aufnahme und Verarbeitung des Moskauer Konzeptualismus in einen formalen künstlerischen Ausdruck, in welchem sich die Mentalität und nationale Kultur widerspiegelt und der Kunst einen eigenen Akzent verleiht. Die Neigung, den Blick in die Vergangenheit zu richten, meist um die Familiengeschichte künstlerisch aufzuarbeiten, ist Ausdruck des Versuchs, sich selbst in Bezug zu den historischen Ereignissen der Epoche zu setzen und eine Orientierung bei der Wahrheitssuche zu finden.

Vor allem die jüngeren Künstler und Künstlerinnen verbinden die konzeptionelle mit der inszenierten Fotografie und gelangen häufig zu einem elegisch-nostalgischen Ausdruck, der dem sehnsuchtsvollen Verlangen nach einer heilen, im Vergangenen liegenden Welt durch ironische Brüche begegnet. Die nötige Distanz und Skepsis wird dadurch wieder hergestellt. Diese Auseinandersetzung mit sich selbst und dem gleichzeitigen Versuch, internationale Tendenzen zu verarbeiten und Anschluß an die internationale Kunstszene zu gewinnen, transponiert die Werke in einen größeren Bedeutungszusammenhang. Es bedarf der ästhetischen und vor allem moralischen Tabuverletzung, um in den allgemeinen Diskurs zu gelangen, da politische Motive diese Funktion innerhalb der russischen Kunstszene nicht mehr erfüllen. Dadurch bekommt der verbreitete Trend der Body-art hier eine eigene politisch-ästhetische Bedeutung. Boris Groys hat die inneren Zusammenhänge dieser Tendenzen dezidiert aus der Sicht des Insiders dargestellt, wobei er weniger als andere russische Autoren davon ausgeht, daß durch die Komplexität ihrer Entwicklungen die gegenwärtige russische Kunst unverständlich sei.[2]

Ungeachtet der Ablehnung und der Zurückweisung westlicher Einflüsse sieht sich die russische Kunst selbst in steter Auseinandersetzung mit der westlichen Kunst. Wladimir Lewaschow schreibt in der jüngsten Veröffentlichung ironisch und doch wahr: „In diesem Paradigma symbolisiert der Westen die Norm, die Rationalität, das Bewußtsein, die Gegenwart, das Erwachsensein; Rußland aber – die Abweichung, die Irrationalität, das Unterbewußtsein, die Vergangenheit und die Kindheit..."[3]

Doch eines bleibt bei diesen Betrachtungen fast immer unberücksichtigt: daß die Kunst, aus ihrem ursächlichen Kontext herausgelöst, ein eigenes und neues Leben beginnt, das geprägt ist durch den neuen Kontext und die mit einem anderen kulturellen Hintergrund versehenen Rezipienten. Dadurch wird sie zwangsläufig einer anderen Sicht und Bewertung unterzogen. Diesem Prozeß kann nur entgehen, wer sich der Herausforderung nicht stellt. Die heutige russische Kunst spricht von der Irritation und dem Versuch der Selbstfindung in der gegenwärtigen Situation, von der Auseinandersetzung mit der Tradition, ihren Werten und moralischen Normen, sie spricht von dem Versuch, durch die Beschäftigung mit der eigenen Familiengeschichte einen Sinn im Gegenwärtigen zu entdecken, aber auch von dem Wunsch, auf dem schmalen Grad von Anpassung an den westlich geprägten internationalen Kunstprozeß und Invididualitätswahrung zu wandeln.

subject-matter no longer serves this function. As a result, widespread movements such as body art assume their own political and aesthetic significance in Russia. Boris Groys has offered a compelling account of the inter-connections of these tendencies from the point of view of the insider, proving that he is less convinced than other Russian commentators that contemporary Russian art has become incomprehensible as a result of the complexity of its development.[2]

Despite the rejection and the repudiation of Western influences, it would be fair to say that Russian art sees itself in constant dialogue with the art of the West. In one of the most recent publications, Vladimir Levashov comments ironically, and yet appositely: 'In this paradigm, the West symbolizes the norm, rationality, consciousness, the present and maturity; Russia, however, [symbolizes] an anomaly, irrationality, the subconscious, the past and childhood.'[3]

One thing, however, almost always remains unconsidered in such accounts: that art in Russia has been removed from its original context and is embarking on a new life, a life informed by the new context established by an audience from a different cultural background. As a result, Russian art will automatically be regarded from another point of view and be assessed in relation to other standards of value. Only those who do not rise to the challenge can escape this process. Contemporary Russian art expresses the irritation of finding oneself in the present situation, and the attempt to find a way out of it. It speaks of engagement with tradition and with its values and moral norms. It articulates the attempt to discover a meaning in the present through investigating the history of one's own family. It also conveys a desire to change, albeit only slightly, in adopting Western practices of making and marketing art and the Western regard for the individual.

Anmerkungen

1. *Jekaterina Djogot, „Die Moskauer Szene". In:* Fluchtpunkt Moskau, *Hrsg. Boris Groys. Aachen 1994, S. 96*
2. *Boris Groys:* Zeitgenössische Kunst aus Moskau. Von der Neo-Avantgarde zum Post-Stalinismus. *München 1991*
3. *Wladimir Lewaschow, „Die Kultur der Kindheit: Zwischen Unvernunft und Begabung. Geschichte der neuen russischen namenlosen Kunst" in:* Configura 2, Dialog der Kulturen. *Erfurt 1995, S. 69*

Notes

1. Yekaterina Dyogot [as Jekaterina Dyogot], 'Die Moskauer Szene', in *Fluchtpunkt Moskau,* ed. Boris Groys (Aachen, 1994), p. 96.
2. Boris Groys, *Zeitgenössische Kunst aus Moskau: Von der Neo-Avantgarde zum Post-Stalinismus* (Munich, 1991).
3. Vladimir Levashov [as Wladimir Levaschow], 'Die Kultur der Kindheit, zwischen Unvernunft und Begabung: Geschichte der neuen russischen namenlosen Kunst', in *Configura 2: Dialog der Kulturen* (Erfurt, 1995), p. 69.

ANGELA LAMMERT

Russian Photography in Context

Russische Fotografie im Kontext

1 *Eine Spielart westeuropäischer Betrachtungsweise von Fotografie ist durch die Befürwortung und Ablehnung der „Wirklichkeitsfotografie" bestimmt.[1] „Im Zuge der digitalen Revolution verliert das fotografische Bild seinen Nimbus der Autonomie und Authentizität", hieß es unlängst in der Zeitschrift „European Photography".[2] Es ist festzustellen, daß gleichzeitig die Wirklichkeitsfotografie zur neuen Museumskunst aufblüht. Von den Kritikern dieses Phänomens wird der voyeuristische Ursprung der Fotos und deren „phallische Präpotenz" betont.*

Demgegenüber stellen Befürworter als besondere Qualität dieser Erscheinung den Unterschied zur Reportagefotografie heraus: „Er fotografiert am Motiv vorbei... Die Rede ist vom Beiläufigen... Das Beiläufige ist nie im Trend".[3] Der Fotograf grenzt sich ab vom „Sozialkitsch" wie vom „Klischee" des Multikulturalismus. In welcher Richtung man auch immer diskutiert – die Modernität von Fotografie wird am Grad der Ablösung vom Dokumentarischen gemessen.

1 Most Western European commentary tends either to endorse or to reject the 'photography of reality'.[1] A recent article claimed that: 'As the digital revolution gathers pace, the photographic image is losing its aura of autonomy and authenticity'.[2] At the same time we have been able to observe the 'photography of reality' blossoming into an art and gaining its rightful place in museums. Critics of this development emphasize the voyeuristic origins of photography and its 'phallic prepotency'. Those, on the other hand, who approve of it, draw attention to the quality that distinguishes the 'photography of reality' from photographic reportage: 'He photographs subjects as they occur... They speak of the incidental... The incidental never constitutes a trend'.[3] The photographer, that is to say, disassociates himself from the criticism of society as he does from the 'cliché' of multi-culturalism. In whatever direction the debate moves however, the modernity of photography continues to be measured by the degree of its removal from the 'merely' documentary.

2 *In der Literatur zur zeitgenössischen russischen Fotografie – ob von russischen oder westeuropäischen Autoren – wird nun im Sinne einer sozialen Fotografie das Dokumentarische als das spezifisch Russische gesehen. Allerdings wäre eine wahrhaft kritische Fotografie in der Sowjetunion erst am Ende der achtziger Jahre möglich geworden, da die politischen Verhältnisse dies vorher nicht anders zugelassen hätten. Die Fotografie als Kunst habe es bis dahin schwer gehabt, das bedeutet: kaum existiert.[4] Die unmittelbaren Erfahrungen der älteren Generation, der jetzt Fünfzig- bis Sechzigjährigen, scheinen diese Beschreibung zu bestätigen. Neuere Äußerungen zur gegenwärtigen russischen Fotografie betonen die Entwicklung zur digitalen Wahrnehmung, die vom Dokumentarischen wegführt. Diese Schlußfolgerung beruht auf faktischen Tendenzen in der jüngsten Fotoszene.*

2 In the writings on contemporary Russian photography – whether by Russians or Western European authors – the documentary, understood as a form of social photography, is regarded as something specifically Russian. It is of course the case that a truly critical form of photography only became possible in the Soviet Union at the end of the 1980s, the political situation not permitting such a development any earlier. Until this point, photography as art had had a very hard time in Russia, that is to say it had hardly existed there.[4] The direct experiences of the older generation of photographers, those now in their fifties and sixties, appear to confirm this claim. Recent texts on contemporary Russian photography have emphasized the development away from the conventionally documentary and towards the digital recording of reality. This line of argument is based on the observation of tendencies in the current Russian situation.

3 *Eine solche Betrachtungsweise geht entweder davon aus, daß das Dokumentarische innerhalb der internationalen Aufmerksameit als konservativ zu bewerten ist oder aber sie betont das Exotische, das „Nicht-mehr-Vorhandene", zumal im westeuropäischen*

3 Such an approach may arise from the assumption that, from the international point of view, the documentary has to be seen as conservative. Alternatively, at least from the Western European point of view, the documentary is seen to emphasize the exotic, the 'no longer existent'. It would therefore seem useful, and perhaps essential, to examine how recent theory has dealt with the subject of Russian photography in the early decades of the twentieth century.

Until recently almost all research in this area was focused on Alexander Rodchenko and the avant-garde photography of the Left Front of Art (LEF). Now, however, there is increasing interest in the contradictory impact of the Pictorial Photographers and the representatives of the avant-garde during the 1920s and 1930s. Photographers such as Georgi Zimin, Moisei Nappelbaum and Yuri Yeremin are being rediscovered. Abram Shterenberg is recognized as a link between the avant-garde and the Pictorialists because his photographic portraits make use of the focusing methods and special printing techniques of the latter. But Rodchenko also hand-coloured some of his prints and signed them. His series of studies 'Glass and Light' (1928) includes close-ups of natural objects of the sort to be found in the work of Nikolai Svistshev-Paola. Rodchenko's pupil Boris Ignatovich used a special type of lens to attain an effect of soft-focus, thereby implementing one of the working principles of the Pictorialists. Although avant-garde photographers consciously sought to disassociate themselves from the Pictorialists, mutual influence was much stronger than either group would readily have acknowledged.[5]

It is precisely in view of such considerations that it appears imperative that we avoid the tendency to explain the character of contemporary Russian photography in terms of the result of the opening up of Russian culture to the West, and that we investigate instead the connections to, and rejection of, elements of the national tradition. The innovative Russian contribution to the history of European photography was already recognized by the late 1920s, even though still regarded, for better or worse, as an exception. The significance of this contribution became clearer, at the latest, in the Stuttgart exhibition of 1929, 'Film und Foto', which included the work of Rodchenko, Ignatovich, El Lissitzky and Arkadi Shaiket. It is nonetheless curious that the innovative achievements of Russian photographers – in, for example, the first photographs to be made in the nineteenth century – were explained, even in the specialist literature, by reference to the immense cold and early nightfall of the Russian winter. It was as if it were only on this account that the Russians might be acknowledged as pioneers, as was later to be the case at Stalingrad.[6]

The question of a national Russian tradition also relates to the use of the documentary photograph. There is no doubt that Rodchenko's 'theory of the snapshot' derives from documentary photography.[7] Rodchenko was here challenging the notion (implicitly supported by art photography and conventional art as a whole) that a human being might be captured in all his or her complexity in a single image. Rodchenko was

Kontext. Es erscheint ebenso sinnvoll wie notwendig, diese Betrachtungsweise zu hinterfragen und zu differenzieren, wie es die Theorie in letzter Zeit für die russische Fotografie vom Anfang dieses Jahrhunderts getan hat.

Standen bis vor kurzem nur Rodchenko und die avantgardistische Fotografie der LEF (Linke Front der Kunst) im Blickfeld der Forschung, ist gegenwärtig das Interesse für die gegenteilige Beeinflussung von Piktoralisten und Avantgardekunst in den zwanziger und dreißiger Jahren gewachsen. Fotografen wie Georgi Zimin, Moisei Nappelbaum und Yuri Yeremin werden wiederentdeckt. Als Bindeglied zwischen Avantgardisten und Piktoralisten ist Abram Shterenberg zu sehen. Er verband seine Porträtfotos mit der Auflösung und speziellen Drucktechnik der Piktoralisten. Aber auch Rodchenko kolorierte einen Teil seiner Abzüge von Hand und signierte diese. In seinen Studien „Glas und Licht" (1928) verwendete er Nahaufnahmen von Naturobjekten, wie sie bei Nikolai Svistshev-Paola zu finden sind. Rodchenkos Schüler Boris Ignatovich benutzte ein spezielles Objektiv, um den Effekt der Weichzeichnung zu erreichen, und nutzte damit ein Arbeitsprinzip der Piktoralisten. Obwohl sich die avantgardistische Fotografie bewußt von den Piktoralisten abzugrenzen versuchte, sind die gegenseitigen Beeinflussungen stärker gewesen, als sie es selbst wahrhaben wollten.[5]

Gerade vor diesem Hintergrund ist es unerläßlich, die zeitgenössische russische Fotografie nicht als ein Ergebnis der Öffnung zum Westen darzustellen, sondern nach der Verbindung und Abstoßung zu den eigenen Traditionen zu fragen. Der innovative Beitrag der Russen zur europäischen Fotogeschichte wurde schon am Ende der zwanziger Jahre erkannt, wenn auch als Sonderleistung betrachtet. Deutlich wurde dies spätestens mit der Ausstellung ‚Film und Foto' 1929 in Stuttgart, auf der Arbeiten von Alexander Rodchenko, El Lissitzky, Boris Ignatovich und Arkadi Shaiket zu sehen waren. Kurios wird es allerdings, wenn innovative Ergebnisse von russischen Fotografen – etwa die ersten Lichtbildaufnahmen im 19. Jahrhundert – in einschlägigen Publikationen mit dem kalten Winter und frühen dunklen Nächten erklärt werden. Nur darum durften die Russen hier die Ersten sein, wie später in Stalingrad.[6]

Die Frage nach der eigenen Tradition betrifft auch die Verwendung des Dokumentarischen. So geht Rodchenkos ‚Theorie des Schnappschusses' zweifellos auf das Dokumentarische zurück.[7] *Er polemisierte gegen die Vorstellung der Kunstfotografie und der konventionellen Kunst, daß ein menschliches Wesen in einem einzigen Bildnis vollständig zu erfassen sei. Durch die Authentizität des Schnappschusses sollte das neue Lebensgefühl Rußlands eingefangen werden.*

4 *Die im Zusammenhang mit der Akademie stehenden Fotografen sind vor diesem Hintergrund interessant, da die Auswahl keiner Stilrichtung folgt.*[8]

Sergei Leontiev entspricht auf den ersten Blick der spezifisch russischen Variante einer sozial ambitionierten dokumentarischen Fotografie. Seine großformatigen Nahaufnahmen von Menschen, die am Rande der Gesellschaft leben, verweisen in beklemmender Strenge des Vortrags auf die Distanz zum Betrachter. Sie wirken nah und dennoch erstarrt – gefangen in der Apathie ihres Zustandes. Leontiev spricht vom Versuch einer Balance zwischen künstlerischer Form und konzeptueller Fotografie. Dabei knüpft er an das hohe Niveau der russischen Porträtfotografie an, radikalisiert und banalisiert aber Motiv und Darstellungsform. Es verbindet das serielle Prinzip Rodchenkos mit dem Individuellen. Es handelt sich weder um einen Typus noch um die mittels Collage gewollte dialektische Sicht einer Persönlichkeit, wie sie in der Fotografie am Anfang des Jahrhunderts gesucht wurde. Das utopische Element der Avantgarde gibt es nicht mehr. Es geht eher um das Klischee der Subkultur, deren Vorführung und Hinterfragung.

Vladislav Efimov baut in der Regel seine Objekte, um sie später als Modelle zu fotografieren. In seiner Rauminstallation „Chinesisches Kino" sind Tierköpfe und Früchte mumienartig eingewickelt – in Todesstarre. Das Nekrophile wird als störend empfunden, als dann doch zu weitgehend in seiner verfremdeten Direktheit und in seinem modrigen Geruch. Die westeuropäische Verarbeitung von Gewalt, Tod und Brutalität erzeugt im Zuge ihres anders gelagerten sozialen Hintergrundes im Gegensatz dazu oftmals eine Ästhetisierung des Toten, eine Gratwanderung zwischen Morbidität und Faszination.[9]

Das Prinzip der Verarbeitung des „Dinghaften" ist bei Efimov und Rodchenko vergleichbar, obwohl sich die beschriebene Motivwahl völlig unterscheidet. Rodchenkos Serien „Glas und Licht", 1928, oder „Antriebsräder", 1930, seien erwähnt. Ebenso scheint die Konzentration auf serielle Fotoreihen einen uneingestandenen Brückenschlag zur Tradition der russischen Avantgarde zu schlagen.

Für Efimov ist die Fotografie ein Mittel seiner „Images" und Installationen. Seit 1994 arbeitet er mit Video und Bildverarbeitung über Computer. In den Videos hält er Fotos fest und variiert sie, um dem zweidimensionalen Bild das Moment der Zeit hinzuzufügen. Es ist in diesem Zusammenhang interessant, daß die Avantgardefotografie in Rußland ihre Ursprünge im Kino hat. Dziga Wertow und die Gruppe Kinoki proklamierten am Anfang der zwanziger Jahre die durch Montage hergestellte Filmchronik des Alltagslebens. Es ging um das „filmische Erleben der Welt". Sie erkannten Fotografie und Kamera als „Foto-glas" und zeitgemäßes Medium ihrer visuellen Aneignung der neuen Welt durch die Montage.[10]

convinced that the new vital consciousness of Russia would be captured through the authenticity of the (serial) snapshot.

4 The Russian photographers currently based at the Akademie are interesting in this context in that their inclusion in the present exhibition does not favour any particular stylistic tendency.[8]

At first glance, the work of Sergei Leontiev would seem to embody the specifically Russian variant of a socially-motivated documentary photography. His close-ups of people living on the periphery of society, printed on a large scale, function with the oppressive severity of a lecture on the theory of the subject's distance from the spectator. These figures seem close to us, and yet they are rigid; ensnared in the apathy of their situation. Leontiev himself speaks of seeking a balance between artistic form and conceptual photography. In this respect he may be seen to draw on the high level of Russian portrait photography, even though radicalizing and banalizing both the motif and its form of presentation. He links the serial principle of Rodchenko with the individual subject. We are no longer presented with a type or with the dialectic imposed by the personality of the photographer by means of a form of 'collage', as was the case in photography at the start of the century. Nor is there anything here of the utopian element found in the work of the avant-garde. We are concerned, rather, with the cliché of the 'sub-culture'; its display and its investigation.

Vladislav Efimov, on the other hand, usually constructs his own subjects, in order then to photograph them. In his room installation *Chinese Cinema,* animal heads and fruit are bandaged up like Egyptian mummies – in all the rigidity of death. This evidence of necrophilia is perceived by the spectator as disturbing, as too extreme in its alienating directness and stench of decay. The Western European treatment of violence, death and brutality by contrast, often emerges, on account of its quite distinct social context, in an aestheticizing of the dead, a tightrope walk between morbidity and fascination.[9]

Efimov and Rodchenko share a commitment to working with objects in an 'objective' fashion, although, as has been indicated, the two differ completely in their *choice* of objects – one need only think of Rodchenko's series 'Glass and Light' (1928) and 'Wheel Mechanisms' (1930). Nonetheless, the concentration on series of photographic images appears to establish an unacknowledged link to the tradition of the Russian avant-garde.

For Efimov, photography is a means to the end found in his 'images' and his installations. Since 1994 he has been working with video and computer-generated images. In his videos he freezes images, then manipulates them in order to add the momentum of time to the two-dimensional image. It is interesting in this connection to recall that avant-garde photography in Russia had its origins in cinema. In the early 1920s Dziga Vertov and the Kinoki Group announced a film chronicle of everyday life produced using the technique of montage. They were concerned with the 'filmic experience of the world'. They saw photography and the camera as a 'photo-glass' and an up-to-date medium for their visual appropriation of the new world by means of montage.[10]

5 Leontiev and Efimov belong to the talented middle generation of contemporary photographers, but they have not been exhibited and promoted by the Western-oriented Regina gallery in Moscow, which has, rather, favoured the photographers of the Fenso-Group, who work with the digitalization of images, video and installation. They seek to create artificial emotional spaces using advertising and the mass media. The trade-name 'Fenso' is a conscious response to the clichés used in such areas. The glossy, large-scale photographs produced by the Fenso-Group evoke the suggestion of secret 'tournaments' or the figures of aggressive 'partisans'.

Nor, however, can Leontiev and Efimov be classified with Igor Moukhin, a photographer who appears to delight in critical reflection on the collapse of the old system. (This, they feel, is enlightening but does not do enough harm to the object thus criticized.) Considered from the formal point of view, Moukhin's works are very close to avant-garde photography. If we trace his subjects over a long period of time we come to his outstanding series 'Benches'. In Russia this subject functions as a symbol of recent historical change much more effectively than its equivalent would in Western Europe.[11] Moukhin himself has observed the connection between his own work and that of Bernd and Hilla Becher. Moukhin's partner, Tatyana Liberman, works with staged photographs, attempting to reconcile images of the human body with graphic or geometric structures, and thereby imbuing a subject central to the Russian avant-garde with the contemporary sense of 'the other'. She also works with video and room installations.

Alexei Goga is interested in spatial sculpture in photography. Using himself as a model, he takes colour photographs of both the whole and fragments of his nude body in a room specially designed for this purpose so that he can be simultaneously lit from many different angles. These photographs are subsequently displayed as large-scale prints. He consciously disassociates himself from the Russian photographic tradition and points to his interest in the work of Josef Sudek, Irving Penn, William Weston, Ansel Adams, Robert Mapplethorpe and, among contemporary Russians, the still virtually unknown Boris Samoilov.

5 *Die genannten Fotografen zählen zur qualitätvollen mittleren Generation, werden aber in der zum Westen ausgerichteten Regina-Galerie in Moskau nicht favorisiert. Diesen Platz nimmt die Gruppe Fenso ein, die mit der Digitalisierung von Bildern, mit Video und Installationen arbeitet. Sie suchen nach der Schaffung emotionaler Räume mit den Mitteln der Reklame und der Massenmedien. Der Warename ‚Fenso' ist ein bewußter Umgang mit diesen Klischees. In brillanten großformatigen Fotos suggerieren sie geheimnisvolle ‚Ritterkämpfe' oder ‚Partisanen' voll aggressivem Potential.*

Leontiev und Efimov gehören aber auch nicht zu denen, die, wie Igor Moukhin, die Lust an der kritischen Reflexion über den Verfall des alten Systems befriedigen. Das erhellt, tut aber nicht weh. Moukhins Arbeiten haben formal gesehen die größten Ähnlichkeiten mit der Avantgardefotografie. Seine Arbeitsweise, bestimmte Motive über einen längeren Zeitraum zu verfolgen, führt zu seiner herausragenden Fotoserie ‚Bänke'. Stärker als in der westeuropäischen Fotografie ist der gewählte Gegenstand ein Zeichen für Geschichte.[11] Moukhin selbst bezieht dies auf Bernd und Hilla Becher. Seine Lebensgefährtin Tatyana Liberman arbeitet mit inszenierten Fotografien und versucht, den menschlichen Körper graphischen oder geometrischen Strukturen anzunähern, indem sie Traditionsmuster der russischen Avantgarde mit zeitgenössischem ‚Anderem' füllt. Auch sie beschäftigt sich mit Video- und Rauminstallationen.

Alexei Goga geht es um räumliche Plastik in der Fotografie. Er arbeitet mit großformatigen farbigen, mehrfachbelichteten Aktbildern und Körperfragmenten, die er in einem eigens dafür gebauten Raum von sich selbst aufnimmt. Er grenzt sich bewußt von der russischen Tradition ab. Ihn interessieren Sudek, Penn, Weston, Adams und Mapplethorpe und der noch zu entdeckende Boris Samoilov.

6 *Samoilov schafft abstrakte Bilder mit dem Medium Fotografie. Er collagiert mit farbigen Partien dinghaft aufgenommene Naturobjekte, die, aus ihrem Zusammenhang gerissen, völlig verfremdet wirken. Seine Arbeiten verbinden sich mit philosophisch-mystischen Gedankengut zu einer bis aufs äußersten konzentrierten meditativen Stimmung. Durch das völlige Fehlen jedweden narrativen Elementes, das in der Avantgardefotografie bestand, muß er für die russische Kunst als Außenseiter gelten. Selbst in Filmen von Eisenstein wird um autonome Sequenzen herum Geschichte und damit Geschichten organisiert. Das gleiche Prinzip fand in der russischen Kriegsfotografie Verwendung. Man denke etwa an das Foto von der geschändeten Zoya Kosmodemyanskaya von Sergey Strunnikow.[12]*

Samoilov hat eine Beteiligung an diesem Ausstellungs- und Publikationsprojekt abgelehnt. Boris Mikhailov ist für ihn der Teufel des westlich orientierten Debakels in Rußland. Die ursprüngliche Grundidee, diese Grenzwerte künstlerischer Haltungen einer älteren Generation vorzustellen – es war in diesem Zusammenhang noch an Alexander Slyusarev und Boris Saveyev gedacht – mußte darum aufgegeben werden. Diese gescheiterte Idee gibt einen trefflichen Eindruck von der Schwierigkeit, Wege zu suchen, die am gegenwärtigen neuen Kunst-Establishment vorbeigehen.

7 *Vor diesem Hintergrund ist Boris Mikhailovs ‚Blaue Serie' bewußt für die Ausstellung gewählt worden. Sie ist in einer Situation entstanden, in der der Fotograf dem gesellschaftlichen Chaos ausgeliefert war. Er konnte nicht konzeptuell zynisch reagieren, wie er es in seinen neuesten Arbeiten von 1995 ‚Wenn ich Deutscher gewesen wäre' wieder versucht. Die ‚Blaue Serie' erlaubt dem Betrachter den Voyeurismus nicht, wird aber bisweilen gerade in Deutschland als folkloristisch abgelehnt. Das Folkloristische als das Gefühlvolle oder Sentimentale kann vor dem geistigen Raum Europa als verdrängtes Pathos angesehen werden. Pathos als Mittel der Entfremdung war in der russischen Avantgarde, etwa bei Rodchenko, seit jeher ein spezifisches Merkmal. Damit ist der Aspekt des sozialen Wirkenwollens in den zwanziger Jahren eng verbunden. Die mit einem alten Apparat aufgenommenen Panoramen sind in ihrer Bildstruktur ähnlich der russischen Konstruktivisten dezentral komponiert.*

8 *Diese unterschiedliche Organisationsform wurde bezeichnenderweise in den dreißiger Jahren Diskussionsgegenstand und politisches Druckmittel. 1928 ging es um einen formalen Vorwurf: Rodchenko und der Gruppe Oktober wurden als Plagiatoren der in Deutschland lebenden Fotografen László Moholy-Nagy und Albert Renger-Patzsch angegriffen.[13] 1931 kommt es zum politischen Vorwurf. Man warf dem Fotomonteur Gustav Klucis vor, durch seine Bildstruktur eine eindeutige politische Aussage zu verhindern. Es handelt sich bei den Arbeiten von Klucis um formstrenge, gegenstandslose Bildkonstruktionen mit linear akzentuierten Strukturen. Die bildhafte Verschmelzung der Montageelemente in einer homogenen Bildstruktur bei John Heartfield wurde Klucis' dezentralem Bildaufbau entgegengehalten.[14]*

Unter anderen Vorzeichen scheint dieses Kompositionsprinzip noch immer in Westeuropa Irritationen auszulösen.

6 Samoilov uses photography to create abstract pictures. He starts by taking 'objective' colour photographs of natural objects and then uses parts of these to make collages. Forcibly removed from their natural context, the original objects are entirely unrecognizable. Samoilov's approach is related to a complex of philosophical and mystical ideas, and his work itself conveys an extremely concentrated suggestion of meditation. On account of the total lack of any element of narrative in this work, Samoilov must be seen as an outsider in the context of Russian art. Narrative was, after all, to be found in avant-garde photography, and even in Sergei Eisenstein's films a sense of history in the making was contrived out of what were originally autonomous sequences of shots. The same principle was applied in Soviet war photography: one recalls, for example, Sergei Strunnikov's photograph of the disgraced Zoya Kosmodemyanskaya.[12]

Samoilov declined to collaborate in the current group exhibition or in the preparation of this volume, objecting both to its approach and to some of the work which was to be included. That of Boris Mikhailov, for example, is in Samoilov's view an epitome of the Western-oriented debacle in Russia. It was also therefore necessary to abandon the basic idea with which we started when planning this event – that of showing the limits of the artistic approach of an older generation. (In this context we had also thought to include Alexander Slyusarev and Boris Savayev.) The failure of this plan leaves little doubt as to the difficulties faced by those seeking to adopt an approach that disregards the current Russian photographic 'establishment'.

7 It is against this background that Boris Mikhailov's 'Blue Series' was consciously selected for the exhibition. It was made at a time when the photographer's own life had been overtaken by social chaos. He was unable to react with cool conceptual cynicism; as he has again tried to do in his latest work, the 1995 series 'If I had been a German'. The 'Blue Series' allows the spectator no element of voyeurism, and yet some commentators in Germany have dismissed it as 'folkloristic'. It is indeed the case that, from the point of view of the spiritual space of Western Europe, the folkloristic, as the emotional or the sentimental, may appear as suppressed pathos. However, pathos has always been a specific characteristic of the Russian avant-garde; for example in the work of Rodchenko, where it was used as a means of achieving alienation. Closely connected with this was the desire of photographers in the 1920s to have an impact on society. The panoramas photographed with an old camera are similar in their decentralized composition to the work of the Russian Constructivists.

8 During the 1930s pictorial organization became a subject of debate and a tool of political pressure; with far-reaching consequences. In 1928 interest was still focused on the formal aspect. Rodchenko and the October Group were attacked as plagiarists of the work of the photographers László Moholy-Nagy and Albert Renger-Patzsch, both then working in Germany.[13] By 1931 however, the matter had assumed a political dimension. The photo-monteur Gustav Klucis was accused of using pictorial structure to obscure a clear political statement. The works concerned were austerely abstract pictorial constructions with emphatic linear elements. The decentralized composition of Klucis's work was unfavourably compared with the pictorial merging of elements of montage into a homogeneous pictorial structure in the work of John Heartfield.[14] This compositional principle still appears to irritate the Western European eye even when encountered in quite another social and political context.

Notes

1 A recent example is the quarrel between Jean Christophe Ammann and Hubertus von Amelunxen concerning the work of Beat Christoph Streuli. See the article 'European Photography', in *Art Magazine*, lvii (1995), pp. 51–58
2 Ibid., p. 51.
3 Ibid.
4 *Die zeitgenössische Photographie in der Sowjetunion: Reportagen sozialer Wirklichkeit*, ed. Victor Misiano (introduction by Eric A. Peschler) (Schaffhausen, 1988) and *Photography in Russia 1840–1940*, ed. David Elliott (London, 1992).
5 *Photography in Russia 1840–1940*, op cit., p. 20 and Inka Graeve in *Sowjetische Photographie der 20er und 30er Jahre* (Cologne, 1991).
6 *Photography in Russia* 1840–1940, op cit., p. 13.
7 Alexander Rodchenko, [Against the Synthetic Portrait: For the Monumental Snapshot] (Moscow, 1928).
8 The Akademie der Künste is organizing a workshop for stipend holders. Each department invites young Russian artists to work for 3 months in Berlin. At the Akademie, Vladislav Efimov and Sergei Leontiev received photography stipends in the Department of Fine Arts, while Alexander Pozharski and Victor Luganski were given stipends in the Department of Film and Media.
9 See, for example, Andres Serrano, *The Morgue*, 1990, in *Gewalt/Geschäfte: Eine Ausstellung zum Topos der Gewalt in der gegenwärtigen künstlerischen Auseinandersetzung*, (Berlin, 1994).
10 Alexander Lavrentiev, 'Photo-Dreams of the Avant-Garde', in *Photography in Russia 1840–1940*, op cit., pp. 61–72.
11 *Kunst im Verborgenen. Nonkonformisten, Russland 1957–1995* (Munich, 1995).
12 Zoya Kosmodemyanskaya was a partisan who was murdered. See *Sowjetische Fotografen 1941–1945* (Leipzig, 1984).
13 László Moholy-Nagy (1895–1946) taught at the Bauhaus in Weimar and Dessau and experimented with photograms. Albert Renger-Patzsch (1897–1966) is regarded as a representative of *Neue Sachlichkeit*. See David Elliott, 'The Photograph in Russia: Icon of a New Age', in *Photography in Russia 1840–1940*, op cit., p. 21.
14 Hubertus Gassner, 'Heartfields Moskauer Lehrzeit 1931–1932', in *John Heartfield* (Cologne, 1991).

Fußnoten

1 *Ein jüngeres Beispiel dafür ist der Streit von Jean-Christophe Ammann und Hubertus von Amelunxen um das Werk von Beat Christoph Streuli, in:* European Photography. Art Magazine. *No. 57. 1995, S. 51–58*
2 *Ebenda, S. 51*
3 *Ebenda*
4 Die zeitgenössische Photographie in der Sowjetunion. Reportagen sozialer Wirklichkeit. *Hrsg. von Victor Misiano. Geleitwort von Eric A. Peschler. Schaffhausen 1988;* Russische Photographie 1840–1940. *Hrsg. von David Elliot. Berlin 1993*
5 Russische Photographie 1840–1940. *Hrsg. von David Elliott. Berlin 1993, S. 20; siehe auch den Aufsatz Inka Graeves in:* Sowjetische Photographie der zwanziger und dreißiger Jahre. *Köln 1991*
6 *Ebenda, S. 13*
7 *Alexander Rodchenko:* Gegen das synthetische Porträt – Für den monumentalen Schnappschuß. *1928*
8 *Die Akademie der Künste organisiert eine Stipendiatenwerkstatt. Alle Abteilungen laden junge russische Künstler zu einem dreimonatigem Arbeitsaufenthalt nach Berlin ein. Als Fotografie-Stipendiaten wurden in der Abteilung Bildende Kunst Vadim Efimov und Sergei Leontiev gewählt, in der Abteilung Film-und Medienkunst Prinz Alexander Pozharski und Victor Luganski*
9 *Andreas Serrano: „Serie Leichenschauhaus. (The Morgue)". 1990, in* Gewalt/Geschäfte. Eine Ausstellung zum Topos der Gewalt in der gegenwärtigen künstlerischen Auseinandersetzung. *Berlin 1994*
10 *Alexander Lawrentjew: „Die Photo-Träume der Avantgarde" in* Russische Photographie 1840–1940. *Hrsg. von David Elliot. Berlin 1993, S. 61f*
11 *Vgl. dazu* Kunst im Verborgenen. Nonkonformisten. Rußland 1957–1995. *Hrsg. v. Andrei Erofeev. München·New York 1995*
12 *Zoyja Kosmodemyanskaya ist als Partisanin ermordet worden. In:* Sowjetische Fotografen 1941–1945. *Leipzig 1985*
13 *László Moholy-Nagy (1895–1946) war Bauhaus-Lehrer in Weimar und Dessau und experimentierte mit dem Photogramm; Albert Renger-Patzsch (1897–1966) gilt als Vertreter der Neuen Sachlichkeit, in: David Elliott: „Die Photographie in Rußland: Ikone eines neuen Zeitalters" in* Russische Photographie 1840 – 1940, *Hrsg. von David Elliott. Berlin 1993, S. 21*
14 *Hubertus Gassner: „Heartfields Moskauer Lehrzeit 1931–1932", in:* John Heartfield. *Köln 1991*

ALEXANDER TOLNAY

Photography: Into the Third Dimension

Fotografie – dreidimensional

In den frühen neunziger Jahren begann eine junge Künstlergeneration in Moskau, die sich ausschließlich oder überwiegend der Fotografie als künstlerisches Medium bediente, ihre Arbeiten in die dritte Dimension zu erweitern. Diese formale Grenzüberschreitung führte, wie bei ihren westlichen Kollegen bereits drei Jahrzehnte davor, zu sogenannten ‚Bindestrich-Kunstformen', von denen das ‚Foto-Objekt', die ‚Foto-Skulptur', die ‚Foto-Installation' oder das ‚Foto-Environment' als weitläufige Bezeichnungen in unseren Sprachgebrauch Eingang fanden. Das Phänomen der Objektwerdung der Fotografie, dem innerhalb des Gemeinschaftsprojekts ‚Zeitgenössische Fotokunst aus Moskau' eine eigene Ausstellung im Neuen Berliner Kunstverein gewidmet ist, soll in diesem Beitrag formal und inhaltlich in Umrissen untersucht werden.

Aus der Geschichte der Fotografie sind einige Experimente bekannt, in welchen durch technische Erfindungen oder optische Effekte versucht wurde, das fotografische Bild in die dritte Dimension auszudehnen. Bereits Ende der dreißiger Jahre kam es zur Produktion von raumplastischen ‚Stereoskop'-Bildern. Zehn Jahre später wurde das Prinzip des dreidimensionalen Fotografierens entdeckt, das unter dem Namen ‚Holografie' in den sechziger Jahren weltweite Popularität erlangte. Der künstlerische Ertrag dieser neuen Fototechnologien war jedoch recht gering, trotz der Errichtung entsprechender Museen, obwohl auch namhafte Künstler, wie z. B. Bruce Nauman, mit Hologramm gearbeitet hatten. Die jüngste Revitalisierung der alten Technik der Stereoskopie unternahm der Deutsche Thomas Ruff mit seiner ‚Schwarzwald'-Serie an der diesjährigen Biennale in Venedig und bewies damit erneut die ungestillte Sehnsucht der Fotografen nach der räumlichen Dimension.

Der Wunsch nach räumlicher Darstellung mit Fotografie ließ in den letzten Jahren auch in Moskau einige Künstler zu stilistischen Mitteln greifen, die lange zuvor im Westen als Folge einer komplexen Wechselwirkung zwischen Fotografie und anderen Kunstgattungen bereits erprobt wurden. Durch die Zunahme der Reise- und Kommunikationserleichterungen ist ihnen der Synchronismus mit der internationalen Kunstentwicklung wieder ermöglicht worden. Auch in Rußland brachen die traditionellen Unterschiede zwischen den einzelnen Medien Malerei, Skulptur und Fotografie auf, und die jungen Moskauer Künstler – zu denen auch die Fotografen im üblichen Sinne zählen –

In Moscow in the early 1990s younger artists working either exclusively or mainly in photography began to extend their work into the third dimension. This crossing of formal boundaries led – as in the West thirty years before – to so-called 'hyphenated' art forms, with umbrella terms (such as 'photo-object', 'photo-sculpture', 'photo-installation' or 'photo-environment') becoming part of the language. This essay seeks broadly to investigate the form and content of the phenomenon of three-dimensional photography, which has a separate exhibition devoted to it in the Neuer Berliner Kunstverein (NBK) as part of the joint project 'Contemporary Photographic Art from Moscow'.

The history of photography records various experiments where attempts have been made to extend the photographic image into the third dimension either by means of technical invention or optical effects. Apparently three-dimensional 'stereoscope' pictures were already being produced in the late 1930s. Ten years later the principle of three-dimensional photography was discovered, becoming popular the world over in the 1960s as 'holography'. But the artistic return on all these new kinds of photo-technology was minimal, despite relevant exhibition spaces being created and well-known artists such as Bruce Nauman having worked with holograms. The most recent revitalisation of the old technique of stereoscopy was by the German Thomas Ruff with his 'Black Forest' series in this year's Biennale in Venice, bearing witness yet again to the unfulfilled longing that photographers have for the third dimension.

Over the last few years in Moscow the desire among artists to work with photography in three dimensions has led to some of them drawing on stylistic means that have long since been tried out in the West as a result of the complex interaction of photography and other art forms. But greater ease of travel and communication have now once again made it possible for Moscow artists to keep in step with developments in the international art world. In Russia, as elsewhere, traditional differences between painting, sculpture and photography have been disintegrating, with young Moscow artists – including photographers in the normal sense – moving freely between various art forms. Their aim was to reconcile the reality of what was being portrayed with the reality of the picture, and to do this they began to use photography in a different way to the generation before them.

The sense that there was something wrong about the practice of presenting photography in exhibitions in the same manner as graphic art led to the creation of 'photo-spaces' and to the construction of 'photo-installations'. In art-historical terms the earliest precursor of photographic installations was the legendary exhibition 'The Family of Man' in 1955 by Edward Steichen in the Museum of Modern Art in New York, in which the photographs, taken out of their frames and down from the wall were strewn all over the floor of the exhibition space. While this extremely effective presentation consisted exclusively of photographs, the next installation exhibition, 'Photography into Sculpture', fifteen years later in the same space, brought together various artistic media with the result that for the first time the viewer was challenged to engage with photographic works as spatial objects. In Moscow the 'founding father' of installations as an art form was Ilya Kabakov, whose international standing was to bear considerable fruit for the next generation of artists.

Where photography becomes three-dimensional it must, by definition, not only do justice to the demands of those 'neighbouring' forms whose criteria it has adopted but must, at the same time, remain true to its own principles. Unlike the two-dimensional photographic image, sculpture confronts the viewer in space as a spatial object, challenging him or her not only as observer but also as bodily presence. In photo-sculptures therefore photographic considerations are of necessity the prime concern: the genesis of the piece by means of light and transparency. Light boxes and transparent film are thus often to be found as constituent parts of photo-objects or photo-installations.

Photo-object, sculptural montage using photographs, and photo-installation are among the different conceptual possibilities for translating the purely optical presence of photography into the tactile fact of sculpture, from surface into the three-dimensional reality of space. The limited perspectivity of the camera's view is no longer at odds with the spatial perceptual horizons humans actually experience. Contemporary art often makes reference to its physical surroundings and is expressed in such a way as to require more from the viewer than an act of passive observation. It invites an interactive response, its aim being to put the viewer into the position of participant, moving in the space around the work of art and assimilating it as time elapses. The development of specific time-space structures goes hand in hand with a new attitude to our social and cultural context, which can no longer be accommodated within traditional thought processes and art forms.

Photography does not only derive its significance as a constituent element in three-dimensional installations from considerations of form. As important are questions of content, such as its experience of the human body, its outside-world context, and its particular capacity to express time and memory. In recent

bewegten sich frei zwischen den verschiedenen Kunstformen. Sie wollten die abgebildete Realität mit der Realität des Bildes auf eine Ebene bringen, indem sie begannen, sich der Fotografie anders als die Generation vor ihnen zu bedienen.

Das Unbehagen über die herkömmlichen Fotoausstellungen im Stile von Grafik-Präsentationen führte zu Inszenierungen von Foto-Räumen, zur Errichtung von Foto-Installationen. Erster kunstgeschichtlicher Vorläufer der fotografischen Installation war die legendäre Ausstellung von Edward Steichen ‚The Family of Man', 1955, im New Yorker Museum of Modern Art, in der die aus dem Rahmen und von den Wänden genommenen Fotos auf die gesamte Fläche des Ausstellungsraumes verteilt waren. Enthielt diese äußerst wirkungsvolle Präsentation noch ausschließlich fotografische Bilder, brachte die nächste ‚Installation'-Ausstellung ‚Photography into Sculpture' im selben Haus fünfzehn Jahre später verschiedene künstlerische Medien zusammen. Mit dieser Methode erreichte man zum ersten Mal, daß die Betrachter aufgefordert wurden, sich mit den Fotoarbeiten als Raumobjekten auseinanderzusetzen. ‚Gründungsvater' der Installation als Kunstform in Moskau war Ilya Kabakov, dessen internationale Anerkennung sich für die nächste Künstlergeneration als äußerst fruchtbar erwies.

Wo die Fotografie zum dreidimensionalen Objekt wird, muß sie zwangsläufig nicht nur den Ansprüchen des ‚Nachbarmediums', dessen Maßstab sie sich zu eigen gemacht hat, gerecht werden, sondern ihnen auch ihre Eigengesetzlichkeit entgegenhalten. Indem die Skulptur, anders als das zweidimensionale fotografische Bild, dem Betrachter im Raum als raumgreifende Gestalt gegenübersteht, fordert sie ihn nicht nur als betrachtendes Gegenüber, sondern auch als körperhaft Anwesenden heraus. Daher stehen bei den Foto-Skulpturen die dem Foto immanenten Eigenschaften notwendigerweise im Vordergrund: die Entstehung der Darstellung durch Licht und Transparenz. Leuchtkästen und durchsichtige Folien sind demzufolge häufig Bestandteile von Foto-Objekten oder Foto-Installationen.

Das Foto-Objekt, die skulpturale Montage von Fotografien oder die Foto-Installation sind unterschiedliche Möglichkeiten konzeptionaler Umsetzung der zweidimensionalen, rein optischen Präsenz der Fotografie in die haptische der Skulptur, von der Oberfläche in die dreidimensionale Realität von Räumen. Die eingeschränkte Perspektivität des Kamerablicks wird mit dem tatsächlichen räumlichen Wahrnehmungshorizont des Menschen in Einklang gebracht. Viele Beispiele der gegenwärtigen Kunstäußerungen formulieren ihre Aussage in bezug auf die räumliche Umgebung und verlangen vom Rezipienten mehr als nur die Erfahrung einer passiven Betrachtung. Sie fordern zum interaktiven Verhalten auf, sie wollen den Betrachter in die Position des Beteiligten versetzen, der sich im Raum bewegt und sich das Kunstwerk im zeitlichen Ablauf aneignet. Die Herausarbeitung dieser spezifischen Zeit-Raum-Struktur geht mit einer neuen Einstellung zu unserem sozialen und kulturellen Umfeld einher, das von den traditionellen Kunst- und Denkformen nicht mehr vollständig erfaßt werden kann.

Die Fotografie gewinnt nicht nur aus formalen Gründen eine Bedeutung für die Einbindung in eine Rauminstallation, sondern auch wegen inhaltlicher Aspekte, wie Körpererfahrung und Außenwelt-Kontext, und wegen ihrer spezifischen Eigenschaften, mit denen sie Zeit und Erinnerung auszudrücken vermag. In den vergangenen Jahren wurden von den Moskauer Fotokünstlern verstärkt ihre zeitgeschichtlich bedingten Erfahrungen verarbeitet. Den restaurativen Bedürfnissen nach alten Ordnungen und dem Trend zur Rückwärtsgewandtheit kommen die Ausdrucksmöglichkeiten der Foto-Installation, wo fotografische Bilder aus historischen Epochen den gewünschten Kontext schaffen, oder umgekehrt, wo der Kontext den Fotografien den historischen Wirkungsraum verleiht, besonders entgegen. Zwischen Stileklektizismus und Reduktivismus, zwischen raffiniertem Manierismus und neoakademischem Purismus führt das Medium Foto-Installation in Moskau ein Doppelleben, das möglicherweise mit dem Allgemeinzustand des heutigen Rußland vergleichbar ist: Prozeß und Statuarik zugleich.

years photo-artists in Moscow have increased their efforts to come to terms with experiences that are both of their past and peculiar to the time in which they happened. The expressive potential of the photo-installation is particularly suited both to these artists' restorative yearning for the old order and to the trend among them of looking to the past, with historic photographs creating the desired context or with the context lending the photographs historical significance. Somewhere between stylistic eclecticism and reductionism, somewhere between subtle Mannerism and neo-academic purism, the photo-installation as a medium leads a double life in Moscow, which perhaps bears comparison with conditions in Russia today: movement and stasis in one.

Artists' Biographies
Künstlerbiografien

AES-GROUP
Группа АЕС

Tatyana Arzamasova
1955 born in Moscow

Lev Evzovich
1958 born in Moscow

Evgeny Svyatsky
1957 born in Moscow

1987 formation of the AES-Group
gründeten die Gruppe AES

Solo Exhibitions (*Einzelausstellungen*)
1989 House 100 Gallery, Moscow
Howard Yezesky Gallery, Boston, MA
Performance at Harvard University, Cambridge, MA
1990 „Pathetische Rhetorik", Inter Art Galerie, Berlin
1991 East West Gallery, London
„Das Irdische Paradies", ifa-Galerie, Berlin
1992 „AES – Drei Künstler aus Moskau", Galerie der Stadt Esslingen
'Children's Bible', Salzau, Kulturzentrum des Landes Schleswig-Holstein
1993 'Art of the Possible', Guelman Gallery, Moscow
„Kain und Abel", Galerie Caspar Bingemer, Hamburg
1994 „Die Narbe", Guelman Gallery, Moscow
1995 'Body Space', Central House of Artists, Moscow
'Family's Portrait in Interior', XL Gallery, Moscow

Group Exhibitions (*Ausstellungsbeteiligungen*)
1986 'Hermitage Society', Beljaevo, Moscow
1987 Exhibition of Young Artists of the Soviet Union, Central Exhibition Hall (Manege), Moscow
1988 'Eidos', Central Palace of Youth, Moscow
18th Exhibition of Young Artists, Central Exhibition Hall (Manege), Moscow
1989 'Drawings of Artists from Moscow' Central House of Artists, Moscow
1990 Tampere Art Museum, Tampere, Finland
'Artists Work with Books', Moscow
'Moscow in Cambridge', Emmanuel College, Cambridge, UK
1991 Exhibition at the Imperial College, London
National Museum, Stockholm
'Exercises Esthétiques', Museum 'Estate Kuskovo of the XVIIth Century', Moscow
„Von Angesicht zu Angesicht" – Ars Baltica Prolog, Kunsthalle Kiel
„Von Angesicht zu Angesicht" – Ars Baltica Prolog, Ausstellungshalle „Latvija", Riga
1992 „Von Angesicht zu Angesicht" – Ars Baltica Prolog, Künstlerhaus Bethanien, Berlin
'Still', Kiev, Ukraine
'Diaspora', Central House of Artists, Moscow

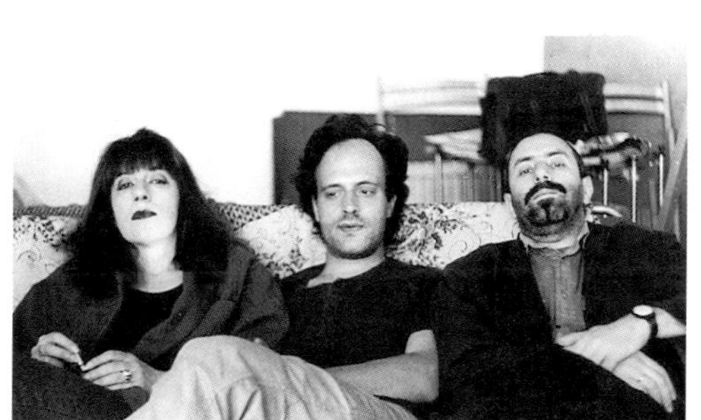

1993 'Conversion', Guelman Gallery, Moscow
'777', Museum of Contemporary Art, Stockholm
Aspex Galerie, Portsmouth
Reykjavik Art Museum
Galerie Nova Bratislava
Kulturzentrum Rheinoper Duisburg
1994 'Conversion', Guelman Gallery, Moscow; ISEA, Helsinki

The AES-Group (Tatyana Arzamasova, Lev Evzovich, Yevgeny Svyatsky) concentrates on photographs of the human body, which, in its view, is the only reality that can be documented. AES photographs superficial fragments of the body as testimony to the disintegration of form and the illusory character of the integral artistic image. AES has been called 'un-Russian' because the basis of its work contradicts current Russian conceptions of the artist. Nonetheless, in the passionless installations created by AES, the body assumes the cold beauty of a museum object.

Die Gruppe AES (Tatyana Arzamasova, Lev Evzovich, Yevgeny Svyatsky) konzentriert sich auf Aufnahmen vom menschlichen Körper, der ihrer Auffassung nach die einzig dokumentierbare Realität bildet. Wenn AES Oberflächenfragmente des Körpers fotografiert, dann bezeugt sie damit den Zerfall der Form, den illusorischen Charakter des ganzheitlichen künstlerischen Bildes. Als 'unrussisch' bezeichnet, da ihre Arbeitsgrundlage gängigen Künstlerauffassungen zuwiderläuft, gewinnt der Körper durch die präsentierte Leidenschaftslosigkeit ihrer Installationen die kalte Schönheit eines Museumobjektes.

YURI BABICH
Юрий Бабич

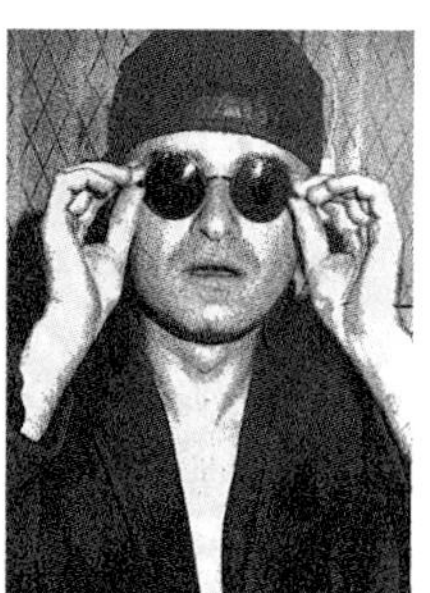

1957 born in Leningrad

Solo Exhibitions (*Einzelausstellungen*)
1991 'Carpets', Shcola Gallery, Moscow
1992 'The Stereotaxic Study', Kritinen Gallery, Helsinki
'The Wedding', Gallery on Trekhprudny Lane, Moscow

Group Exhibitions *(Ausstellungsbeteiligungen)*
1986 Festival in Valka, Russia
1987 Festival in Krasnogorsk, Russia
Private Action Show in Uglich, Russia
'Representation', Hermitage Association, Moscow
Autumn Show, Moscow
17th All-Union Exhibition of Young Artists, Central Exhibition Hall (Manege), Moscow
1988 Hippolite Gallery, Helsinki
'Contemporary Soviet Photography', Museet for Fotokunst, Odense, Denmark
1988/89 'Say Cheese!', Galerie Comptoir de la Photographie, Paris; Portfolio Gallery, London; Museum of Cinema, Moscow
1989 Contemporary Photography, Stockholm
Action Show, Copenhagen
Performance Festival, Roskilde, Denmark
Video Festival of the Nordic Countries, Copenhagen
'150 Years of Photography', Central Exhibition Hall (Manege), Moscow
1990 'Society for Lovers of Letter Reading', Kashirka Gallery, Moscow
'Towards Culture and Recreation', Kashirka Gallery, Moscow
1991 'Monochrome', Kashirka Gallery, Moscow
1992 New Russia's Art Festival, Finland
Vanha Gallery, Helsinki
1993 'Baroque at the End of the Century', V.Kh.P.U., named after Moukhina, St. Petersburg
1994 'Reproduction', Center for Contemporary Art, Moscow
'Art of Contemporary Photography-Russia, Ukraine, Belorus', Central House of Artists, Moscow
1994/95 „Neue Fotokunst aus Rußland", Badischer Kunstverein, Karlsruhe; Kunsthaus Osterfeld, Pforzheim
1995 Show in Club 'Manhattan Express', Moscow

In his work Babich emphasizes the artist's responsibility for his actions. Babich shows a reality that has 'suffered', been ransacked and degraded to meaningless decoration by the endless image-generating capacity of the computer culture of the West. In Babich's view, the artist is ever less the self-determined creator of his images. In the process of cultural transformation, these assume an autonomous dynamism.

Babich unterstreicht in seinen Arbeiten die Verantwortlichkeit des Künstlers für sein Tun: Er zeigt eine Realität, die „gelitten" hat, umgestülpt wurde und von der Endlosbilder generierenden Computerkultur des Westens zur sinnentleerten Dekoration degradiert wird. Der Künstler ist immer weniger selbstbestimmter Gestalter der Darstellung; vielmehr entwickelt diese im Prozeß des kulturellen Wandels eine autonome Dynamik.

GOR CHAHAL
Гор Чахал

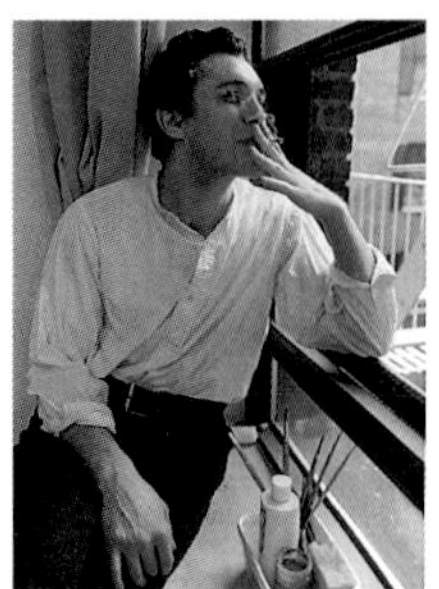

1961 born in Moscow

Solo Exhibitions (*Einzelausstellungen*)
1990 1.0 Gallery, Moscow
1991 'Black Light', Gallery on Trekhprudny Lane, Moscow
1992 'On bottom', 1.0 Gallery, Moscow
Sprovieri Gallery, Rome
1993 'The Fields', Central House of Artists, Moscow
1995 Shcola Gallery, Moscow

Group Exhibitions (*Ausstellungsbeteiligungen*)
1986/88 Author and participant of many performances with the groups 'Parallel Actions' and 'Post'
1988 'Novue Peredvizniki', luggage boot of automobile 'Volga'-GAZ 24, Moscow-Leningrad
'The Labyrinth', Central Palace of Youth, Moscow
18th All-Union Exhibition of Young Artists, Central Exhibition Hall (Manege), Moscow
'Unfinished Works', Furmannaja Gallery, Moscow
'Anti Sotheby's', S. Shutov Studio, Moscow
1989 'Inexpensive Art', 1.0 Gallery, Moscow
1990 „Inspiration", Messegelände Hannover
'For Cultural Rest', Exhibition Hall Kashirskaya, Moscow
1991 'Modern Moscow Art', Seibu Art Forum, Tokyo
'Rome-Moscow', Sprovieri Gallery, Rome
'Aesthetic Experiment', Kuskovo Museum, Moscow
1992 'A Mosca ... a Mosca', Villa Compolletto Ercolano; Galleria Communale d'Arte Moderna, Bologna
'Moscow Romanticism', Central House of Artists, Moscow
1993 Collection Rinaco, Central House of Artists, Moscow; Caisse des depots et consignation, Paris
4th Annual Jury Exhibition, Synchronicity Space, New York
1995 'Winter Garten', Exhibition Hall 'Feniks', Moscow
'View behind the Horizon', Exhibition Hall in Belyaevo, Moscow

Chahal addresses the contemporary problem of the artist's self-identification in a period of the 'erosion' of traditional values in art as a result of the mass-production of images in advertising and on computer screens. The construction of his images leads the artist to investigate the possibilities of creating fashion and re-defining the laws of the impact of advertising.

In seinen Arbeiten analysiert Chahal das aktuelle Problem der Selbstidentifikation des Künstlers in einer Situation der „Erosion" traditioneller Werte in der Kunst durch massenhafte Bilderproduktion in der Werbung und auf Bildschirmen. Der Aufbau eines Images führt den Künstler zur Untersuchung der Möglichkeiten, Mode zu gestalten und die Gesetze der Einwirkung von Reklame neu zu bestimmen.

OLGA CHERNYSHEVA
Ольга Чернышева

1962 born in Moscow

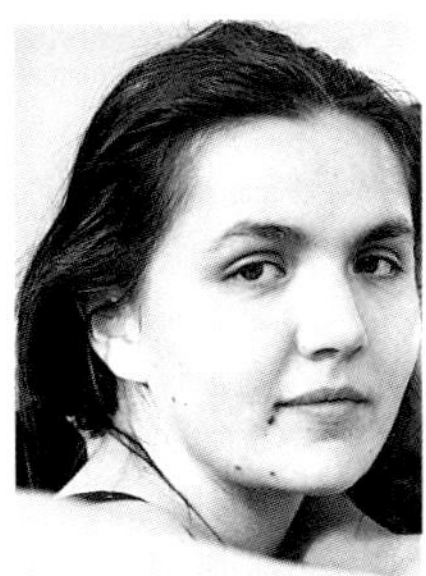

Solo Exhibitions (*Einzelausstellungen*)
1992 1.0 Gallery, Moscow
1993 'Anton Olshvang, Olga Chernysheva', Museum of Cinema, Moscow
1994 'Anton Olshvang, Olga Chernysheva', Galerie Krings-Ernst, Köln
'Pro Portsii', State Russian Museum, St. Petersburg

Group Exhibitions (*Ausstellungsbeteiligungen*)
1987 17th Exhibition of Young Artists, Central Exhibition Hall (Manege), Moscow
1989 Furmanny Lane, Novitzy Gallery, Warsaw
1990 ZHEN, Sadovniki Gallery, Moscow
'Towards the Object', Tsaritsyno Contemporary Art Museum, Moscow
'In de Ussr en erbuiten', Stedelijk Museum, Amsterdam
'Over There, Over Here', Avantgardist Club, Moscow
'Furmanny in Factory', Salzmann Kulturzentrum, Kassel
„Künstler der Furmannstrasse, Russland zu Gast", Limburg
1991 'Weight and Madness', Galeria Fernando Duran, Madrid
'Solitary Pursuits', Center for Contemporary Art, Moscow
'No Vacio. (In Emptiness)', Santiago de Compostela, Spain
'Hinderloppet', Tomililla, Sweden
'Aesthetic Experiences', Kuskovo Country Palace-Museum, Moscow
'Novecento', Central House of Artists, Moscow
'V izbah (in Rooms) Dom kultury', Bratislava
1992 'A Mosca ... A Mosca ...', Villa Compolletto Ercolano; Galleria Communale d'Arte Moderna, Bologna
Festival of Moscow Contemporary Art, Helsinki
'Humanitarian Aid for Germany', Moscow, Berlin
'New Works', Storm Gallery, Amsterdam
1993 „Prospekt 93", Frankfurt am Main
„Kontext Kunst 90", Künstlerhaus Graz
1994 'Watt', Witte de With, Rotterdam
„Fluchtpunkt Moskau", Ludwig Forum, Aachen
'Reproduction', Center for Contemporary Art, Moscow
'Biennale Contemporary Art', Contemporary Art Museum, Cetinje, Montenegro
'Dacha', Amsterdam-Russia project
'Open atelier', Rijksacademie, Amsterdam
1995 „Kunst im Verborgenen", Wilhelm-Hack-Museum, Ludwigshafen; Documenta-Archiv, Kassel; Lindenau-Museum, Altenburg
„Kräftemessen-Contending Forces", Künstlerwerkstatt Lothringerstraße, München
'I Don't Actually Have To Go', Lumen Travo Gallery, Amsterdam

Chernysheva often makes use of found photographs that, after retouching, take on an anonymous, impersonal character. She has adopted the black-and-white aesthetic of Moscow Conceptualism, though not its propensity for verbalization. In her work there is always a balance between 'positive notions' (originality, nature, authenticity) and scepticism with regard to the possible results of any undertaking.

In ihren Arbeiten verwendet sie oft gefundene Fotos, die in der Kombination mit auktorialen Retuschen einen anonym-unpersönlichen Charakter annehmen. Vom Moskauer Konzeptualismus hat sie die Schwarz-Weiß-Ästhetik übernommen, nicht allerdings die Neigung, ihre Kunst zu verbalisieren. Olga Chernysheva balanciert in ihren Arbeiten ständig zwischen „positiven Ansätzen" (Originalität, Natur, Authentizität) und der Skepsis gegenüber möglichen Resultaten.

VLADISLAV EFIMOV
Владислав Ефимов

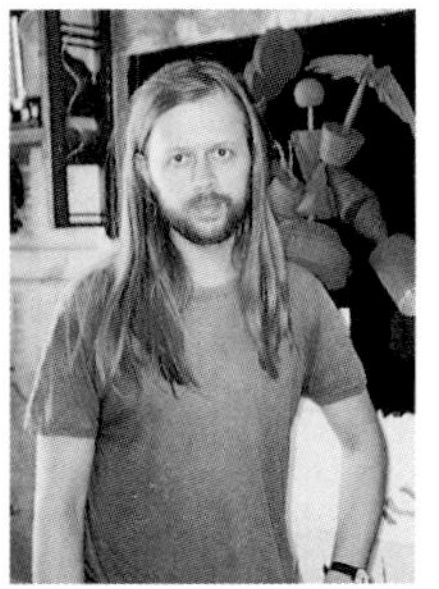

1964 born in Moscow

Solo Exhibitions (*Einzelausstellungen*)
1991 'Untitled', Center for Contemporary Art, Moscow
Shcola Gallery, Moscow
1993 'Nature Morte: Arcadia', New Space Gallery, Odessa
1994 'Untitled', Center for Contemporary Art, Moscow
Studio 20 Gallery, Moscow
'Tables', Video Studio TV Gallery, Moscow
1995 'Vladislav Efimov & Oleg Migas, Dis(crete) Moving Pictures or Chinese Cinema', 1.0 Gallery, Moscow
'The High', Studio 20 Gallery, Moscow

Group Exhibitions (*Ausstellungsbeteiligungen*)
1987 'Presentation', Exhibitions of the Union 'Hermitage'/Exhibition Hall, Moscow
'Photoexposition', Exhibition Hall in Belyaevo, Moscow
1988 Photosalon on Malaja Grusinskaja Street, Moscow
'Exhibition of Moscow Photograph', Photography Museum, Lvov, Russia
1989 '150 Years of Photography', Central Exhibition Hall (Manege), Moscow
1990 'Contemporary Photography from the USSR', Walker, Ursitti & McGuinniss Gallery, New York
1991 'Presentation of Contemporary Art', Center for Contemporary Art, Moscow
'Solitary Pursuit. Center for Contemporary Art', Moscow
1.0 Gallery, Moscow
1992 'Vladislav Efimov – Yuri Babich', Vanha Gallery, Helsinki
1993 'Kunst-Kammer', 1.0 Gallery, Moscow
'Bestiarium', Navicula-Artis Gallery, St. Petersburg
1994 'Art of Internal Space – 1st Exposition: Yuri Albert, Vladislav Efimov', 1.0 Gallery, Moscow
'Art of Contemporary Photography: Russia, Ukraine, Belarus', Central House of Artists, Moscow
'Surface of Sense. Laying Covers', Central House of Artists, Moscow
'Final Show of Curatorial Development Workshop', Center for Contemporary Art, Moscow
„Europe '94", München
Festival of Contemporary Art, Sochi, Russia
'New Media Tropia', Central House of Artists, Moscow
1995 „Configura 2, Dialog der Kulturen", Erfurt

Efimov's work represents an especially striking and characteristic tendency in contemporary Russian photography: that of exploiting the associative capacity of the individual consciousness. Using negative prints, he creates a psychedelic world. Efimov rejects both the planar reproduction of outer reality and the symbolic character of the modern culture of interpretation.

Efimov repräsentiert eine besonders markante und charakteristische Tendenz in der zeitgenössischen russischen Fotografie, die mit Assoziationsreihen des individuellen Bewußtseins operiert. Mittels Negativabdruck erschafft er eine psychedelische Welt. In seinen Arbeiten wird die plane Abbildung der äußeren Wirklichkeit ebenso abgelehnt wie die Zeichenhaftigkeit der modernen Interpretationskultur.

FENSO-GROUP
Группа Fenso

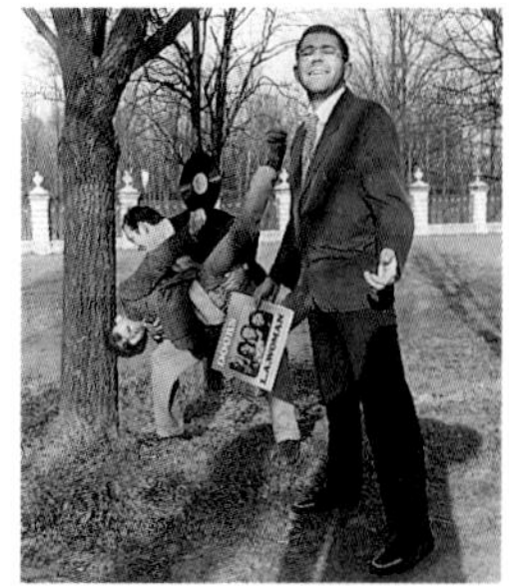

Denis Salautin
1968 born in Moscow
Vasily Smirnov
1970 born in Moscow
Anton Smirnsky
1970 born in Moscow

In 1993 the Fenso project was begun
1993 begann das Fenso-Projekt

Solo Exhibitions (*Einzelausstellungen*)
1993 'Fenso Lights', 1.0 Gallery, Moscow
'Fenso Lights', Shcola Gallery, Moscow
'Fenso Lights', Philippe Briet Gallery, New York

Group Exhibitions (*Ausstellungsbeteiligungen*)
1993 'Exchange', Center for Contemporary Art, Moscow
1994 Festival of Contemporary Art, Sochi, Russia
'Exchange-2', Amsterdam
'The artist instead of the artwork', Central House of Artists, Moscow
'Multi media', Central House of Artists, Moscow
Regina Gallery, Moscow

This artists' group (Denis Salautin, Vasily Smirnov, Anton Smirnsky) belongs to the generation that is exploiting new technologies, both organically and naturally, as artistic tools. The 'magical' character of its images is conveyed through their presentation in photography or on the computer screen. The group translates its romantic fantasies through the sign systems associated with the mass media (including video recordings and computer manipulation).

Diese Künstlergruppe (Denis Salautin, Vasily Smirnov, Anton Smirnsky) gehört der neuen Generation an, die neue Technologien organisch und natürlich als Kunstmittel ausnutzt. Der magische Charakter ihrer Arbeiten wird durch die Darstellung auf der Fotografie oder dem Bildschirm übermittelt; in diese medialen Zeichensysteme (u.a. Videoaufzeichnungen und Computermanipulationen) übersetzen sie ihre romantischen Phantasien.

VADIM FISHKIN
Вадим Фишкин

1965 born in Pensa

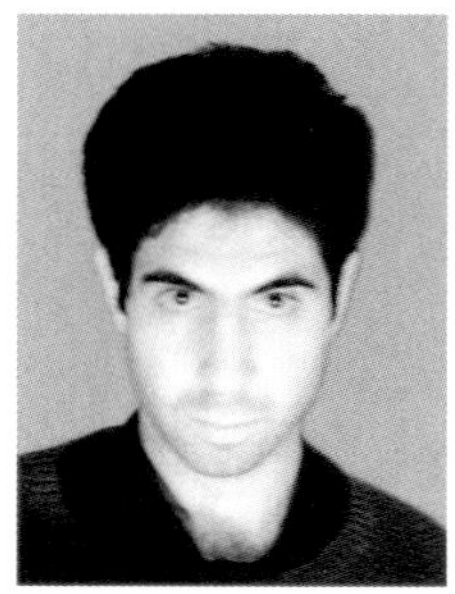

Solo Exhibitions (*Einzelausstellungen*)

1991 Galerie Polaris, Paris
Boycott Galerie, Bruxelles
Gallery on Trekhprudny Lane, Moscow
1992 Regina Gallery (within the Animalist Project), Moscow
Shcola Gallery, Moscow
1993 Gallery on Trekhprudny Lane, Moscow
'Sunset Orbit': Guelman, Dar, 1.0, Shcola Gallery and Center for Contemporary Art, Moscow
1994 'Orbit S', XL Gallery, Moscow

Group Exhibitions (*Ausstellungsbeteiligungen*)

1986 'Artist and Children's Drawings', Central House of Artists, Moscow
1987 'Painting', House of the Architects' Union, Moscow
1988 'The Labyrinth', Central Palace of Youth, Moscow
18th exhibition of Young Artists from Moscow, Central Exhibition Hall (Manege), Moscow
1989 'Precious Art', Central Palace of Youth, Moscow
'Dialogue', Centre Boris Vian, France
'Rauschenberg-us, we-Rauschenberg', 1.0 Gallery, Moscow
'Unfinished Works', Zvezdochotov Studio, Moscow
'Little Works', Shutov-Studio, Moscow
'Little Creations', 1.0 Gallery, Moscow
'World Champion', Plehanov Institute, Exhibition Hall, Moscow
'Furmany Pereulok', Modern Art Center, Warsaw
'Les Champions du Monde', Art 2 Gallery, Paris/Espace 'Transit', Strasbourg
'The Other Side of Terms', Central Palace of Youth, Moscow
'L'art est libre, le livre comme l'art', C. Corre Gallery, Paris
Iskusstvo, Linden Gallery, Melbourne
Workshop Furmany Pereulok, Monastery of Martigny, Switzerland
'Red and White', The Netherlands
1990 'To and Fro', Moscow
'Green Exhibition', ART Gallery, New York
„Furmanys in Fabrik (Soviet Avantgarde)", Kulturfabrik Salzmann, Kassel
„Künstler der Furmannstraße", Stadt-Galerie, Limburg
'Young Art from Eastern Europe', Rotterdam
'New and Recent Works', Exhibition Hall Kashirskaya, Moscow
'The Alps of Moscow', Mars Gallery, Moscow
F.I.A.C 90, Gallery Polaris, Paris (fair booth)
1991 'Moscow-Ticino', Lugano
'Novicento', Central House of Artists, Moscow
1992 'Art from Previous Owners', Regina Gallery, Moscow
1993 'Virtual Garden', WdnH, Moscow
Festival 'New Territories of Art', Krasnojarsk, Russia
'House' Project (with Andrei Sumatochin and Robert Philipini Europäer), City Museum, Moscow; Kunstverein Graz
1994 'Hamburger Project', Center for Contemporary Art, Moscow
'Transitions', Medium Gallery, Bratislava, Slovakia; Budapest Gallery, Budapest
„Europe '94", München
'Proektika', Center for Contemporary Art, Moscow
1995 ARS 95, Aiteen Museo, Helsinki
Biennale, Russian Pavillion. Venice

Fishkin's work reflects an orientation to the metaphysical and an absorption in a primitive world of the psyche that are characteristic of contemporary Russian art. Photography here appears as the projection of an individual perception of the world, an adaptation of the 'cosmic' to the consciousness and the imaginative power of man.

Fishkins Werk reflektiert die für die zeitgenössische russische Kunst charakteristische Ausrichtung auf das Metaphysische und die Versunkenheit in eine eigene Welt der Psyche. In seinen Arbeiten erscheint Fotografie als Projektion einer individuellen Wahrnehmung von Welt, einer Adaption des „Kosmischen" an das Bewußtsein und die Imaginationskraft des Menschen.

ALEXEI GOGA
Алексей Гога

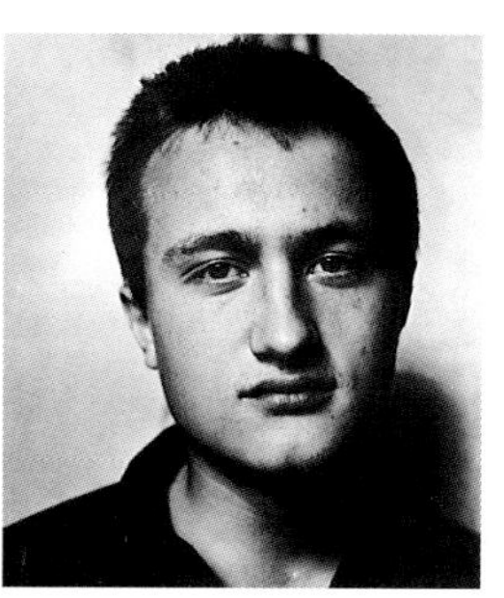

1970 born in Krasnogorsk

Solo Exhibitions (*Einzelausstellungen*)
1994 Theatre Metropol, Moscow
1995 'Gender' (in collaboration with Irina Klopova), Museum of Humanitarian Culture, Russian State Unviersity for the Humanities, Moscow

Group Exhibitions (*Ausstellungsbeteiligungen*)
1994/95 „Neue Fotokunst aus Moskau", Badischer Kunstverein, Karlsruhe; Kulturhaus Osterfeld, Pforzheim
1995 „Fototage", Herten, Germany
Show in theatre Kinoaktera, Moscow
Show in Club 'Manhattan Express', Moscow

Goga experiments with wide-angle lenses and a 'camera obscura' of his own construction, with which he is able to stage and record a photographic representation of the human body, himself functioning as both model and photographer. By means of combining several posed images within a single negative, he brings an original approach to the problem of 'artist and model'.

Goga experimentiert mit Breitformat-Kameras und einer eigens konstruierten „Camera obscura", mit der er eine Fotodarstellung des menschlichen Körpers inszenieren und realisieren kann, in der der Fotograf Modell und Darsteller ist. Durch Fixierung verschiedener Standfotos auf dem selben Negativ thematisiert er das Problem „Künstler und Modell" auf originelle Weise.

VLADIMIR KUPRIYANOV
Владимир Куприянов

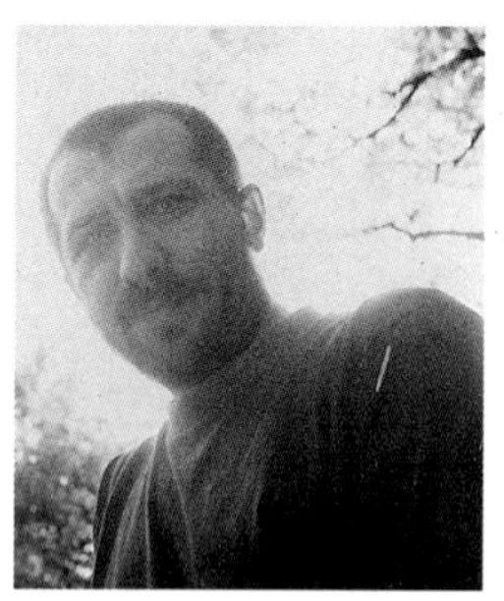

1954 born in Moscow

Solo Exhibitions (*Einzelausstellungen*)
1983 Strajitelnaja Gasjeta, Moscow
1990 „Mittelrussische Landschaft", InterArt Agentur für Kunst, Berlin
1992 Forum Stadtpark, Graz
Shcola Gallery, Moscow
1994 Shcola Gallery, Moscow
1995 21 Galerie, Hamburg
„Photoarbeiten 1981–1995", Haus am Waldsee, Berlin
„Miniaturen", Art 5 III Galerie Inge Herbert, Berlin

Group Exhibitions (*Ausstellungsbeteiligungen*)
1987 Heremitage Artists' Group, Moscow
Kupriyanov and Sherbakov, Sculptor House, Moscow
1988 'Contemporary Soviet Photography', Museum for Photography, Lausanne
Graphic arts in books, Central House of Artists, Moscow
1989 'Photo Bridge', Avantgardist Club, Moscow
I. Internationale Foto-Triennale, Villa Merkel, Esslingen
'150 Years of Photography', Central Exhibition Hall (Manege), Moscow
1990 'The Logic of the Paradoxical', Central Palace of Youth, Moscow
'Contemporary Photography from the USSR', Walker, Ursitti & McGuiness Gallery, New York
'Oppositions: Commitment and Cultural Identity in Contemporary Photography': II. International Biennale of Photography, Center for Photography, Rotterdam
'The Missing Picture – Alternative Contemporary Photography from the USSR', MIT List Visual Arts Center, Cambridge, MA
1991 „Heimat", Galerie Wewerka & Weiss, Berlin
Long Island University, Southampton
1992 Rauma Biennale Balticum '92, Art Museum Rauma
'Contemporary Portrait Photography from Russia, Belorussia and the Ukraine', Amsterdam
1993 Österreichische Triennale zur Fotografie: Krieg, Neue Galerie am Landesmuseum Joanneum/Forum Stadtpark, Graz
1994 'Photo-Reclamation: New Art from the Former Soviet Union', John Hansard Gallery; Photographers' Gallery, Southampton
„Europe '94"
'The Art of Contemporary Photography', Central House of Artists, Moscow
„Für F. N. Nietzsche in der bildenden Kunst der letzten 30 Jahre", Stiftung Weimarer Klassik, Schloß Belvedere, Weimar
1995 ARS '95, Museet for Nutidskonst, Helsinki
'Where Is Your Brother Abel?' Sacheta Gallery, Warsaw
„FotoRäume", Landeskulturzentrum Salzau, Kiel

The phantasmagorical and immaterial character of Kupriyanov's photographs can be associated with his concern with the formal perfection of the image, its sculptural compactness and the aesthetic value of its installation. Kupriyanov ensnares reality in the 'net' of his artistic vision. In presenting his images on transparent photographic film and photographic glass plates, he demonstrates their transparency.

Die Phantasmagorik und Immaterialität seiner Fotoarbeiten verbindet sich mit der Ausrichtung auf formale Vollendung des Bildes, die plastische Geschlossenheit und den ästhetischen Wert der Installationen. Kupriyanov legt ein Netz des auktorialen Sehens über die Realität. Indem er die Darstellungen auf durchsichtigen Fotofilmen und Fotogläsern präsentiert, stellt er ihre Transparenz unter Beweis.

SERGEI LEONTIEV
Сергей Леонтьев

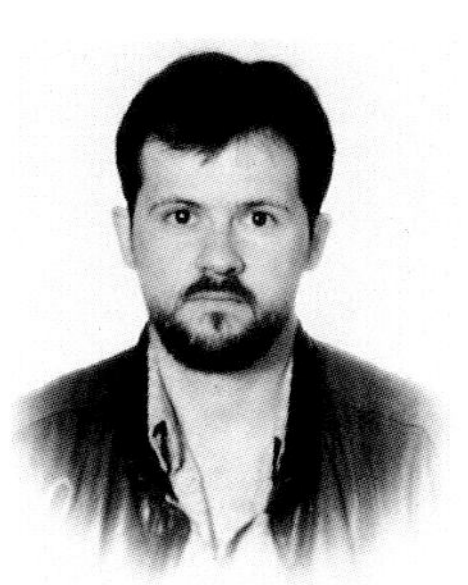

1962 born in Moscow

Solo Exhibitions (*Einzelausstellungen*)

1989 'The Life of a Photographer' (with A. Shulgin), Exhibition Hall, Kashirskaya, Moscow
1993 Untitled Installation (with A. Shulgin), Russian-Dutch project 'Exchange', Moscow

Group Exhibitions (*Ausstellungsbeteiligungen*)

1987 'Representation', Exhibitions of the Union ‚Hermitage'/ Exhibition Hall Belyaevo, Moscow
Autumn Photo Show, Malaya Gruzinskaya, Moscow
1988 'Contemporary Photography in the Soviet Union', Museum of Photography, Lausanne
1988/89 'Say Cheese!', Galerie Comptoir de la Photographie, Paris; Portfolio Gallery, London; Museum of Cinema, Moscow
1989 'Photomost' (Photobridge), Avtozavodskaya Hall, Moscow
'150 Years of Photography', Central Exhibition Hall (Manege), Moscow
Art Museum, Cheboksary, Russia
1990 Photoclub 'Egzva', Syktyvkar, Russia
'Contemporary Photography from the USSR', Walker, Ursitti & McGuinness Gallery, New York
'Oppositions: Commitment and Cultural Identity in Contemporary Photography': II. International Biennale of Photography, Center for Photography, Rotterdam
1991 'Photo Manifesto', Fine Arts Gallery & Avram Family Gallery, Fine Arts Center, Long Island University, New York
'Photoproject Zurich-Moscow',Taganka Theatre, Moscow; Photo Forum Gallery, Zürich, University of Zürich; Photo Center, Moscow
1992 Albrecht Galerie, München
'Litsa (Faces): Contemporary Portrait Photography from Russia, Belorussia and Ukraine', Foundation CIRC, Amsterdam
2. Internationale Foto-Triennale, Esslingen
1993 'What Am I? The Art of Making a Choice', Shcola Gallery; Union Gallery, Moscow
„Über die Großen Städte", NGBK-Akademie-Galerie, Berlin
1994 'Art of Contemporary Photography. Russia, Ukraine, Belarus', Central House of Artists, Moscow
1994/95 „Neue Fotokunst aus Rußland", Badischer Kunstverein, Karlsruhe; Kulturhaus Osterfeld, Pforzheim

As a follower of the Moscow School of 'direct photography', Leontiev firmly rejects staged photography and image manipulation. The directness of his photographs — seen at its most emphatic in his 'Study in Hard Photography' — is achieved through the intervention of the photographer, who uses his camera like a surgical instrument.

Als Anhänger der Moskauer Schule der „unmittelbaren Fotografie" lehnt Leontiev Inszenierung und Manipulation strikt ab. Die Unmittelbarkeit der Aufnahme – in seinen „Versuchen in harter Fotografie" extrem zugespitzt – wird zur direkten Einmischung des Fotografen, der die Kamera „hart", als chirurgisches Instrument einsetzt.

TATYANA LIBERMAN
Татьяна Либерман

1964 born in Moscow

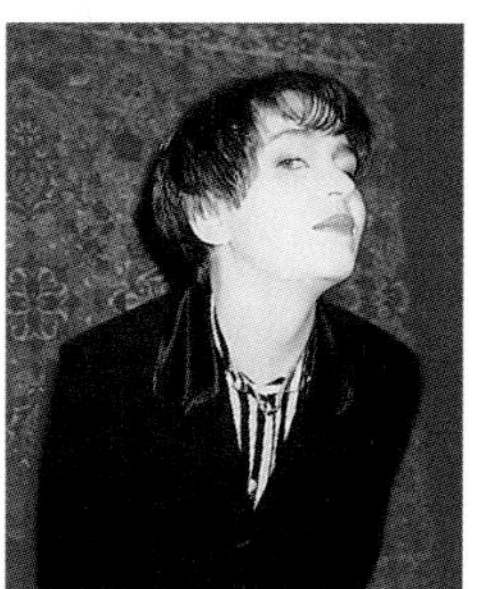

Solo Exhibitions (*Einzelausstellungen*)
1994 'Projection', XL Gallery, Moscow
1995 'Reconstruction', Goethe Institut, Moscow

Group Exhibitions (*Ausstellungsbeteiligungen*)
1987 Student club of Moscow University, Moscow
1990 'Igor Moukhin and Tatyana Liberman', Photo Gallery, St. Petersburg
'Towards Culture and Recreation', Exhibition Hall, Kashirskaya, Moscow
1991 'Photo Manifesto', Museum for Contemporary Art, Baltimore
'Svalbart-Fotografiske Fragmenter', Kristiansand, Norway
1993 'Sextinian Chapel', Teatro/Art & Design Center, Moscow
'Young Talents', Photocenter, Moscow
'Vadim Gippenreiter and Tatyana Liberman', Teatro/Art & Design Center, Moscow
1994 'Art of Contemporary Photography-Russia, Ukraine, Belorus', Central House of Artists, Moscow
Russian Union of Art Photographers, Annual Exhibition: 'Photography by Women', Ryazan Museum, Ryazan, Russia
'Surface of Sense: Laying Covers', Central House of Artists, Moscow
Second Moscow Photography Festival, Gallery Na Solyanke, Moscow
1994/95 „Neue Fotokunst aus Moskau", Badischer Kunstverein, Karlsruhe; Kulturhaus Osterfeld, Pforzheim
1995 'Visual Concept', ADC and Tampa Museum of Art, Tampa

For Liberman, staging is indispensable to photography, and she exploits the full range of its technical possibilities. Photography offers her the chance to 'document' her inner world. The body, Liberman's principal subject, is for her something self-contained, but also something that can be recorded through the fantasies she sets in motion. In her view, her 'work' is over long before the photographs are printed, even before the negatives are developed.

Der Inszenierungscharakter ist für Liberman unabdingbare Eigenschaft der Fotografie, die sie in allen technischen Facetten einsetzt. Fotografie bietet ihr die Möglichkeit, die Innenwelt zu „dokumentieren". Der Körper als Hauptmotiv ist für sie etwas in sich Geschlossenes, das die Projektion ihrer Fantasien, die sie in Szene setzt, aufnehmen kann. Für sie sind ihre Arbeiten lange vor Abdruck und sogar schon vor der fotografischen Fixierung abgeschlossen.

BORIS MIKHAILOV
Борис Михайлов

1938 born in Kharkov, Ukraine

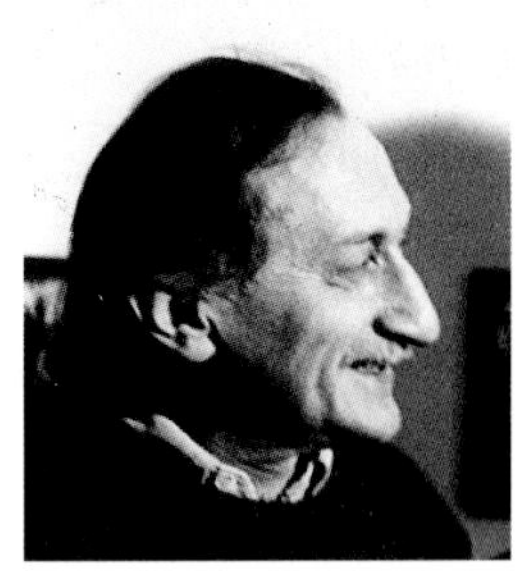

Solo Exhibitions (*Einzelausstellungen*)
1989 Museum of Contemporary Art, Tampere, Finland
1990 Museum of Contemporary Art, Tel Aviv
1992 Forum Stadtpark, Graz
1993 Photoscriptum Place, St. Petersburg
1994 Fotogalerie Kulturamt Friedrichshain, Berlin
XL Gallery, Moscow
1995 The Photographer's Gallery, London
Galerie in der Brotfabrik, Berlin
Galerie Andreas Weiss, Berlin
Marat Guelman Gallery, Moscow
ART Museum, Kharkov, Ukraine
Walters Hall Gallery, Douglas College. New Brunswick, NJ

Group Exhibitions (*Ausstellungsbeteiligungen*)
1989 '150 Years of Photography', Central Exhibition Hall (Manege), Moscow
'150 Years of Photography', Prague
'Contemporary Soviet Photography', Kunsthuset, Stockholm
'Say cheese!', Comptoir de la photographie, Paris; Portfolio Gallery, London; Museum of Cinema, Moscow
1990 'The Missing Picture – Alternative Contemporary Photography from the USSR', MIT List Visual Art Center, Cambridge, MA
'Erosion', Amos Anderson Art Museum, Helsinki
'Photography of Kharkov and Ukraine', Kunsthuset, Stockholm
'Oppositions: Commitment and Cultural Identity in Contemporary Photography': II. International Biennale of Photography, Center for Photography, Rotterdam
1991 Carnegie International, Pittsburgh
'Photo Manifesto', Museum for Contemporary Art, Baltimore
1992 'Herbarium', Fotogalerie Wien/Kunsthalle Exnergasse, Wien
1993 'New Photography 9', Museum of Modern Art, New York
Dom Hodozhnik, Moscow
1994 Photographers' Gallery, London

Mikhailov was the first Russian photographer to integrate texts into his photographs (the 'Lurik' cycle); his work nonetheless resists every attempt at classification. He often combines emotionally affecting everyday scenes with stylizing and alienating technical processes that place the resulting photographic images mid-way between the qualities of proximity and distance, immediacy and decoration.

Mikhailov hat als erster russischer Fotograf das konzeptuelle Verfahren der Integration von Textinformation angewandt („Lurik"-Zyklus); allerdings weichen seine Arbeiten jedem Einordnungsversuch aus. Oft koppelt er emotional wirkungsstarke Alltagsdarstellungen mit stilisierenden und verfremdenden Verfahren, die die Aufnahmen in ein Beziehungsnetz von Nähe und Ferne, Unmittelbarkeit und Dekoration setzen.

IGOR MOUKHIN
Игорь Мухин

1961 born in Moscow

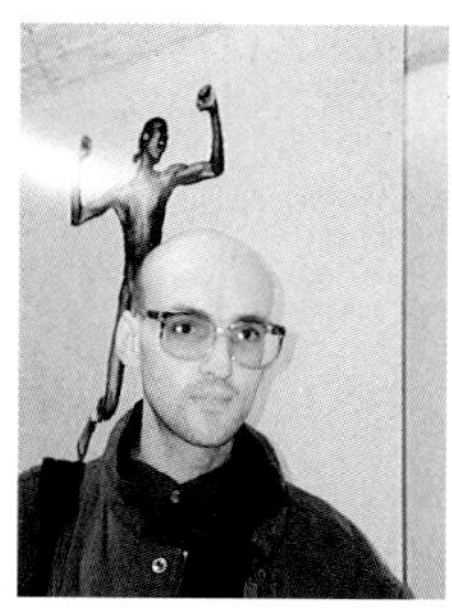

Solo Exhibitions (*Einzelausstellungen*)
1987 Moscow State University, Moscow
1988 URALMASH Factory Club, Sverdlovsk, Russia
1989 Photo Gallery, Kujbyshev, Russia
Photo Reporters Club, Ukhta, Russia
1990 Photo Gallery, Leningrad
1993 'A Research into the Soviet Monumental Art', Mary Photo Art Society Exhibition Hall, Yoshkar-Ola, Russia
1994 'Benches: Transformation for the Future', XL Gallery, Moscow
1995 '40 Photographs', Museum of Revolution, Moscow

Group Exhibitions (*Ausstellungsbeteiligungen*)
1986 'Photo '86', Malaya Gruzinskaya, Moscow
1987 'Photo '87', Malaya Gruzinskaya, Moscow
'Photoexposition', Hermitage Association, Moscow
1988 'Contemporary Soviet Photography', Museet for Fotokunst, Odense, Denmark
'Contemporary Soviet Photography', Stockholm
1988/89 'Say Cheese!', Comptoir de la Photographie, Paris; Portfolio Gallery, London; Museum of Cinema, Moscow
1989 'Russian Show', Soho Photo Gallery, New York
Art Museum, Cheboksary, Russia
'Photobridge', Avantgardist Club, Moscow
'150 Years of Photography', Central Exhibition Hall (Manege), Moscow
'Exposition des photographes Sovietiques', Theatre de Cherbourg, France
1990 'Looking East', Image Gallery, Aarhus, Denmark
'Changing Reality', Corcoran Gallery of Art, Washington, D.C.
'Photo Manifesto', Museum for Contemporary Art, Baltimore
'Towards Culture and Recreation', Kashirka Gallery, Moscow
1991 'Photo Manifesto: Photography of Perestroika', Long Island University, Fine Arts Gallery, New York
'RUSSIE – USSR, 1914–1991. Changements de regards', Paris Foto Forum, Zürich; Moscow
1992 Galerie Albrecht, München
'Litsa (Faces): Contemporary Portrait Photography from Russia, Belorussia and the Ukraine', Foundation CIRC, Amsterdam
'Experiences Photographiques Russes', L'Atrium de Grand Ecran (Mois de la Photo), Paris
'Premier Photographie', Galerie du Jour (Mois de la Photo), Paris
2. Internationale Foto-Triennale, Esslingen
1993 'A la recherche du père', Espace Photographique de Paris, Paris
'What Am I? The Art of Making a Choice', Shcola Gallery; Union Gallery, Moscow
Presentation of Photographic Collections Museum, ROSIZO State Museum and Exhibition Center, Moscow
1994 'Art of Contemporary Photography-Russia, Ukraine, Belarus', Central House of Artists, Moscow
'Who Is Who: Celebrities of New Russia', Central House of Actors, Moscow
'Le Sault dans le Vide'. Central House of Artists, Moscow
'Artist Portraits', ADC/TEATRO, Moscow
'Monuments and Memory: Reflections on the former Soviet Union', Gallery of Sacred Heart University, Bridgeport, CT
'Sense of Surface: Laying Covers', Central House of Artists, Moscow
1994/95 „Neue Fotokunst aus Moskau", Badischer Kunstverein, Karlsruhe; Kulturhaus Osterfeld, Pforzheim
1995 'Vision of Russia', Photofestival Naarden, Holland
'Visual Concept', ADC and Tampa Museum of Art, Tampa
„Kunst im Verborgenen. Nonkonformisten Rußland 1957–1995", Wilhelm-Hack-Museum, Ludwigshafen; Documenta Archiv, Kassel; Lindenau-Museum, Altenburg

Moukhin has no interest in recording the passing moment as a document of the age; his work lacks any element of reportage. The metamorphoses of a Soviet bench against the background of the changes brought by the seasons offer a critique of society, exposing the degeneration of the symbols of the Soviet Union. Time is clearly present in Moukhin's work, the dynamism of destruction making itself felt despite the rigidity of his subjects.

Das Festhalten des Augenblicks als Zeitdokument interessiert Moukhin nicht; seinen Arbeiten mangelt jeder Reportagecharakter. In Metamorphosen einer sowjetischen Sitzbank vor dem Hintergrund des Wechsels der Jahreszeiten läßt sich Sozialkritik wahrnehmen, die die Degeneration der Symbole des Sowjetsystems enthüllt. Die Kategorie der Zeit artikuliert sich unmittelbar durch die erstarrten Objekte hindurch, in denen die Dynamik der Zerstörung zutage tritt.

ILYA PIGANOV
Илья Пиганов

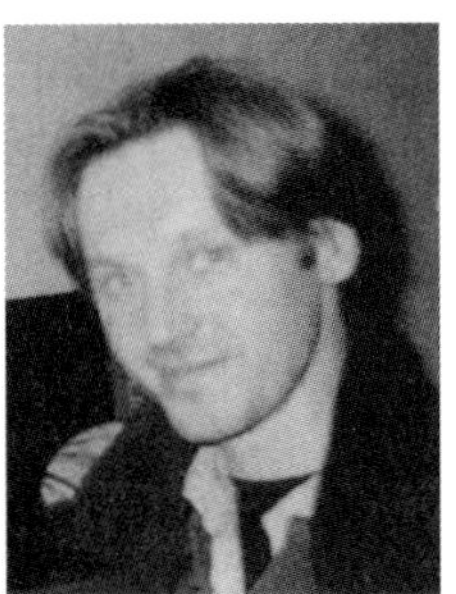

1962 born in Moscow

Solo Exhibitions (*Einzelausstellungen*)
1989 City exhibition hall, Nikolaev, Russia
Finnphoto Gallery, Helsinki
1992 Studio 20 Gallery, Center for Contemporary Art, Moscow
1993 Pont Neuf, Paris
Laboratory Gallery, Center for Contemporary Art, Moscow

Group Exhibitions (*Ausstellungsbeteiligungen*)
1987 'Representation', Hermitage Association, Moscow
Autumn Photosalon, Malaya Gruzinskaya, Moscow
'Photo 87', Malaya Gruzinskaya, Moscow
1988 Spring Photosalon, Malaya Gruzinskaya, Moscow
'Say Cheese!', Comptoir de la Photographie, Paris; Portfolio Gallery, London; Museum of Cinema, Moscow
1989 'Photo Bridge', Avantgardist Club, Moscow
'Alternative?', Glinka Music Culture Museum, Moscow
„Moskau-Wien-New York", Messepalast, Wien
'150 Years of Photography', Central Exhibition Hall (Manege), Moscow
1990 'The Logic of the Parodoxical', Central Palace of Youth, Moscow
'Catalogue', Central Palace of Youth, Moscow
'The Missing Picture – Alternative Contemporary Photography from the USSR', MIT List Visual Art Center, Cambridge, MA
1993 'Baroque at the End of the Century', V.Kh.P.U., named after Moukhina, St. Petersburg
'New Territory of Art', Culture Center Krasnojarsk, Russia
1994 'Art of Contemporary Photography-Russia, Ukraine, Belorus', Central House of Artists, Moscow
'Surface of Sense: Laying Cover', Central House of Artists, Moscow

Piganov is above all concerned with cultural archetypes, rather than with reality. In his earlier work he employed processes of ideographic provocation, combining religious imagery with erotic subjects. More recently concern for decorative qualities has lost the character of pure simulation and allowed Piganov to concentrate on a process of formal aestheticization. In his latest work he uses images taken from a computer screen, thus definitively freeing himself from the 'world of things'.

Ilya Piganov beschäftigt sich primär mit kulturellen Archetypen, nicht mit der Realität. Während er in älteren Arbeiten Verfahren der ideographischen Provokation nutzte, indem er religiöse Darstellungen mit erotischen Sujets verquickte, so verliert in seinen Arbeiten jüngeren Datums das Bemühen um Dekorativität den Charakter reiner Simulation und wird zur Konzentration auf formale Ästhetisierung. In seinen neuesten Werken verwendet er Fotos vom Monitor, womit er sich endgültig von der „Welt der Dinge" löst.

MARIA SEREBRIAKOVA
Мария Серебрякова

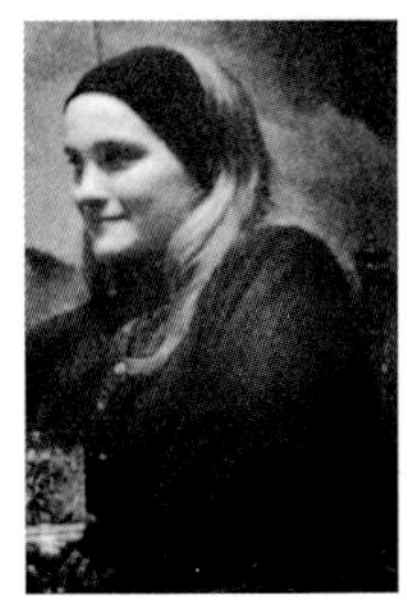

1965 born in Moscow

Solo Exhibitions (*Einzelausstellungen*)
1991 Shcola Gallery, Moscow
1992 Zeno X Gallery, Antwerp
Galerie Giorgio Persano, Turin
Künstlerhaus Bethanien, Berlin
1993 Zeno X Gallery, Antwerp
1994 'Le Creux de l'Enfer', Centre d'Art Contemporain, Thiers, France
1995 'La Base', Centre d'Art Contemporain, Levallois, France

Group Exhibitions (*Ausstellungsbeteiligungen*)
1987 'Representation', Exhibition of the Union 'Hermitage', Exhibition Hall of the Union, Belyaevo, Moscow
'Retrospective Exhibition of Moscow Artists 1957–1987', Exhibition of the Union 'Hermitage', Exhibition Hall of the Union, Belyaevo, Moscow
1988 'The Labyrinth', Central Palace of Youth, Moscow
18th All-Union Exhibition of Young Moscow Artists, Central Exhibition Hall, Moscow
1989 'Dorogoje Iskusstvo', Central Palace of Youth, Moscow
'Serebriakova, Shuravlev, Kirzova', Student Culture Center, Belgrad
'Installation', Garage Gallery, Belgrad
'Moscow-New Jerusalem', One-day exhibition in the landscape in New Jerusalem near Moscow
'Group Exhibition of Moscow Artists', Gallery Monumentalis Oporto, Lisbon
'Inexpensive Art/Exhibition of Little Creations' (Nedorogoje Iskusstvo) 1.0 Gallery, Moscow
'The Exhibition of Unfinished Works', Furmannaya Gallery, Moscow
„Moskau-Wien-New York", Wiener Messepalast, Wien
1990 „Maria Serebriakova & Anatoli Shuravlev. Malerei und Objekte", Inter Art Gallery, Berlin
'Mosca-Moscow-Mockba '90', Sala Umberto Boccioni, Milan; Prov. Museum Mod. Kunst, Ostend
'Towards the Object', Exhibition Hall Kashirskaya, Moscow; Stedelijk Museum, Amsterdam
'Catalogue', Central Palace of Youth, Moscow
'Between Spring and Summer: Soviet Conceptual Art of the Epoch of late Communism', Tacum Museum, Seattle; ISA, Boston
'The Work of Art in the Age of Perestroika', Phillis Kind Gallery, New York
'Art Summer', Split
'Artedomani, 1990 punto divista', Ex-Ospedale San Matteo degli Infermi, Spoleto
'Da Mosca', Unione Culturale/Mostre, Turin
'Shizokity', BC, Moscow
'Wystavka-Zasada', Moscow
'The Missing Picture – Alternative Contemporary Photography from the USSR', MIT List Visual Art Center, Cambridge, MA
1991 'Perspectives of Conceptualism'; University of Hawaii, Honolulu; P.S.1, The Clocktower, New York
'Serebriakova, Rezun-Zvezdotsjotova, Turnova', Picaron Editions/Circ, Amsterdam; Cult. Centrum, Antwerp
'Private work', Soljanka, Moscow

'Optika Vzglyada, Ida Applebroog, Maria Serebriakova', Avtozovodskaja, Moscow
'Unknown Europe', Kraków
1992 „Documenta IX", Kassel
1993 'In Extenso / 1989–1992', Museum van Hedendaagse Kunst, Gent
'The Memory of the Future', Kunsthalle Lophem, Belgium
'Collection Rinaco', Moscow; Caisse des Dépôts, Paris
1995 'International Zomerproject 1995', Kunsthalle Lophem, Belgium
'Pour un Cocteau', Le Creux de l'Enfer, Centre d'art Contemporain, Thiers, France

For Serebriakova the photographic image is of significance above all as the bearer of information about its object in the form of a 'memory' of reality. Photography preserves the integrity of the transformed aura and reproduces archetypes in the form of fragments. Serebriakova boldly selects and re-combines these to form a bizarre world of her own.

Die Fotodarstellung ist für Maria Serebriakova vor allem als Träger von Information über das Objekt in Form von „Erinnerung" an die Realität von Bedeutung. Die Fotografie bewahrt die transformierte Aura ihrer Geschlossenheit und reproduziert im Fragment Archetypen, mit denen sie souverän umgeht und mit ihnen eine eigene bizarre Welt formt.

ALEXEI SHULGIN
Алексей Шульгин

1963 born in Moscow

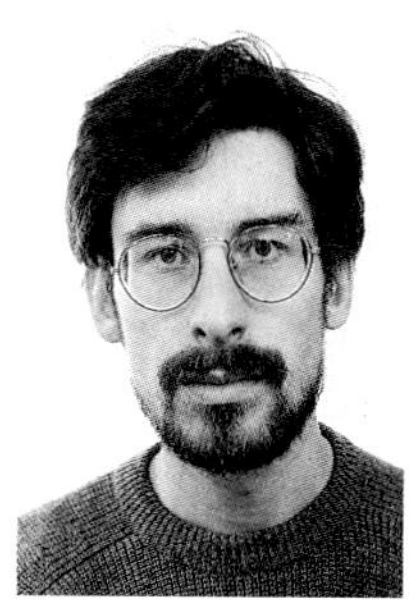

Solo Exhibitions (*Einzelausstellungen*)
1984 Elena Selina apartment, Moscow
1988 'Others' Photographs', Ukhta, Russia
1989 'The Life of a Photographer' (with Sergei Leontiev), Exhibition Hall Kashirskaya, Moscow
Finnfoto Gallery, Helsinki
1992 '10 Years on the Art Scene', Gallery on Triokhprudny Lane, Moscow
1993 'What Am I? The Art of Making a Choice', Shcola Gallery; Union Gallery, Moscow
Untitled Installation (with Sergei Leontiev), Russian-Dutch project ‚Exchange', Moscow
1994 'Televisions', 1989–1993', XL Gallery, Moscow
'Others' Photographs', Central House of Artists, Moscow

Group Exhibitions (*Ausstellungsbeteiligungen*)
1987 Photofestival, Krasnogorsk, Russia
'Representation', Exhibitions of the Union 'Hermitage'/ Exhibition Hall Belyaevo, Moscow
'Photoexposition', Exhibitions of the Union 'Hermitage'/ Exhibition Hall Belyaevo, Moscow.
17th All-Union Exhibition of the Young Artists, Exhibitions of the Union 'Hermitage'/Exhibition Hall Belyaevo, Moscow
1988 „Die Zeitgenössische Photographie in der Sowjetunion", Photographiemuseum, Lausanne
'Contemporary Soviet Photography', Museet for Fotokunst, Odense, Denmark
1989 'Contemporary Soviet Photography', Kunsthuset, Stockholm
'Photobridge', Exhibition Hall of Avtozavodskaja, Moscow
'The Exhibition of the Unfinished Works', Furmannaya Gallery, Moscow
„Moskau-Wien-New York", Wiener Festwochen, Messepalast, Wien
'150 Years of Photography', Central Exhibition Hall (Manege), Moscow
1990 'The Logic of the Paradoxical', Central Exhibition Hall, (Manege) Moscow
'Mosca-Moscow-Mockba '90', Scala Umberto Boccioni, Milan
'Da Mosca', Unione Culturale/Mostre, Turin
'Art Summer '90', Split
'Contemporary Photography from the USSR', Walker, Ursitty & McGuinness Gallery, New York
'Artedomani, 1990 punto di vista', Galleria Communale d'Arte Moderna, Spoleto
'Oppositions: Commitment and Cultural Identity in Contemporary Photography': II. International Biennale of Photography, Center for Photography, Rotterdam
'Erosion: Soviet Conceptual Art & Photography of the 1980s', Amos Anderson Art Museum, Helsinki
'The Missing Picture – Alternative Contemporary Photography from the Soviet Union', MIT List Visual Arts Center, Cambridge, MA
1991 'Photo/Manifesto', Fine Arts Gallery & Avram Family Gallery, Fine Arts Center, Long Island University, New York; Museum for Contemporary Arts, Baltimore
1992 Galerie Albrecht, München
„Herbarium. Die photographische Reflexion in der zeitgenös-

sischen russischen Kunst", Kunsthalle Exnergasse & Fotogalerie Wien, Wien
„Die Andere Malerei. Moskauer Avantgarde der 50er bis 80er Jahre. Sammlung Talotschkin", Kunststation, Kleinsassen, Fulda
'Waist', Center for Contemporary Art, Moscow
2. Internationale Foto-Triennale, Esslingen
1993 'Magazine/Shop', Furniture Store 'Konstantin', Moscow
'New Territories of Art', State Museum of Arts, Krasnojarsk, Russia
1994 'Art of Contemporary Photography. Russia, Ukraine, Belarus', Central House of Artists, Moscow.
'Hamburg Projekt', Center for Contemporary Art, Moscow
'Despository', Exhibition Hall on Solyanka, Moscow
Spring Exhibition of the Moscow Union of Artists, The House of Artists, Moscow
'Escape', Center for Contemporary Art, Moscow
'The Night of the Art', 'Pilot' Night Club, Moscow
'PHOTO-reclamation: New Art from Moscow & Saint Petersburg', John Hansard Gallery; University of Southampton; Street Level Gallery, Glasgow
'Surface of Sense. Laying Cover', Central House of Artists, Moscow
Contemporary Art Festival, Sochi, Russia
'Minima Media', 2. Medien Biennale Leipzig
'Exchange-2', Amsterdam
1994/95 „Neue Fotokunst aus Rußland", Badischer Kunstverein, Karlsruhe; Kulturhaus Osterfeld, Pforzheim
1995 'PHOTO-reclamation: New Art from Moscow & Saint Petersburg', The Photographers' Gallery, London
'No Man's Land: Art from Near Abroad', Nikolaj Contemporary Art Center, Copenhagen

Shulgin sees his photographic work as concerned with two problematic areas: that of his self-identification as a photographic artist and that of the notion of authorship in contemporary mass media culture. Each of his earlier projects ('Alien Photographs', 'Televisions' and 'Rotating Old Photographs') clearly articulates his view that the process of 'fixing' that occurs in photography does not elucidate the significance of the fixed image. Only reflection on this image offers the possibility of individual creation.

Sein fotografisches Werk sieht Shulgin in der Beschäftigung mit zwei Problemfeldern: dem der Selbstidentifikation als Fotokünstler und dem der Autorschaft in der zeitgenössischen Massenmedienkultur. In jedem seiner jüngeren Projekte („Fremde Fotografien", „Fernseher" und „Rotierende alte Fotografien") manifestiert sich seine Auffassung, daß die Fixierung in der Fotografie die Bedeutung der Darstellung nicht erhellt: Nur die Reflexion auf die Darstellung enthält eine Möglichkeit für individuelles Schaffen.

ANATOLI SHURAVLEV
Анатолий Журавлев

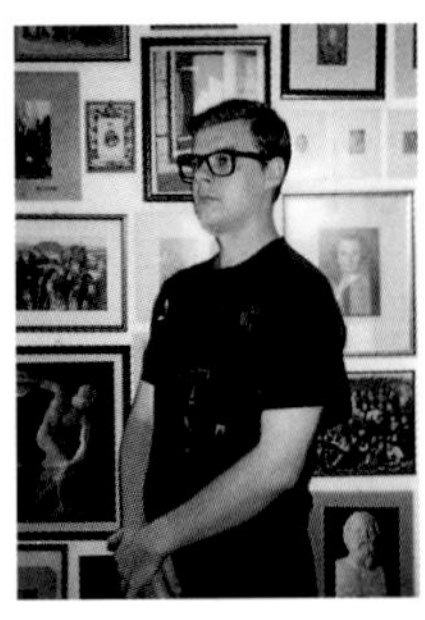

1963 born in Moscow

Solo Exhibitions (*Einzelausstellungen*)
1990 „Maria Serebriakova & Anatoli Shuralev. Malerei und Objekte", Inter-Art-Galerie, Berlin
1992 „Anatoli Shuralev in den Arbeitsräumen des Senators für Kulturelle Angelegenheiten", Berlin
Künstlerhaus Bethanien, Berlin
Galleria Giorgio Persano, Turin
1993 'Ignotiom per Ignotius', 1.0 Gallery, Moscow
'Attempt to see' (in der Reihe „Alltagsgeschichten – objektiv gesehen"), Galerie im Literaturforum Brecht-Haus, Berlin
1994 Collection René Steiner, Erlach, Switzerland (with permanent installation)
'Ad Realibus ad Realiora', Kunst-Werke Berlin; State Russian Museum, St. Petersburg
New Academy of Fine Arts, St. Petersburg
1995 La Base, Centre d'Art Contemporain, Levallois/Paris
Schauraum Specks Hof, Leipzig
Galerie Otto Schweins, Köln

Group Exhibitions (*Ausstellungsbeteiligungen*)
1985 An Autumn Exhibition, Malaya Gruzinskaya, Moscow
Central House of Artists, Moscow
1986 17th Exhibition of Young Moscow Artists, House of Artists, Moscow
'Art Against Commercialism', Bitza Park, Moscow
Exhibitions of the Union 'Hermitage', Exhibition Hall Belyaevo, Moscow
1987 'Representation', Hermitage Association, Moscow
'Retrospective Exhibition of Moscow Artists 1957–1987', Moscow
1988 'The New Artists', Palace of Culture M.E.L.S., Moscow
In the Bath-Houses, Avantgardist Club, Moscow
'The Labyrinth', Central Palace of Youth, Moscow
18th All-Union Exhibition of Young Artists, Central Exhibition Hall (Manege), Moscow
1989 'Precious Art', Central Palace of Youth, Moscow
'Serebrjakova, Shuravlev, Kirzova', Student Culture Center, Belgrad
'Installation', Garage Gallery, Belgrad
'The Exhibition of Unfinished Works', Furmannaya Gallery
'Inexpensive Art: Exhibition of Little Creations', 1.0 Gallery, Moscow
'10+10: Travelling Exhibition 1989–1990', Forth Worth, San Francisco, Buffalo, Milwaukee, Washington, D.C.; Moscow, Leningrad
„Moskau-Wien-New York", Wiener Festwochen, Wien
1990 'Mosca, Moscow, Mockba '90', Sala Umberto Boccioni, Milan
P.M.M.K. Ostend, Belgium
'In the Direction of Object', Exhibition Hall Kashirskya, Moscow
'In the USSR and beyond', Stedelijk Museum, Amsterdam
'Catalogue', Central Palace of Youth, Moscow
'Artedomani, 1990 punto di vista', Ex-Ospedale San Matteo degli Infermi, Spoleto
'Da Mosca', Unione Culturale/Mostre, Turin
'Shizo-China', Avantgardist Club, Moscow
Art Summer, Split

1991 'Ambush', Studio House Tschistye Prudy, Moscow
'Perspectives of Conceptualism', The Honolulu University Gallery, Honolulu
P.S.1, The Clocktower, New York
'Passionate', 1.0 Gallery, Moscow
'Private Occupations', 1.0 Gallery, Moscow
'Europe Unknown', Palace of Arts, Kraków
'Contemporary Soviet Art', Setagaya Art Museum, Tokyo
'Novocento', Central House of Artists, Moscow
'In Rooms', House of Artists, Bratislava
'Russian Art', Rotunda, Hong Kong
1992 „37 Räume", Kunst-Werke Berlin
'The Fall: The One and the Other', Immo Art Gallery, Antwerp
1992/93 A Mosca..., A Mosca..., Villa Campolleto, Ercolano; Galleria Communale d'Arte Moderna, Bologna
1993 'Orlov, Lebedev, Shuravlev, Kulik', Center for Contemporary Art; Collection Rinako; Central House of Artists, Moscow; Caisse de dépots et consignation, Paris
„Privat", Kunst-Werke Berlin
„Spurlos", Altes Rathaus, Potsdam
'Konversia', Central House of Artists, Moscow
1994 „6 Moskauer Konzeptualisten (Maria Serebriakova, Anatoli Shuravlev, Vadim Zakhorov, Medizinische Hermeunetik)", Galerie Rigassi, Bern
„Kunst: Sprache" Kunst-Werke Berlin
'Towards the Moscow Biennale', Central House of Artists, Moscow
'Resistance and Renaissance', State Russian Museum, St. Petersburg
2. Biennale of Contemporary Art, Cetinje, Montenegro
XXII. Biennale de São Paulo, Brazil
„Project For Europe. Engel heute", Galerie Gottfried Hafemann, Wiesbaden
1995 „Das Medium der Photographie in der zeitgenössischen Kunst", Galerie Dacic, Tübingen
„Kunst im Verborgenen. Nonkonformisten 1957-1995", Wilhelm-Hack-Museum Ludwigshafen; Documenta Archiv Kassel; Lindenau-Museum Altenburg
'I is Another', Institute of Theore(c)tical Painting, Kunst-Werke Berlin
„Configura 2, Dialog der Kulturen", Erfurt
International Festival of Photography, Arles

The basis of Shuravlev's work is always a rational idea and the precisely defined means of its visualization. At the same time, the embodiment of this idea always assumes a form that repudiates the rationalization of conceptual analysis. Shuravlev's principal concern is the opposition between the concepts of the real and the illusory, the visible and the invisible, the possible and the impossible. Art itself, in his view, is evidence of the indestructibility of these opposed categories.

Die Grundlage der Arbeiten Shuravlevs ist immer eine rationale Idee und die genau festgelegten Mittel ihrer Visualisierung. Gleichzeitig nimmt die Verkörperung dieser Idee stets eine Form an, die den Rationalismus der konzeptuellen Analytik desavouiert. Die künstlerische Problematik Shuravlevs bewegt sich um die Oppositionen der Begriffe von Realem und Illusorischem, Sichtbarem und Unsichtbarem, Möglichem und Unmöglichem. Die Kunst selbst demonstriert dabei die Unzerstörbarkeit dieser Oppositionen.

IV VYSOTA-GROUP
Группа IV. Высота

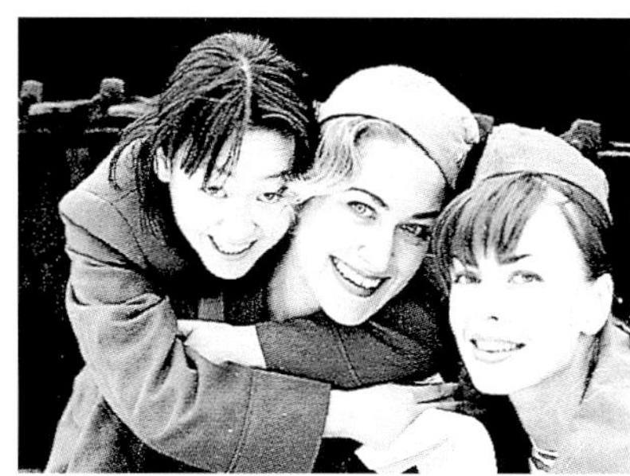

Galina Smirnskaya
1967 born in Rjazan

Katya Kameneva
1971 born in Moscow

Dina Kim
1970 born in Moscow

In 1994 they formed the Group IV. Vysota.
1994 gründeten sie die Gruppe IV. Vysota.

Solo Exhibitions *(Einzelausstellungen)*
1994 'Vchuvstvovanie 1931–1939', Yakut Gallery, Moscow
1995 'Strategy and Tactics', Yakut Gallery, Moscow

Group Exhibitions *(Ausstellungsbeteiligungen)*
1995 'The Art of Dying', Central Exhibition Hall (Manege), Moscow; Yakut Gallery, Moscow

This group (Dina Kim, Galina Smirnskaya, Katya Kameneva) is perhaps the only women artists' group in Moscow not to assume a fundamentally feminist stance. It uses photography for purely simulatory ends, creating the space of an illusion that has been developed out of girlish 'heroic fantasies', Soviet children's literature and transformation games. There is here no subtle play of ideas; we find instead the open display of a 'female logic', of a consciously naïve desire for the materialization of personal fantasies.

Diese Gruppe (Dina Kim, Galina Smirnskaya, Katya Kameneva) ist vielleicht die einzige Künstlerinnenvereinigung in Moskau ohne feministische Grundposition. Sie benutzt die Fotografie zu rein simulatorischen Zwecken und schafft den Raum einer Illusion, der aus mädchenhaften „heroischen Phantasien", aus sowjetischer Kinderlektüre und Verwandlungsspiel geboren ist: kein feinsinnig konzeptuelles Spiel, sondern eher die offene Demonstration einer „Frauenlogik", der absichtlich naive Wunsch einer Materialisierung der eigenen Fantasie.

Compiled by Irina Bazileva, Moscow
(Erstellt von Irina Bazileva, Moskau)

List of Illustrations
Abbildungsverzeichnis

27 From the series 'Fenso Lights' *(Aus der Serie „Fenso Lights“)*, 1993

Black-and-white photographs, each 100 x 100 cm *(Schwarz-Weiß-Fotografien)*

28 From the series 'Fenso Lights' *(Aus der Serie „Fenso Lights“)*, 1993

Black-and-white photographs, each 100 x 100 cm *(Schwarz-Weiß-Fotografien)*

VADIM FISHKIN

29 From the series 'Orbit 2' *(Aus der Serie „Umlaufbahn 2“)*, 1993

Black-and-white photograph, 30 x 40 cm *(Schwarz-Weiß-Fotografie)*

30 From the series 'Orbit 2' *(Aus der Serie „Umlaufbahn 2“)*, 1993

Black-and-white photograph, 30 x 40 cm *(Schwarz-Weiß-Fotografie)*

31 *Orbit S (Umlaufbahn S)*, 1994

Installation. Mixed media *(Installation. Mischtechnik)*

32 Untitled *(Ohne Titel)*, 1991

Black-and-white photograph, 30 x 40 cm *(Schwarz-Weiß-Fotografie)*

33 Untitled *(Ohne Titel)*, 1991

Black-and-white photograph, 30 x 40 cm *(Schwarz-Weiß-Fotografie)*

ALEXEI GOGA

34 *Self-Portrait (Selbstportrait)*, 1993

Colour photograph, 150 x 100 cm *(Farbfotografie)*

35 *Self-Portrait (Selbstportrait)*, 1993

Colour photograph, 150 x 100 cm *(Farbfotografie)*

36 Untitled *(Ohne Titel)*, 1994

Colour photograph, 60 x 80 cm *(Farbfotografie)*

37 Untitled *(Ohne Titel)*, 1994

Colour photograph, 60 x 80 cm *(Farbfotografie)*

VLADIMIR KUPRIYANOV

38 'The Three Graces' *(„Die drei Grazien“)*, 1993–95

Transparent film, plastic, 3 parts, 365 x 55 cm *(Positivfilm, Plastik, 3 Teile)*

39 'The Three Graces' *(„Die drei Grazien“)*, 1993–95

Transparent film, plastic, 3 parts, 365 x 55 cm *(Positivfilm, Plastik, 3 Teile)*

40 From the series 'The Hamlet' *(Aus der Serie „Das Dorf“)*, 1992–95

Transparent film, wood, 90 x 120 cm *(Positivfilm, Holz)*

41 From the series 'The Hamlet' *(Aus der Serie „Das Dorf“)*, 1992–95

Transparent film, wood, 90 x 120 cm *(Positivfilm, Holz)*

42 'On the Phantasmagorical' *(„Über das Phantasmagorische“)*, 1994

Photo glass, 6 parts, 30 x 72 x 24 cm *(Fotoglas, 6 Teile)*

SERGEI LEONTIEV

43 From the series 'Study in Hard Photography' *(Aus der Serie „Versuche in harter Fotografie“)*, 1990–91

Black-and-white photograph, 50 x 60 cm *(Schwarz-Weiß-Fotografie)*

44 From the series 'Study in Hard Photography' *(Aus der Serie „Versuche in harter Fotografie“)*, 1990–91

Black-and-white photograph, 50 x 60 cm *(Schwarz-Weiß-Fotografie)*

45 From the series 'Study in Hard Photography' *(Aus der Serie „Versuche in harter Fotografie“)*, 1990–91

Black-and-white photograph, 50 x 60 cm *(Schwarz-Weiß-Fotografie)*

46 From the series 'Study in Hard Photography' *(Aus der Serie „Versuche in harter Fotografie“)*, 1990–91

Black-and-white photograph, 50 x 60 cm *(Schwarz-Weiß-Fotografie)*

47 From the series 'Study in Hard Photography' *(Aus der Serie „Versuche in harter Fotografie“)*, 1990–91

Black-and-white photograph, 50 x 60 cm *(Schwarz-Weiß-Fotografie)*

48 From the series 'Study in Hard Photography' *(Aus der Serie „Versuche in harter Fotografie“)*, 1990–91

Black-and-white photograph, 50 x 60 cm *(Schwarz-Weiß-Fotografie)*

49 From the series 'Study in Hard Photography' *(Aus der Serie „Versuche in harter Fotografie“)*, 1990–91

Black-and-white photograph, 50 x 60 cm *(Schwarz-Weiß-Fotografie)*

TATYANA LIBERMAN

50 From the series 'Living Monument' *(Aus der Serie „Lebendes Monument“)*, 1993

Black-and-white photograph, 50 x 60 *(Schwarz-Weiß-Fotografie)*

51 From the series 'Man and Mirror' (with G. Vinogradov) *(Aus der Serie „Mensch und Spiegel“ [zus. mit G. Vinogradov])*, 1993

Black-and-white photograph, 50 x 60 *(Schwarz-Weiß-Fotografie)*

52 From the series 'Man and Mirror' (with G. Vinogradov) *(Aus der Serie „Mensch und Spiegel“ [zus. mit G. Vinogradov])*, 1993

Black-and-white photograph, 50 x 60 *(Schwarz-Weiß-Fotografie)*

53 From the series 'Man and Mirror' (with G. Vinogradov) *(Aus der Serie „Mensch und Spiegel“ [zus. mit G. Vinogradov])*, 1993

Black-and-white photograph, 50 x 60 *(Schwarz-Weiß-Fotografie)*

BORIS MIKHAILOV

54 From the series 'Ground Bound' *(Aus der Serie „Bodenständig"),* 1991

Sepia-toned black-and-white photograph (approx. 200 works in the series), each approx. 12 x 24 cm *(Sepia-getönte Fotografien [ca. 200 Bilder])*

55 From the series 'Ground Bound' *(Aus der Serie „Bodenständig"),* 1991

Sepia-toned black-and-white photograph (approx. 200 works in the series), each approx. 12 x 24 cm *(Sepia-getönte Fotografien [ca. 200 Bilder])*

56 From the series 'Ground Bound' *(Aus der Serie „Bodenständig"),* 1991

Sepia-toned black-and-white photograph (approx. 200 works in the series), each approx. 12 x 24 cm *(Sepia-getönte Fotografien [ca. 200 Bilder])*

IGOR MOUKHIN

57 'Examination of a Soviet Bench' *(„Erforschung einer sowjetischen Parkbank"),* 1993–95

12 black-and-white photographs, each 30 x 40 cm *(12 Schwarz-Weiß-Fotografien)*

58 From the series 'Last Soviet Monumental Art': *Hand, Moscow (Aus der Serie „Letzte sowjetische Monumentalkunst": Hand, Moskau),* 1988–95

Black-and-white photograph, 30 x 40 cm *(Schwarz-Weiß-Fotografie)*

59 From the series 'Last Soviet Monumental Art': *Tractor Driver, Shukov (Aus der Serie „Letzte sowjetische Monumentalkunst": Traktorist, Shukov),* 1988–95

Black-and-white photograph, 30 x 40 cm *(Schwarz-Weiß-Fotografie)*

ILYA PIGANOV

60 Untitled *(Ohne Titel),* 1994

Colour photograph, mixed media, 160 x 130 cm *(Farbfotografie, Mischtechnik)*

61 Untitled *(Ohne Titel),* 1994

Colour photograph, mixed media, 160 x 130 cm *(Farbfotografie, Mischtechnik)*

62 Untitled *(Ohne Titel),* 1994

Colour photograph, mixed media, 160 x 130 cm *(Farbfotografie, Mischtechnik)*

MARIA SEREBRIAKOVA

63 Untitled *(Ohne Titel),* 1994

Glass, wood, film, 2 parts, each 180 x 50 x 120 cm *(Glas, Holz, Film, 2 Teile)*

64 Untitled *(Ohne Titel),* 1993

Glass, wood, transparent film (bed: 103 x 208 x 80 cm; table: 112 x 68.5 cm) *(Glas, Wood, Positivfilm)*

65 Untitled *(Ohne Titel),* 1992

Wood, glass, film, plaster, textiles, 6 parts), each 180 x 50 cm *(Holz, Glas, Film, Gips, Textilien, 6 Teile)*

ALEXEI SHULGIN

66 From the series 'Rotating Old Photographs' *(Aus der Serie „Rotierende alte Fotografien"),* 1992–95

Original old photograph, frame, electric motordrive, remote detector, 18 x 24 x 6 cm *(Alte Fotografie, Rahmen, elektronischer Antrieb, Ferndetektor)*

67 From the series 'Rotating Old Photographs' *(Aus der Serie „Rotierende alte Fotografien"),* 1992–95

Original old photograph, frame, electric motordrive, remote detector, 18 x 24 x 6 cm *(Alte Fotografie, Rahmen, elektronischer Antrieb, Ferndetektor)*

68 From the series 'Rotating Old Photographs' *(Aus der Serie „Rotierende alte Fotografien"),* 1992–95

Original old photograph, frame, electric motordrive, remote detector, 40 x 30 x 10 cm *(Alte Fotografie, Rahmen, elektronischer Antrieb, Ferndetektor)*

69 From the series 'Rotating Old Photographs' *(Aus der Serie „Rotierende alte Fotografien"),* 1992–95

Original old photograph, frame, electric motordrive, remote detector, 40 x 30 x 10 cm *(Alte Fotografie, Rahmen, elektronischer Antrieb, Ferndetektor)*

70 From the series 'Televisions' *(Aus der Serie „Fernseher"),* 1989–93

Colour photograph, TV frame, 47 x 50 x 7 cm *(Farbfotografie, Gehäuse eines Fernsehers)*

ANATOLI SHURAVLEV

71 Untitled *(Ohne Titel),* 1992

Black-and-white photograph, mixed media, 70 x 50 cm *(Schwarz-Weiß-Fotografie, Mischtechnik)*

72 Untitled *(Ohne Titel),* 1995

C-Print, 150 x 100 cm

73 Untitled *(Ohne Titel),* 1995

C-Print, 150 x 100 cm

IV VYSOTA-GROUP

74 *Front Friends (Frontfreundinnen),* 1995

View of the exhibition room *(Blick in die Ausstellung)*

75 *Front Friends (Frontfreundinnen),* 1995

Object. Black-and-white photograph, fabric *(Objekt. Schwarz-Weiß-Fotografie, Gewebe)*

76 'Strategy, Tactics' project *(Projekt „Strategie, Taktik"),* 1995

View of the exhibition room *(Blick in die Ausstellung)*

Selected Bibliography
Auswahlbibliographie

1986 D. Mrazkova, V. Remes (eds.), *Another Russia,* exh. cat., Oxford.

1987 *A Day in the Life of the Soviet Union,* exh. cat., New York.

1988 Eric A. Peschler, Viktor Misiano (eds.), *Die zeitgenössische Photographie in der Sowjetunion* (Zürich: Edition Stemmle).
Say Cheese! Un Regard sur la Photographie Sovietique Contemporaine 1968–1988, exh. cat., Paris.

1989 *Moskau, Wien, New York: Kunst zur Zeit,* exh. cat., Vienna.
150 Years of Photography, exh. cat., Moscow.
Photostroika: New Soviet Photography, exh. cat., New York.
1. Internationale Foto-Triennale, exh. cat., Esslingen.

1990 *Erosion: Soviet Conceptual Art and Photography of the 1980s,* Helsinki.
Yekaterina Dyogot, Vladimir Levashov (eds.), *Catalogue,* exh. cat., Moscow.
Valeria Stigneev, Andrei Baskakov (eds.), *Photo Art of Russia* (Moscow: Verlag Planeta).
The Missing Picture: Alternative Contemporary Photography from the Soviet Union, exh. cat., Cambridge, Mass.

1991 *Solitary Pursuits,* exh. cat., Moscow.
Photo Manifesto: Contemporary Photography in the USSR, exh. cat., New York.

1992 *Herbarium: The Photographic Experience in Contemporary Russian Art,* Vienna.
Faces (Litsa): Contemporary Portrait Photography from Russia, Belorussia and the Ukraine, exh. cat., Amsterdam.
2. Internationale Foto-Triennale, exh. cat., Esslingen.

1993 *Art Hamburg,* exh. cat., Hamburg.
Krieg. 1. Österreichische Triennale zur Fotografie, exh. cat., Graz.

1994 *Art of Contemporary Photography: Russia, Ukraine, Belorussia,* exh. cat., Moscow.
PHOTO-reclamation: New Art from Moscow and St. Petersburg, exh. cat., Southampton, London.
Surface of Sense: Laying Covers, exh. cat., Moscow.
Postphotography (conference texts), Moscow.
Boris Groys (ed.), *Fluchtpunkt Moskau* (Ostfildern and Aachen: Cantz Verlag).
Kathrin Becker, Barbara Straka (eds.), *Selbstidentifikation: Positionen, St. Petersburger Kunst von 1970 bis heute,* exh. cat., Kiel, Berlin.

1995 Andrei Erofeev, Jean-Hubert Martin (eds.), *Kunst im Verborgenen. Nonkonformisten Rußland 1957–1995* (Munich and New York: Prestel-Verlag).
Configura 2: Dialog der Kulturen, exh. cat., Erfurt.

PHOTOGRAPHIC CREDITS
Fotonachweis

Le Creux de l'Enfer: S. 85
Enno Kaufhold, Berlin: S. 63, 64
Galerie Otto Schweins, Köln: S. 92, 93
ZENO X Gallery, Antwerp: S. 86